GOING DIGITAL

GOING DIGITAL

A MUSICIAN'S GUIDE TO TECHNOLOGY

Brad Hill

Schirmer Books
An Imprint of Simon & Schuster Macmillan
NEW YORK

Prentice Hall International
LONDON   MEXICO CITY   NEW DELHI   SINGAPORE   SYDNEY   TORONTO

Schirmer Books
An Imprint of Simon & Schuster Macmillan
1633 Broadway
New York, New York 10019

Library of Congress Catalog Number: 97-47311
Printed in the United States of America
Printing number
1 2 3 4 5 6 7 8 9 10

Library of Congress Cataloging-in-Publication Data

Hill, Brad, 1953–
    Going digital : a musician's guide to technology / Brad Hill.
        p.   cm.
    Includes bibliographical references and index.
    ISBN 0-02-864513-8
    1. Computer sound processing. 2. Microcomputers. 3. MIDI
(Standard). I. Title.
    MT723.H538 1998   97-47311
    780'.285—dc21   CIP
                                                        MN
This paper meets the requirements of ANSI/NISO Z39.48–1992
(Permanence of Paper).

CONTENTS

PREFACE

This is a nontechnical book about technology. I have written it for musicians of various kinds—performers, composers, teachers, and recreational players—who are not entirely comfortable with the new digital tools of the past 15 years.

It has been an enormously eventful decade and a half. In those short years the digital frontier has been glimpsed, approached, and embraced. Not by everyone, of course. As promising and intriguing as technology is for some, it is confusing, intimidating, or seemingly undesirable for others. This book seeks to create a bridge of understanding between the digitally reluctant musician and the potential of new tools, based on examples of how modern technologies help musicians create music, run their businesses, and expand their reach in the global musical community.

TECHNOLOGY'S CURVE

Of all the changes we face in a breathlessly accelerated world, technological change is both the most insistent and the least clearly necessary. In most areas of life, we have moved far beyond survival technology. Medicine will always be engaged in developing the cutting edge of life-and-death science, but most people don't often need to cope with modern machines of healing. Such technology does not usually intrude in our days, forcing us to adjust habits, reconsider our methods of basic living, or challenge the conceptions of our professions and social lives. The new inventions that create these disruptions in our regular lives tend to be oriented around entertainment, communication, and personal productivity. They don't represent crucial, bottom-line issues of life, least of all for those who are not attracted to technology for its own sake. For some people, tomorrow's glitzy devices are today's feverish anticipation; but for others, 500 channels of digital TV is already a few hundred channels too many.

Technology settles into our lives along a curve of acceptance. The path from resistance to reliance passes through stages we have seen over and over. Significant inventions, requiring deep changes in our daily patterns, have historically required many years to become thoroughly integrated into our lives. The telephone marched slowly into our homes over the roughly six decades following its invention in 1876. The compact disc player is one of the technologies of our time that has caught on more quickly, with production efficiencies reducing prices and marketing efficiencies spreading the word. Yet technological innovations still take a while to catch on, especially the big ones. The larger the challenge to our lifestyle habits, the harder it is to win our acceptance. Furthermore, most new technology needs underlying support before it can really worm its way into our lives. The telephone needed a network of lines and switches. CD players relied on the recording industry to supply the marketplace with a large enough library of CD products to make the purchase of a player worthwhile. Television needed broadcast stations and programming content. The phonograph needed records. Railroad trains needed tracks. And in all cases, technology needs our compliance, in the form of a willingness to take on new habits and new expectations.

BIG SHIFTS, LITTLE SHIFTS

An underlying infrastructure of technology supports new inventions as the ocean supports boats. Once afloat, a new invention will usually launch smaller, related inventions in the form of improvements and minor innovations. So it may go for generations, until, in an epochal blaze of genius and ingenuity, a new technological infrastructure is discovered or developed—a new ocean. So it was that we moved from land and water travel into the air, from muscle power to electrical power, from horseback courier to broadcast signal. Each shift to a new infrastructure, a new medium of development, brings a rush of invention, inspiration, and adjustment that is simultaneously frightening and exhilarating, sometimes trivial, but often bearing unexpected jewels of new possibility for improved life.

We are witnessing such a shift now. We stand at a juncture. We are straddling two technology infrastructures, and as the market-driven pioneers of invention push us insistently from the old to the new, our lives will be affected in ways predictable and unforeseeable, gross and subtle, clearly marked and seamlessly woven. We are a society going digital, and although the ramifications may not yet seem extraordinary, neither did they at the first advent of the printing press or electricity. In fact, nobody really knows what an increasingly digital world will mean to us and require of us. But we do know the advantages and possibilities that have opened into reality for the present, as a result of what is already, and aptly, called the digital revolution.

INTRODUCTION

What does *digital* mean? To make something digital is to translate it into bits of data; "zeroes and ones" is the informal rendition of this binary translation. What undergoes this translation? Primarily, what we perceive with ears and eyes. The other senses (touch, taste, and smell) are too mysteriously complex to yield their secrets to any sort of recording process, digital or nondigital. But what we see and what we hear can be broken down into tiny constituent parts and assigned numbers. These numbers, when reconstituted through the proper machines, approximately reproduce the original sight or sound. It is paradoxical that something as fluid as perception can be quantified, and it is compromise that enables us to do it. Digitization almost never provides the same fidelity as the real thing. Depending on the quality (in particular, the degree of resolution) of the technology used, digitization leaves out some of the details of a sound that give it its full character. For example, some frequencies or overtones may be eliminated when making a digital recording, creating a sound lacking the tonal fullness of the original. But generally, our eyes and ears can be fooled by the digital compromise when it is done well.

But why compromise our perceptions? Because it is, in a word, convenient. That may not seem like a good enough reason. Well, it's powerfully convenient. Digitization allows transmission and manipulation of sight and sound in ways that extend our potential of communication and creation. A digital world is a smaller one, and in a way a more personally empowered one. Calling the digital revolution an Information Superhighway reflects the utilitarian role of technology in an industrial society. But as we move from an industrial age to an information age, we need only shift lanes to travel on what I call the Creation Highway. And this justifies the compromises of going digital, compromises we'll look at more deeply in this book, as we also consider the potentials. Digital tools—inventions that are spinning out of the new oceanic, digital infrastructure—can make us more creative, more expressive, and more communicative.

HOW IS MUSIC AFFECTED?

It is strange that artistic pursuits, immune as they seem to any kind of incremental analysis, dissection, or quantification, have been served so vigorously by the tools of digitization. Music in particular has been embraced by the digital revolution. It's not overstating to say that personal musical power has been reborn through the midwifery of computers. The development of MIDI (Musical Instrument Digital Interface) systems enabling manipulation of sound is a milestone in the history of music technology: Its impact can be compared to the emergence of music notation. Besides MIDI, a specifically musical application of the Creation Highway, general-purpose computer and online technologies advance the professional and lifestyle goals of working musicians in various ways. We'll look at them, too.

THINKING ABOUT TECHNOLOGY

We live in an age of abundant technology, so much so that we may have a glib understanding of what it is. We certainly don't relate well to what it *was*. The technologies of past generations and centuries seem to us, accustomed as we are to shining, scientific, finely mechanized technology, to be the primitive meanderings of a pretech culture. If we turn our attention to nonartistic fields for a moment, we can see the truth of this. To a doctor, ancient healing arts seem more like voodoo than medicine. To an astronomer, Earth-centric models of the universe are laughably provincial. We hesitate to assign the word *technology* to civilization's beginnings because that word carries a sheen of modernity, a connotation of silicon smoothness, not to mention an arrogant correctness. Technology is of the moment; in the information-age perspective that sees yesterday as old news, technology is intrinsically high-tech.

But if we are to relate to high technology as a useful adjunct to our creative and communicative lives, we must take a different view of technology in general. No matter what age we live in, technology is any tool; it brings us closer to our goals. If our goal is to grow more food, then irrigation is technology as it furthers that goal, propelled by mules and wooden troughs.

All this may seem obvious. Technology builds upon itself, evolving as it furthers social evolution. What are the age-old goals of musicians? What primal musical endeavors remain constant through the ages, and are continually furthered by evolving music technology?

THE ENDURING GOALS OF MUSIC TECHNOLOGY

CREATIVITY

Composers in particular need creative tools. But all performers making music and teachers interpreting it need to tap into the deep well of human creativity. Every interpretation—of a classical piece played by the note, or an exact cover of a pop tune— engages the creative impulses of the performers.

INSTRUMENTS

Composers want better ones to spark their imagination, performers want constant refinement to better express their instrumental art, and audiences are rewarded by instruments that stay in tune and stretch their sonority to the far corners of concert halls.

ACCESSIBILITY AND DISTRIBUTION

It almost goes without saying that we must have access to music if we are to enjoy it, practice it, and share it. This is as true for music lovers (maybe even more so) as for vocational musicians. Accessibility and distribution are the two sides of a single technology coin. None of us lives in a vacuum, and certainly no creative musician wants to feel isolated from the listening community. Composed, performed, printed, and recorded music must be distributed if the art and craft of music is to survive.

EDUCATION

The tradition of teaching music is only one generation newer than the history of music itself. Anyone who appreciates music at any level is invested in music education.

REAL WORDS

Technology has changed my life for sure! I was an independent producer/recording engineer who got tired of great music not making it through the record company funnel (too many artists funneled down to too few good labels). So I opened the anti–record company Artist Underground. We take the best music we can find, in all genres, and promote it and make available for sale on the Web—straight from the artist to the people!

Joe Seta
Artist Underground
http://www.aumusic.com

With each of these goals, the primary benefit is empowerment. Personal musical empowerment exists in two flavors, or directions:

- **Inner-directed.** Tools that enable the individual musician to practice, perform, compose, teach, and evolve as a musical being are basically directed inward. These are creative tools, better instruments, and in the case of music lovers, all inventions that bring music more effortlessly into the home.

- **Outer-directed.** Any modern development (regardless of the time period) that conveys music from the musician's conception to wide appreciation is an outer-directed technology. This includes education technologies and distribution media such as recordings, broadcasting, and the development of performance traditions.

AN INFORMAL HISTORY

This book introduces modern tools of musical empowerment, and describes the *why* and *how* of our empowerment through them. In this section we look at a few *whens* of musical technology, to set the stage. This is not a history course, and we're not concerned with names or dates—and definitely not quizzes. Looking back gives us perspective on the present. If we can see that the inventions of the past, which seem folksy to our modern sensibilities, are actually examples of technology in action, then our perspective on modern technology shifts. If the primitive, easygoing past seems too friendly and low-tech to be called technology, but in fact is such, then perhaps the highly quantified, seemingly cold, apparently inartistic digital tools of our cutting-edge present are really friendlier than they appear. Besides, it's always fun to take a fond look back at bygone eras.

NOTATION

What was composition like before music was written down? Less organized, that's for sure. We can't know for certain how far back in time the urge to create organized music might stretch, but it has probably beaten strongly in the musical souls of all people who had the leisure time to indulge it. Folk tunes of many cultures were developed before musical notation was standardized, and in fact still are, without the assistance of notation technology. A shepherd watching his flock on a hillside with only the company of his wooden flutes is more than a romantically pastoral image; this was a particularly boring occupation for generations of land-dwelling folk. They created simple, repetitive melodies, strung variations together to form coherent pieces, and introduced those pieces to neighbors and family at village gatherings; dances were created to accompany those pieces, and other musicians, playing other folk instruments, adopted the melodies. This traditional process organically brought together social filaments that could weave a tapestry of community, dance, celebration, ritual, song, and ensemble musicianship.

It's not surprising that nonnotated music is difficult to notate; in fact, that is part of its signature sound and appeal. Native folk music traditions tend to be stylistically ornate, reflecting the elaborate variations and ornaments added to simple melodies by composers who had huge expanses of time for refinement. Primitive music is usually not lengthy, but makes up for it in detail. Grace notes, trills, accents of breath, imitations of prevailing vocal technique, and other subtle minutiae are embedded inextricably in old folk melodies; you may not notice them on first hearing, but the music is naked, unnatural, and incomplete without them. Such stylistic detail defies documentation, creating an ironic historical situation: The lack of notation actually can be said to have furthered musical expression in certain ways, and the introduction of notation technology strips indigenous music of its essential texture. There are many people of the contemporary age, some of whom may be holding this book, who will say that technology generally strips the depth from human expression. Although that is not my viewpoint, it is a question that comes up again and again in examinations of modern music technology. Ultimately, we must each find a personal balance of soul and machine.

If music notation is an inadequate technology for capturing essential details of folk traditions, it makes up for it by advancing the goals of musical technology as follows:

- **Transmission of music.** As music is a language, folk music is an oral tradition, and music notation is a written language. Notation has not meant the death of transmission through listening and copying by any means: Grassroots folk music continues today to be shared, often with the help of tape recorders and published collections of tunes.

- **Preservation of music as it was originally composed** (as opposed to nuances of performance better preserved orally, as stated above). This is a gain for composers, naturally. Not bad for music lovers, either, who benefit from the safekeeping of centuries of musical creativity. Oral tradition is a selective and unreliable preserver of music.

- **Evolution of musical form.** Notation's biggest impact might lie in the relief of memory. Once a composer can write down a melody, it frees the creative impulse to begin building larger architectures of music. Furthermore, other musicians can learn new and more complex pieces at their leisure.

HOME INSTRUMENTS

Certain instruments have always existed in the home, of course, from tribal drums to Irish fiddles, African rattles to Balkan bagpipes. A quantum leap of music accessibility was made when harpsichords and fortepianos (the first pianos) made their entrance to parlors in private houses; their eighteenth-century migration from public concert hall to living room shifted the balance of musical power fairly drastically, and combined with music notation to create new interest, creativity, and skill in nonprofessional musicians.

Keyboard instruments that play simultaneous melodies and chords bear a certain stretched resemblance to computers. (Bear with me on this comparison.) By this I mean that each has a general ability to process music. A computer can run many software programs, and is not limited to a single style of processing (math, for example, or word processing, or music sequencing, or telecommunications). By the same token, the harpsichord and the fortepiano brought flexible music processing into the home for the first time. With the "software" of sheet music, and the fact that keyboards can play melody and chords at the same time, these instruments could play any style of composition. They even allowed more creative people to "program" (compose) their own "software" (music).

Orchestral Instruments Through the Centuries

Pianos, harpsichords, claviers, and fortepianos, being fairly complicated machines, show a steeper technology development curve over the last couple of centuries than simpler instruments such as flutes, viols, and horns. Nevertheless, orchestral instruments have benefited from the advance of music technology. A quick listen to an "original instrument" recording of Baroque or pre-Baroque music reveals that significant changes affecting the tuning and sonority of single-note instruments have taken place. For an even more drastic comparison, listen to the older, folk incarnations of wind and string instruments as heard in the indigenous recordings of various ethnomusical regions.

Modern wind instruments relying on keys and valves to determine pitch have much more advanced mechanics than earlier versions. In fact, ancient horns had no valves at all (witness the ceremonial shofar used for thousands of years in synagogues at high holy days, or the hunting horn), depending on nothing more than changes in breath pressure to sound different notes in the natural series of overtones. Obviously, such a limitation sharply constricted their melodic potential! Primitive flutes had finger holes, unadorned with keys and pads. The modern flute achieves chromaticism with a key system that can cover and uncover more holes than is practically manageable using only a standard supply of fingers. Additionally, the evolution of material, from simple reed (made from the stem of a grass) flutes, to wooden Irish valve flutes and European recorders, to metal orchestral flutes and piccolos, has endowed the instrument with a sharper, clearer, more embossed tone. Finally, the switch from end-blown designs to transverse (sideways-blown) makes intonation more accurate, not to mention giving the modern player more room on stage to accommodate the flung-out elbow.

Bowed string instruments attained sophistication early in the European classical tradition, and the changes to date have been more subtle than with some other instrument classes. However, a glance back to eastern European instrumental tradition reveals a primitive type of viol whose strings were touched by the finger but not pressed against the neck, resulting in much less accurate intonation. Sonority was accomplished partly through the use of sympathetically vibrating strings placed underneath the main strings (a version of which today enjoys a distinguished life in the folk music of Sweden). There weren't nearly as many sizes of instrument as we enjoy today with violins, violas, cellos, and contrabasses. The formal demands of written European music, beginning in the Renaissance, catalyzed the evolution of bowed instruments.

Even percussion instruments, seemingly too simple to allow much technological development, have grown in variety and refinement. The question of variety is crucial, as the typical modern orchestra is equipped with a huge assortment of objects waiting to be struck in the service of an evocative tone poem or symphony. And nothing typifies music technology as applied to percussion more than timpani, whose pitched, almost melodic potential removes them far from their primitive, hollowed-log ancestors.

The refinements of instruments in general are not as fundamental as the quantum technological leap represented by fortepianos in the home, but they result in greater satisfaction for the player, and sometimes more affordable choices. The latter is certainly true in the case of upright pianos, which must have seemed an outlandish technological application when they appeared near the beginning of the nineteenth century. Closer to our era, the introduction of electronic instruments, especially in portable forms, has brought a new age of convenience and availability. And most recently, the digital MIDI interface has had a revolutionary effect.

PRINTED MUSIC

This is primarily a technology of distribution—the main one, in fact, before recording technology, when sheet music was the only music distribution avenue available to publishers, and the release of a new classical folio or, especially, a popular song in sheet form was greeted with anticipation and excitement, as a CD album or single is today.

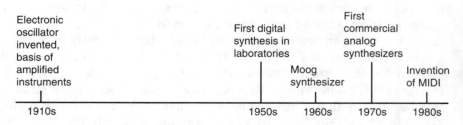

The development of electronic music.

Printed music is a follow-up technology to the more basic notation technology. There is nothing to print without a written musical language. Before the printing press, notation was distributed in the form of hand-created manuscripts. This was very handy for communicating parts to an orchestra, for example, but did nothing for bringing music into the home. Printed music shrank the world as dramatically as the phonograph would some four centuries later. And of course it would be an invaluable technology of education.

RECORDED MUSIC

This is a technology of popularization. It's hard for us to imagine the impact of the phonograph, accustomed as we are to recording and broadcast technologies filling our ears with stimulation almost constantly. Cultural overload is a contemporary problem, but before the phonograph, the only way to hear an organized musical presentation was to attend a concert. Folk music was played informally in communal gatherings, and in the home to a degree. But hearing an orchestra was a climactic sensory experience to be sought, anticipated, and remembered.

Knowing that, it can better be imagined why concerts were such focal events in earlier centuries. The modern analog is perhaps the stage productions of pop stars, who imbue their presentations with enough high-sensory multimedia spectacle to distinguish their performances from the fastidiously produced albums on which they're based. Because the music doesn't usually undergo much variation from CD to concert (or MTV video), lights and choreography are used to keep us interested.

Recording technology and the phonograph created a huge shift in music accessibility. Suddenly opera, symphony, chamber music, and virtuoso solo performances could be experienced in the home. Music appreciation, awareness, and education grew staggeringly. Eventually, as sound production and media manufacturing technologies made the recording process more available to independent musicians, it became a technology of distribution as well as of accessibility.

DIGITAL INSTRUMENTS

As we moved into the 1950s and 1960s, a whole technology of timbre became represented by electronically amplified instruments. This was not altogether welcome at the time—in fact, the pop genres that were propelled by loudly amplified instruments were often reviled and helped define the fabled generation gap—and it might not be clear even now how this technology empowers musicians. Most obviously, it resulted in loud music, initiating a tradition of huge concerts, a form of mass distribution in which thousands could sit together and listen to and watch musicians.

More importantly, plug-in instruments set the stage to launch us into the age of digital music.

The manifestations of music digitization are still emerging, and nobody can see clearly down this road and all its branching avenues. Digitized music is compact and accessible. By translating music to the zeroes and ones of binary data, we gain the ability to manipulate those zeroes and ones more freely. Tools are developed that take advantage of that malleability, and so enhance creative possibilities.

Digitization shrinks the musical world in a number of ways. Musicians can easily share their personal software (that is, the musical files they have created in the digital realm). Instruments and instrument types can be connected together in systems that add up to more than the sum of their parts. Computers offer personalized control, a wealth of sonic timbres and textures, organizational and processing power, and the ability to notate and print music.

Digital technology is today's manifestation of the tradition of individual musical empowerment, accelerating our empowerment through the mechanisms of an information-age culture.

The goal of this book is not to provide an instruction manual in different technologies, but to chart their possibilities while outlining what you need to get them. I'm not out to make you an instant expert in MIDI production, for example, or computers in general, but to reassure technology-resistant musicians that there is something worthwhile in the modern tools of the trade, perhaps even unglimpsed benefits. In the best spirit of the information age, we should all be able to find what we want in a shrinking world; to take what we each need of technology, and leave the rest. In so doing, we encourage technology to fulfill its mandate, which is to promote, not hinder, our creative happiness.

As we begin a venture into the digital realms of music, we should meet two musical people who are destined to take the digital path in two different directions.

Penelope Envelope is a professional musician working in the front lines of the business. She survives handily by doing a little bit of everything: teaching piano in her home, playing jazz gigs in restaurants a couple of times a week, performing studio dates when she can get them, and picking up a smattering of composing and arranging commissions. She recently released a CD of innovative arrangements of piano standards.

Pat Chedit, bass player for the Silicon Transplants, wants to keep rocking but doesn't like the instability of pro music. Stockbroker by day, club artist by night (on the weekends, anyway), he keeps his band on its toes with original grunge and hip covers.

PART ONE
COMPUTERS AND MUSIC

Our intrepid Penelope Envelope has become interested in computers for distinctly nonmusical reasons. She wants to be able to promote her business activities without running to the computer/copy shop every two days. She's just landed a steady four-night-a-week solo gig at a nearby jazz club, and wants to build a computerized mailing list, figuring that she can sell her CD to her audience through the mail. She's thinking ahead to the next CD, too, and wants to be up to speed with computer art programs for cover layout by the time she records it.

Pat Chedit uses computers at work, and wants to promote his band gigs just as Penny does, using a mailing list. He's also vaguely aware of MIDI and going online, but first things first. Before getting fancy with musical tools, Pat plans to do some serious game-playing.

Penny and Pat both buy new computers with the one peripheral that really helps with promotion: a printer. Penelope goes for the gold (and red, yellow, green, and other colors) with a color printer, and Pat, who envisions nothing more glamorous than printing labels, picks up an inexpensive black-and-white laser printer.

1

THE DIGITAL
FACE OF MUSIC

When was the last time you heard computer music? Chances are good it was within the past hour. Almost certainly in the past day, unless you live a remarkably quiet and undisturbed life. If you heard a snatch of commercial radio, spent a little time in a room with a TV playing, went to a movie, or listened to a pop CD, your sensibilities have probably been affected by the digital revolution. Computer music—or, more accurately, computer-age music—is no longer confined to exotic, artistically questionable blips and squeaks of the early experimentalists in the 1960s and 1970s.

So if computer music is so transparent, so easily mistaken for "real" instruments and acoustic timbres, some questions arise. Why is it revolutionary? What do we mean by the **digitization** of music? What is the result of making music digital; how does it affect creative quality? How does it help or hinder the objectives of musicians and music lovers?

HOW DO WE HEAR?

To understand digitizing music, it helps to know something of the nature of sound itself.

Sound is merely patterns of air molecules that have been pushed. This process is always initiated by vibration of some sort: a plucked guitar string, the vibrating vocal chords of a singer, a struck tuning fork, a hit drum. The vibration may be short or sustained, fast (high pitched) or slow (low pitched), broad (producing a loud sound) or narrow (producing a soft sound), even or uneven (producing tonal quality). Different sounds come from vibrations varying in size, shape, speed, and duration. As the vibrating object moves back and forth, it pushes the air around it, setting up waves of molecules known as sound waves.

These air wave patterns, the sound waves, spread out from the vibrating physical object (or instrument). The wave pattern

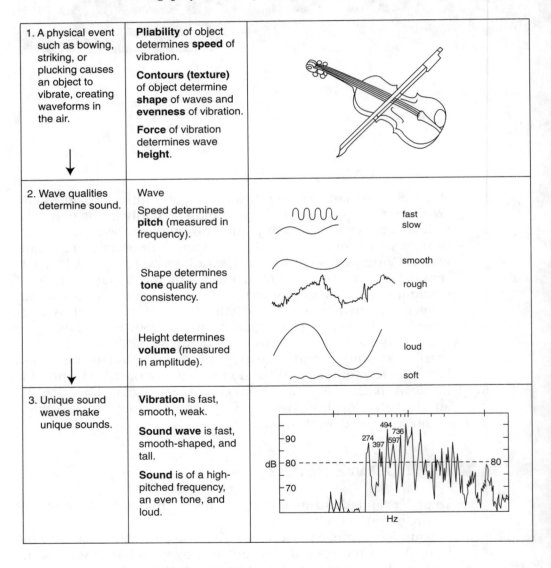

1. A physical event such as bowing, striking, or plucking causes an object to vibrate, creating waveforms in the air.	**Pliability** of object determines **speed** of vibration. **Contours (texture)** of object determine **shape** of waves and **evenness** of vibration. **Force** of vibration determines wave **height**.	
2. Wave qualities determine sound.	Wave Speed determines **pitch** (measured in frequency). Shape determines **tone** quality and consistency. Height determines **volume** (measured in amplitude).	fast slow smooth rough loud soft
3. Unique sound waves make unique sounds.	**Vibration** is fast, smooth, weak. **Sound wave** is fast, smooth-shaped, and tall. **Sound** is of a high-pitched frequency, an even tone, and loud.	

From vibrations to sounds.

spreading out in one direction may change, making it different from those spreading in other directions. Think of the circular waves of water that ripple out from a rock dropped into a still pond. The wave may look identical around its circumference, but in fact contains many small variations depending on how the rock entered the water, small objects already in the water, and innumerable other variables. Similarly, airborne sound waves moving away from the source interact with objects in the environment. Meeting with smooth surfaces, they reflect in new directions. Colliding with porous and uneven objects, they are broken up, absorbed, and partially reflected in new patterns. If portions of the expanding spherical wave of sound do not meet anything in their path, they simply continue, but with a deteriorating effect: Interaction with molecules along the path degrades the purity of the original wave pattern until it gradually loses its shape.

The pulsating air patterns become sound, in a way we can relate to, when they meet one particular physical object: an eardrum. Our eardrums are designed to vibrate with great sensitivity to waves of air molecules, and the rest of the ear is built to translate those patterns into an auditory sensation we call sound. The closer we are to the source of the sound wave, the more accurately we perceive it because the air patterns have not had the time (and space) to change or degrade very much. If we are farther away, the sound is distorted to some degree in volume, tone, and pitch.

This book is not an anatomical text, nor is it about acoustical science. The important point here is that sound travels in vibration-induced waves and is perceived through sympathetic vibrations in our ears.

SOUND WAVES HAVE SHAPE

When something vibrates, creating patterns in the air (or any other medium, but for our purposes we'll think about sound moving through the air), there are three ways in which that vibration can occur:

- **Width of vibration.** The force with which an object moves back and forth determines sound wave width. For example, if you pluck a guitar string lightly you'll see a narrow vibration, and a more assertive pluck yields a broader vibration and a broader sound wave. The width, or amplitude, of the sound wave determines the volume of the sound.

- **Speed of vibration.** How fast the vibrating object moves back and forth, or frequency, depends on the physical qualities of the object (its size, texture, and so on), not on how it is struck, plucked, or breathed into. Speed of vibration determines pitch.

■ **Consistency of vibration.** The smoothness and evenness with which something vibrates throughout the life of the vibration determines the tone of the sound. Pliable substances tend to vibrate smoothly, whereas more rigid ones offer shorter, harder-edged vibrations. You can alter the smooth vibration of a pliable object, such as a guitar string, by holding something lightly against it during its movement, such as a coin. The change in tonal quality is obvious, and is caused by the changing shape of the sound wave. In the case of a coin held against a vibrating guitar string, an angular, jagged wave shape introduced by interrupting the smooth vibration of the string produces a buzzing tone.

These vibrational variables produce corresponding movements of air molecules. Wide vibrations push the air hard, creating wide sound waves; fast vibrations pulse the molecules quickly, creating rapidly moving sound waves; smooth and rough vibrations create rounded or jagged sound waves. When these different patterns of air movement enter our ears and push against the eardrum, vibrating the eardrum in a way that corresponds to the impulse that began the vibration, we hear sounds of varying volume, pitch, and tone.

HOW IS SOUND DIGITIZED?

Sound waves can be visualized and diagrammed into standardized shapes. These visual waves can be charted, with their frequency (speed) and shape (height, width, consistency) representing the characteristics of the vibration that produced them.

When a sound is digitized, its characteristic shape is recorded and stored as a collection of numbers. These numbers, when translated back into wave form with certain circuitry, become once again the actual sound wave, ready to be heard by our ears. A digitized sound is a snapshot of one moment of sound. Of course, sound is constant, proceeding seamlessly from moment to moment. To digitize a sustained sound, a process is used similar to that of recording motion pictures. A sequence of snapshots is taken, each very close in time to the next; the result is a quick succession of audio snapshots that results, when they are translated back to their original natural state, in a continuous sound. The process doesn't necessarily produce more pleasing results than a nondigital tape recorder, but the result is more portable and more easily alterable.

The digitizing process is accomplished with two specific types of equipment:

- **A/D converters.** Analog-to-digital converters are hardware devices that treat sound waves much as video cameras record visual information. A/D converters record a real-world (analog) sound by translating it into a series of data equivalents that represent the sound wave's shape.

- **D/A converters.** Digital-to-analog converters reverse the digitizing process by retranslating the digitized wave back into an analog sound.

A/D and D/A converters are the heart of all sampling devices (instruments that digitize sound input, then turn it into sound output across the range of their playable keyboards). Other circuitry is involved in the hardware equation, but the converters are responsible for the digitizations and dedigitizations.

The conversion of sound from wave form into a series of numbers and back again might seem like translating a work of literature from English to Portuguese, then back into English. But sound dig-

---

REAL WORDS

In my opinion, the debate between digital and analog is silly. These are two formats that are entirely different, and it seems to me that what analog does, it does much better than digital, and vice versa. Neither medium accurately captures what is going in—it really comes down to a matter of preference, and what the user's needs are.

Ken Lee/Eleven Shadows
Burglar@primenet.com

REAL WORDS

My first digital recorder was a PCM F1-compatible recorder, and it completely changed the way I made music. It did that because up until that point, the recorders I was using changed a fundamental character of the sound. That was always disappointing, knowing that I could never hear what I had recorded. But when I heard the F-1, even though it wasn't perfect (especially by today's standards), it gave me back the same character that I had put into it. There were still a few things I wanted to change in the way it sounded, but it was the first time I didn't feel like I had to overcompensate some facet of the mix to allow for the recorder. I was reborn!

Craig Patterson
midigod@aol.com

---

itization is tremendously significant for both music consumers and producers. The CD would be impossible without it, as would realistic MIDI production. It's also important to look at spin-off technologies that have resulted from sound digitization, or sampling.

WHAT IS SAMPLING?

Sampling is the process of digitizing sound, and a sample is simply a digitized sound wave. Within those broad definitions there is a huge range of examples. A CD can be considered one huge sample; at the opposite end of the spectrum, a 2-second instrument digitization of a violin note is also a sample. In the spirit of practical categorization, here are three main types of sample, divided by size and intent:

■ **Instrument samples.** Short digitizations of single-instrument notes, recorded and used by samplers, represent the most typical use of the word *sample*. Such recordings are samples in the dual sense of being digitizations and, more literally, samples of an instrument's tone and range. Usually, instrument samples are repeated every few half-tones throughout the instrument's pitch range and stored for playback in the sampler's memory circuits.

■ **Production samples.** In the course of producing a song, sampling can be used as a convenient and effective way of storing tracks that are repeated throughout the song. For example, the vocal hook of a song's chorus might be heard eight times. Having recorded a perfect take of that hook, there is no reason to test fate by having the vocalist attempt to perform seven additional perfect takes when one can be digitized, stored in memory, and inserted (played back) at the appropriate moments during the song. Production sampling is used in many ways; in addition to vocal tracks it can be applied to instrumental takes, eight-bar rhythm grooves, and sound effects. Contemporary pop songs, especially urban music tracks, often use production samples as raw material from which bits and pieces are cut and spliced into the songs, creating a tapestry of prerecorded sound, the audio version of modern multimedia art.

▪ **Sampled masters.** The largest kind of digital sample is an entire work that is mastered as a digitization, either in preparation for CD reproduction or simply as a convenient, portable alternative format to analog tape. The advent of digital audiotape (DAT) machines, hard disk recording programs, and, more recently, writable CD devices, has made digital mastering fairly common.

Sampling in Daily Life

Almost everyone uses sampling-enhanced products and services, often without knowing it. Though usually invisible, sampling technology helps make daily life a bit more convenient and flexible. These examples illustrate the degree to which the technology has affected various aspects of daily life.

- *Telephone voice-mail systems and digital answering machines.* For some people, the abolition of tape-based technology is never more welcome than when it comes to delivering and receiving phone messages. Digital message devices mean the end of mangled and stretched tape that can make you sound like an extraterrestrial. Corporate voice-mail systems, with menus of selections and options, also use sampling.

- *Talking toys.* Barbie need never suffer the plastic indignity of a stretched, s-l-o-w internal tape lowering her voice two octaves.

- *Voice-delivered information.* Whether you consider them annoying or helpful, all kinds of talking devices, such as automobile alarms, use sampling.

- *Electronic books.* If you've ever watched the delight and wonder of a child's face as an interactive storybook plays across a home computer screen, you can thank sampling for a new field of "edutainment."

WHAT HAS SAMPLING DONE TO MUSIC?

Everyone has heard the results of sampling technology, without necessarily knowing it. Sampled sounds and instruments are heard every day in commercials, pop songs, and television soundtracks. But sampling's effect is more than mere ubiquity. The modern producer's ability to digitize sound has had an effect on the quality of music that ranges from subtle to genre-shaping.

The modern reliance on sampled instruments, as opposed to real instrumentalists, has given much contemporary music a static sound. Sampled tones taken from acoustic instruments are realistic, but the way in which they are played ("controlled," as producers say) doesn't do a good job of emulating the constantly changing timbres of a real instrument. When a violin is bowed, for example, there are many variations in bow pressure and speed, not to mention vibrato on the fingerboard, that influence the consistency of the tone. Although these variables can be mimicked to some degree through digital manipulation of the violin sample, the result is never as vibrant, unpredictable, or realistic as the original article.

The widespread availability of all kinds of samples has lent a startling instrumental scope to pop music. It's not unusual to hear orchestral textures in a pop recording (orchestral hits are especially popular in urban music) that wouldn't have been possible in the old days without hiring an orchestra. Now, previously unfeasible production decisions are easy to carry out with one sampler and a good library of sampled sounds. Pop music and jazz, even when produced under limited budgets, are more lush than they ever were before digital music technology. Consider that $10,000 can buy a very nice digital music setup with more than one sampler or synthesizer, a good mixer, speakers, and a computer with software to run the whole thing as often as you want, for as long as you want. (Even half that amount of money could buy a computer, basic sampler, and mixer.) But $10,000 wouldn't buy a single day in a recording studio with an orchestra. Even without the orchestra, the cost of studio time alone is daunting, running up to $250 per hour for the best facilities.

As sampling has become a production technique, more than just a tool for getting acoustic instrument sounds into the mix, all kinds of strange results have been heard. Sample rip-offs are all the rage in certain types of pop music as short excerpts from one song are grafted into another. In this context, sampling has reduced pop music to material that can be cut, sewn, and woven together into patchwork quilt songs made up of other artists' grooves and licks. Such practices have bent copyright laws out of shape.

Copyrights and Wrongs

The principle of copyright is fairly simple. Copyright enforces the notion that the creator of something is the only person empowered to duplicate and distribute it. Within the copyright code there is a built-in allowance for "fair use," which enables anyone to use a very short excerpt of the created work for illustrative purposes. Fair use is invoked, for example, when quoting a book to illustrate a point in another book. In music, audio excerpts can be used in the same way if they are under 29 seconds.

Sampling throws a wrinkle into the copyright formula. What happens when a MIDI composer, equipped with a sampler, records a four-measure excerpt from a current pop music hit and incorporates it into the foundation rhythmic groove of an original work? In that case, the purpose of the quote is not illustrative; instead, the sampled excerpt becomes an important musical element in a new piece of music. How much of an excerpt, if any, should be allowed for this type of use? How much must it be altered in order to be considered legally original? These are the copyright gray areas currently being worked out on a case-by-case basis.

OTHER SIDES OF MUSIC'S DIGITAL FACE

Sampling isn't everything in digital music, but one species of a world inhabited by all computer-based production tools, a rich world that will unfold for you as you read this book. Most prominently, digital music production tools are as follows:

- **Musical Instrument Digital Interface** (MIDI) is the computer **language** (a set of instructions used to build programs) that represents the functions of musical instruments. It enables keyboards and computers to work together, providing an easy way to record and manipulate keyboard performances. MIDI is not a software program that you load into a computer, nor is it an operating system; it is a computer standard built into a digital instrument's processor and used in certain **music software** programs. MIDI processes keystrokes, pedal movements, and other mechanical aspects of performance by reducing them to computer information. By recording notes as numbers, MIDI **sequencing** (data recording) is extremely flexible, although to some degree MIDI-recorded music usually sounds artificial.

- **Hard disk recording.** Sampling technology turns computers into enhanced multitrack recorders. Blending the multitrack capacity of traditional studio tape recorders with the data-processing power of a computer, **hard disk recording**, a form of sampling, has ushered in the era of the tapeless studio.

■ **Sound synthesis.** An entirely new, infinitely expandable sound canvas has become available to composers since synthesizers hit the scene. The early uses of synthetic sound were obvious, academic, or garish. Now, though, synthesis plays a subtler role in creating atmosphere in songs and musical underscoring.

2

UNDERSTANDING COMPUTER BASICS

Despite the headlong rush to embrace the information age, many people haven't bought into the computer generation by purchasing the most obvious and visible emblem of it: a computer. Each year of this decade has been a banner year for computer manufacturers as new machines have been sold at a dizzying clip. With new types of computing machines on the horizon as we approach the end of the century, it's impossible to predict how sales will proceed, but at this writing about 70 percent of the U.S. population has yet to purchase a computer.

So if you haven't yet bought a computer, you are in the majority. For many intelligent, creative folks, the reasons for going digital haven't been compelling enough. Computers, though increasingly friendly, are hardly transparent in their interfacing. (We have a long way to go before reaching *Star Trek* levels of computer friendliness.) There is also the widespread impression that though intriguing, computers are essentially impractical high-tech toys that don't really save time, increase productivity, offer more pleasing recreation than traditional social activities—in short, they don't offer much to anyone not attracted to computing for its own sake.

There is some truth to this impression. But as the technology scene continues its rapid evolution, computers are becoming both friendlier and more useful in ways that matter to productive people. For the musician approaching technology as a beginner, it's important to remember that computers are simply tools, so they're only as creative as the person using them.

GEEKHOOD NOT REQUIRED

If you get nervous when you see an automatic teller machine, you refuse to use computerized card catalogs in the library, or entering your PIN at a gas pump pushes the limits of your technical experience, this segment is for you. It's a bare-bones description of some words and concepts that will introduce you to what computers are and how they work. Following that is an explanation of software and hardware. Later chapters delve deeper into the specific relationships between computers, music, and musicians.

The computer's fearsome reputation used to be well deserved. Some models were easier than others, but nothing was as simple as it is today. This is not to say that computing is necessarily trouble-free, but neither are cars. The computer may not be as easy to use as a television, but it offers much more interaction. People do, in a sense, create relationships with their computers, and relationships are never without rough spots.

Computer manufacturers have learned that people want the benefits of computers without having to learn a new language or develop technical repair skills. User-friendliness has long been an industry ideal, and quite a bit has been accomplished in that respect. You relate to a computer through its interface, and a lot of technological development has gone into making that interface as transparent and natural as possible. Any machine or program that is particularly friendly, with an interface that can be figured out with minimal help, is called intuitive.

Today's most intuitive computers are still a far cry from the smart machines of *Star Trek*. By and large, we still have to talk to computers by typing, they are still slow when performing difficult tasks, and they sometimes run out of memory. But the tools they present on the screen are easy to use with a little practice. The graphical user interface (GUI), developed in the 1980s concurrently by a few manufacturers, has made all the difference. Typed commands have been replaced with attractive menus and the keyboard has been largely usurped by the point-and-click mouse. Using this graphic interface, anybody who has mastered the mouse can use a well-designed program immediately.

To Stay or to Go?

Computers used to be enormous. In the earliest days of computing machines, a device that filled a room had less computational power than the average hand-held calculator of today. Following the trend of the information age, smaller became more powerful, and we have arrived on the doorstep of the new millennium with astonishing machines that can be packed in a briefcase. Portability is another bias of modern life, one that has created a demand for portable computers. So, when considering buying your computer, you are faced with the first big decision: Desktop or laptop?

Desktops take more room and give you more features. They almost always have larger monitors, and usually contain more memory, more disk drives, and better multimedia features. They are also quite a bit cheaper than laptops.

Laptops sacrifice power and features for portability. But they are hardly weaklings, and are getting stronger all the time. If you can live with a small screen and keyboard and higher cost, you may appreciate their convenience.

WHAT IS AN OPERATING SYSTEM?

If you are beginning, you'll be glad to know that you need very little technical information about operating systems. The **operating system**, or **OS**, is the software that runs your computer's basic functions. It is the set of instructions that determines internal routines such as how files are saved and retrieved, how programs will appear to the user, and how data pathways will be routed. Without an operating system, your computer would just be a blank screen. For the most part, you can ignore the operating system as long as it does its job, permitting you to do yours. (That's as technical as we need to get.)

If you begin reading computer magazines (definitely not a requirement!), you'll notice continuing debate about whether one operating system, or **platform**, is better than another. This is because in many computers the operating system can be changed at any time. But to be practical, there are only a few words and bits of crucial knowledge that a beginner needs to know.

■ **Windows.** Even computer haters have heard of Windows 95 if they listen to the news. It is one of a series of operating systems authored and marketed by the Microsoft Corporation, and it is by far the most common OS in the world. The overwhelming majority of new computers sold in the United States are equipped with Windows 95 built in. It is the successor to **Windows** (without the *95*), which is still used quite a bit in computers that came with that older version built in.

■ **Macintosh.** Macintosh, or **Mac**, is the name of a computer made by Apple, and also the name of its operating system. Although it was more popular in the mid-1980s than other computers, it has been surpassed in popularity by machines that use Windows. Clones of the Mac have begun to appear in the late 1990s.

In considering a computer, keep in mind that Windows-compatible computers, also called **PCs**, are made by many different companies, but none of them run the Macintosh operating system. Some Macintosh computers can run Windows, however. The decision boils down to what software programs you want to run because, although many programs are available in both Mac and PC versions, programs designed for one OS are not compatible with another. Macintosh programs cannot be loaded into Windows (but some Macintosh computers accept Windows programs).

Which is the better choice for musicians? The answer is far from definitive. Windows, the most popular operating system in the world, has a vast selection of software. However, the Macintosh holds a special place in the music world as the preeminent studio computer. Generally speaking, Macs (and the software written for them) have a strong reputation as a computer for the arts. Windows wins more points for business and productivity software. If there are particular Macintosh programs you know you want to use, then the answer is clear; if you will want to sample a broad selection of programs from the enormous variety of Windows packages, then you'll also find good music tools.

Q & A: OPERATING SYSTEMS

Q Is it important for a musician to know much about operating systems?

A A few crucial pieces of knowledge are important to avoid making costly mistakes at the beginning. Hands-on experience with different computing systems is always best, but lacking that, talking with experienced computer musicians is advisable. Musicians are largely immune to the drawbacks that plague the larger Macintosh community, which finds it increasingly hard to locate software. Because Macintosh computers are venerable music studio components, software companies that create music programs for them are authoring and distributing their products through the same music-oriented channels as always. But musicians who want a computer whose operating system supports a wide range of other programs should think twice. Aside from this consideration, the choice depends on how the OS looks and feels to the user. All contemporary versions of both Windows and Macintosh OSs are user-friendly and fairly easy to learn.

Q How can a musician assess an operating system?

A If a local music store displays different kinds of computers, operating systems, and music programs, the best plan is to spend some time getting familiar with how they all work. Talking with experienced users also helps. An operating system should be easy to use and intuitive in its basic operations (making menu choices, opening and saving files, starting programs), with a friendly screen environment.

It should also look nice and give the user some control over screen elements such as the size, design, and color of windows. With music programs, the operating system determines how the screen windows appear and operate, and how music files (MIDI compositions, for example, or synthesizer sound creations) are stored to and accessed from the computer's hard drive.

Q If a musician has a Windows computer, is it important to upgrade to Windows 95?

A It's more important in some cases than others. Windows 95 quickens basic computer operations such as starting programs, opening files, and saving files. If you are dealing with large blocks of data, as with a hard disk recording system, upgrading the operating system can have real benefits and make life easier. However, Windows 95 also has requirements of its own, and shouldn't be used in machines that can't support it. Check to see whether you have enough hard drive capacity for the larger operating system, and make sure you have at least 16 megabytes of RAM. A fast **video card** is also advisable. If you are using a computer primarily as a **sequencer** (to record music with digital instruments), and are comfortably productive with an earlier version of Windows (preferably 3.1), there may be no reason to rock the boat because sequencing is a light-memory activity that won't be appreciably quickened by an OS upgrade.

Q Besides Windows and Macintosh, can musicians choose from other operating systems?

A A field once quite highly populated has been reduced to the giant Windows and Mac choices, with a few less-prominent choices lingering on the sidelines. The most popular of the nonmainstream operating systems is OS/2, created by IBM. OS/2 has a few different versions, and runs on IBM and **clone** machines (that is, computers that can also run Windows and Windows 95). A small cadre of OS/2 loyalists maintains that OS/2 is superior to Windows in stability (crashes less often), design, and multitasking ability. OS/2 users are not limited to software written for their system: OS/2 is compatible with Windows.

UNIX is a venerable operating system that remains popular among technically oriented computer users. UNIX is the original OS of the Internet, and those who know the system have a head start in understanding online structures from the inside out. However, learning UNIX is not very intuitive to most people in this day of drop-down menus and picturesque GUIs. UNIX is strictly a command-based system, similar to **DOS** (the underlying OS of Windows). UNIX aficionados can relate to server technology (the skeletal technology of the Internet and other computer networks) from the ground up, but there is little practical reason for a musician to use it these days. Even cutting-edge musicians who are aggressively using the Internet and World Wide Web to promote their careers have access to friendlier tools for setting up and maintaining a Web site.

Q How can you tell what operating system a computer is using?

A Usually, when you start the computer, a banner displays what operating system is in use. If you are still in doubt, almost every piece of software used by that computer mentions the operating system in its Help files and version notices.

Q Can any operating system be put into any computer?

A No. The Macintosh operating system cannot be loaded into a Windows computer, and vice versa. However, Windows and Windows 95 can be used in all IBM-clone computers, regardless of the brand name. OS/2, an alternative operating system, can also be used by any Windows-compatible machine. Macintosh operating systems must be used by Apple Macintosh computers or the new breed of Mac clones being manufactured by other companies.

MULTIMEDIA: WHAT'S THE BIG DEAL?

It's one of the most prominent concepts, and biggest buzzwords, in the computer world. What is **multimedia**, how is it different from what went before, and what does it look like?

Before multimedia, computers operated in a single medium: static image. You can do a lot with screen images that don't move, such as write books, design illustrations, build mailing lists, print letters, balance a checkbook, create a newsletter, and all the other tasks that motivated the personal computer revolution. You can compose and record music, too. Even today, many of the most popular and productive computer programs such as music sequencers or word processors provide largely static, nonmultimedia screen environments.

Multimedia computers bring sound and video to the computer speakers and screen. This turn of events was launched by the invention of the **CD-ROM** in the 1980s (although computer CDs didn't start getting popular until about 1993), which enabled programmers to include sounds, videos, and animation in their programs. They needed CD-ROM for this because it has a much larger storage capacity than the diskettes that programs used to be packaged on. **Multimedia files** (the sound and video portions of a program) take much more memory and storage space than the static image elements.

Multimedia is finding its way into daily productivity programs such as word processors, music recorders, and databases. Almost all programs have a Help section that explains the program's functions, and multimedia can make such explanations much clearer with pop-up pictures, animation, and even on-screen videos. Wizards (built-in, automated Help subprograms that walk the user through the program's features) are greatly enhanced by multimedia. In many cases, small multimedia touches make the program more realistic and fun; one common example is a clicking sound that occurs when a screen button is activated with a mouse click. Taking this to an extreme, there are multimedia operating system enhancements that manifest sounds every time you save a file or open a window and replace static screen items with animated versions; the result is a busier (and noisier) computer presentation. It's not always very useful.

More significantly, multimedia has given birth to a whole new type of computer program. Once CD-ROM drives began appearing in new computers, programmers and publishing companies began flooding the marketplace (computer and book stores) with CD-ROM disks. These disks contain elaborate multimedia programs presenting a wide range of information and entertainment. Multimedia encyclopedias have perhaps garnered the most attention. CD-ROM shelf space is also crowded with history titles, virtual reference books, interactive children's books, pictorial travelogues, music videos, and games of increasing sophistication and realism. The CD-ROM caught the imagination of the computer marketplace, and seemed to be the guardian and promoter of multimedia technology. Until the Internet came along.

Multimedia has changed the face of telecommunications and online interaction drastically. The online universe has abruptly commandeered the attention of the computing world, raising some questions about the role of CD-ROMs.

Q & A: MULTIMEDIA FOR MUSICIANS

Q Is multimedia the same as MIDI?

A No, they are entirely different. The Musical Instrument Digital Interface (MIDI) is a computer language; multimedia is digitized sound and video. MIDI functions as a series of commands used to play a digital instrument; multimedia is a data stream organized into computer files that play sounds or display images. MIDI is used with specialized instruments and other components networked together into a MIDI studio. Multimedia doesn't need components or instruments separate from the computer and its sound card, CD drive, and speakers.

Q Can multimedia be used to compose or play music?

A Multimedia is for the display of images and the playing of sounds, but it is not primarily a creative tool. Musical compositions are featured in some multimedia presentations, but that music is created apart from the computer multimedia domain, using MIDI.

Q What do you need to get multimedia on a computer?

A You can get multimedia upgrade kits to turn a nonmultimedia computer into a multimedia machine. They include a CD-ROM drive, sound card, and speakers. You can also buy those components separately. Using multimedia online requires a modem, preferably a very fast one. A multimedia computer must have a modern display system with at least 256 colors on the screen; older systems need an upgraded video card and perhaps a new monitor.

Q How does multimedia help musicians?

A Multimedia computing offers a new frontier for composers, producers, teachers, and performers. Composers and producers can create music for multimedia products such as CD-ROM games and entertainment. Performers can share digitized versions of their recordings with other computer users by networking their computers together via the Internet and e-mail systems. Teachers benefit from computer-based educational products that use sight and sound to teach young people the basics of music.

SOFTWARE

Computers are similar to phonographs, CD players, and tape machines in at least one respect: They don't do a thing until you put something in them. As machines, they stand ready to perform a variety of functions and assist in all kinds of creative endeavors. But without a set of instructions, they are helpless. These instructions are the software that bring the hardware to life.

The computer **hardware** is the actual machine, made of metal, plastic, silicon chips, and other firm materials. **Software** is made up of stored coded instructions written using one of a huge assortment of computer languages. Loaded into the computer via disk, it gives the hardware specific abilities, transforming it from a generalized processing machine to a specific creative tool. Operating systems are a special software category.

PROGRAMS

Software generally refers to programs. **Programs** are loaded into a computer (you are guided through this process by little automated subprograms called installers), where they determine what the screen will look like and how the computer will function according to your commands. The screen environment includes certain windows designed to help with your task, menus that provide selections you'll need, and the means to save your work. Software programs turn your computer into a specialized tool for creating words, music, art, or databases.

Overview of Programs

▦ Many competing programs are available for most popular music functions, such as recording or building a concert mailing list.

▦ You can acquire software from at least two sources: stores and online. Software stores sell packaged programs on floppy disks and CD-ROMs. Inexpensive titles can cost as little as $15.00, whereas full-featured professional programs sell for hundreds of dollars.

▦ Software programs are written and made available for the type of operating system you have, and cannot be used in another type. For example, a Windows 95 program will not work in a Macintosh computer. A version of the program may be available for the Macintosh user, however, and certain operating systems are cross-compatible, such as OS/2 and Windows.

▦ Programs are stored permanently on your computer's hard drive. You don't have to enter them into the computer every time you want to use them, but you do need to activate them when you turn the computer on. This is called booting up the program, or running it.

FILES CAN BE PROGRAMS

Programs aren't the only kind of software. In fact, any coherent collection of data that is used by a computer is software. In computer-speak, a **file** can be anything from a music recording program to a recording made with that program; from a MIDI sequence to a mailing list database. MIDI itself is not a file or a program; it is a **standard**, or a software language from which certain programs are built, and it is used to operate digital instruments.

Computers work with files (programs) to create files. One creates **MIDI files** with programs that use the MIDI standard.

The MIDI standard is discussed in detail beginning on page 89.

What Are Files?

■ The file you create can be incomplete or tiny; it is still a file.

■ Programs load files that you have saved and named, enabling you to alter or continue a work in progress.

■ Created files can be shared with people who have the same program you used to create the file. In some cases, created files are generic, and can be loaded, viewed, and altered by many programs.

Q & A: COMPUTER FILES

Q Can computer files be taken out of the computer?
A Yes, files can be removed using a floppy disk and loaded into a different computer (if it has a compatible operating system) that also has a floppy disk drive. Files can also be backed up (archived for safety) onto tape or specialized external hard disk drives. Text and music notation files can also be removed in the form of printouts if the computer is equipped with a printer.

Q When a file is moved to a disk, is it taken from the original computer?
A Usually not. Files are generally copied to a floppy disk or a backup disk drive, so a copy still remains on the original internal hard drive.

Q How many files can fit in a computer?
A That depends on the size of the computer's hard drive, which is

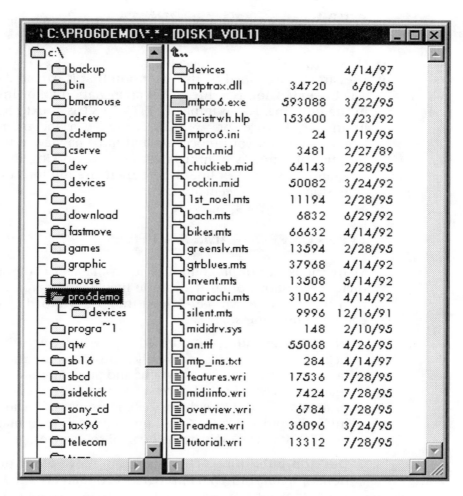

Different file types are known by their extensions (the three-letter suffix after the dot). In this folder, the .exe file is a sequencer program (Master Tracks Pro) and the .mts files are music pieces created with that program.

where files are stored. It also depends on the size of the files. In other words, there is no simple answer, but larger hard drives store more files than smaller ones. Most modern computers, equipped with very large hard drives, store hundreds or thousands of program and saved files.

Q Are there many different file types?

A Yes. The main types are program files that let you create and save files, the saved files themselves, **sound files**, **graphic** (picture) **files**, movie files, and compressed files that can be downloaded from online sources. But within each of those categories there are many types of file.

Q How can you tell what type a file is?

A Files are distinguished by the extension that is part of their name. The **file extension** is a three-letter abbreviation following a period in the filename. For example, LETTER4.TXT is a text file, readable in any word processor. ANNCMNT.DOC is a document file specific to a certain word processor, and must be viewed within that specific software. As beginners get used to working in individual programs or surfing online, where there are millions of files, the extensions begin to seem less cryptic.

TYPES OF PROGRAMS AND FILES

Many thousands of program files are available for computers, and there are millions of created music files floating around. But the wealth of software can be divided into a few broad categories of computer usefulness.

- **Word processing.** As a glorified typewriter, a **word processor** helps you write words, not music. Musicians use them to write business letters, concert programs and program notes, lyrics, and many other word-based necessities. The files you create can be printed and saved in either a generic format that can be loaded into all word processors, or a program-specific format that can be reliably viewed only in the original software program.

- **Desktop publishing.** The next step above word processing, desktop publishing (DTP) programs contain art and layout features that let you create posters, flyers, concert programs, newsletters, and other promotional items.

- **Music.** There is a broad range of educational, recording, and MIDI software that takes advantage of the modern computer's multimedia capacity.

- **Art.** Design, drawing, photo retouching, and painting programs abound. These can be used to add graphic elements to concert announcements and other promotions, or to design album covers.

- **Online access.** Some software is designed to work with a computer's modem and connect you with an online service, the Internet, or your e-mail box.

- **Database.** Database programs keep lists. These are good for maintaining mailing lists for advertising concerts, selling recordings, recruiting students, and any other customer contact. Many such programs have features that make it easy to print address labels and sort them by state or zip code.

■ **Education.** The emergence of multimedia computing has brought a whole new look to educational software. The flagships of the new fleet of programs are interactive multimedia encyclopedias. Music learning and appreciation are enhanced considerably by multimedia computers.

■ **Games.** Who doesn't want to have fun? Computer games range from checkers to high-tech flight simulators.

■ **Spreadsheets.** These programs facilitate complex calculations such as balancing a checkbook, creating a budget, or performing a cost–benefit analysis or project analysis (plugging in variables such as the cost of upgrading equipment or renting a studio).

HARDWARE

Considering their formidable appearance (not to mention price), you'd be surprised to look inside a computer and see how simple they can be. A computer is basically a big circuit board connected to devices that store information. There's also a power source that gets plugged into the wall. Things do get complex within the circuits themselves, where millions of digital pathways are carved out of silicon. Understanding a computer's creative usefulness will come easier if you can conceive, in a general way, how a computer is constructed. What follows is not a computer science course, nor will it get too technical; it's merely an overview of what a computer is made of and what those components do.

BRAINS OF THE OPERATION

The central processing unit (**CPU**), also known as the processing chip, is the brain of the machine. Entire industries rise and fall on the fortunes of companies that invent and develop these small, square wafers. Most consumer computer models are defined by the type and brand of central processing chip they contain. Examples you may have heard of include 486, Pentium, Pentium Pro, and Power PC machines.

The processor is attached to the main circuit board (called the motherboard), and performs the computations that create digital music, art, and manuscripts. It is usually removable and replaceable. This means that a computer's power and speed can be upgraded for the cost of replacing the single central chip (usually a couple hundred dollars). Processing chips are defined in three ways:

- **Brand name.** This is simply the company that made the chip. Some of the biggest chip makers are Intel, Cyrix, IBM, and Motorola.

- **Generation.** Chip development proceeds in quantum leaps. When a chip can be made that represents a large enough improvement over previous generations to become a useful enhancement to computer owners, it is manufactured, marketed, and built into new models. The 486, **Pentium**, Pentium Pro, and Power PC chips are examples of generational levels.

- **Speed.** Also known as cycle speed, this is the swiftness with which a bit of computer information can cycle in and out of a processing chip. A chip's speed is measured in **megahertz** (MHz). The higher the number, the faster the chip.

These three features combine to define a processing chip, and therefore the speed and power of a computer using that chip. This is why computers are advertised with descriptions of the processing chip. People even talk about their computers strictly in terms of the chip characteristics, regardless of the model of the computer itself, as in, "I just got a great deal on an Intel Pentium 133 machine." Translation: "I hope I got a decent deal on a computer that uses a processing chip built by Intel, Pentium model, running at 133 MHz."

STORING THE GOODS: DRIVES

In order to be useful as a creative tool, the computer must give you a way to store what you make. The technology wouldn't be worth much if you lost your work every time you turned the machine off. Every computer comes with at least one drive, which is basically a data recorder. A computer drive lets you record, or write, your work to a location you can find again later. (You don't need to know anything about data to do this; the Save feature is built into every computer program that exists.) Computers have historically offered two basic options: hard drives and floppy drives.

HARD DRIVES

Hard drives usually exist within the computer, out of sight. They are the main storage drive of a computer. They offer a couple of advantages:

■ **Speed.** Hard drives operate faster than floppy drives. This swiftness shows up when you are saving and retrieving your work. Most people save their ongoing computer projects often, so that if the computer loses power suddenly, a recently updated version is available when the power is restored. It would be frustrating to have to pause for long every few minutes when saving, as is the case when writing a large work-in-progress file to a floppy drive. Hard drive speed is also noticeable when you start software programs because they are usually stored on the hard drive.

■ **Lots of storage space.** The size of a hard drive is defined by how much data it can hold. Data is measured in bits and bytes (bytes are groups of bits, just as words consist of letters), and hard drive capacity is measured in **megabytes** (MB). (One megabyte equals a million bytes.) During the last couple of years, hard drives have gotten huge because the programs that must fit on them have become huge and the advent of multimedia computing has given us creative files that are huge. Before 1995, a 500-megabyte hard drive was considered ample; now it is barely adequate. The good news for consumers is that prices have plummeted accordingly, and computer owners can upgrade for a couple of hundred dollars to a hard drive that holds thousands of megabytes of information. (A **gigabyte**, abbreviated GB, is one thousand megabytes, and hard drives storing up to 2 gigs are common.)

Buried as they are in the computer, hard drives cannot easily be removed and placed in another computer (although there is a special breed of removable hard drive, sometimes used in laptops). They can be removed to be replaced by another hard drive, but this requires performing surgery on the computer; many people leave such upgrades in the hands of qualified technicians.

FLOPPY DRIVES

Before there were hard drives, there were floppies. The original floppy disks didn't look exactly like modern floppies, though. They were larger, and flopped around if you waved them. Today's standard is a smaller disk (3.5 inches in diameter), housed in a rigid plastic container that is reassuringly firm. The earliest personal computers exclusively used floppies for storage; hard drives were considered exotic and unnecessary at that time. Despite the reliance on hard drives these days, floppy drives are still included in computers, and can be found on the front panel. There is a slot for placing a floppy disk in the drive; the format is completely standardized, so every brand of disk works with every brand of drive.

Floppy Features

■ **Backup.** Hard drives may be quicker and larger, but they're neither infallible nor immortal. They break and wear down, just like any machine. Saving crucial files to floppy disks is a security measure, like keeping valuable documents in a fireproof safe.

■ **Portability.** Floppy disks are conveniently small and interchangeable. You can copy files to one or more of them, insert the disks into another computer, and use those files in the second machine. This is great for sharing files between two people, or for one person who has more than a single computer.

The big disadvantages to floppy drives are their small storage capacity and slow speed. It can take several times as long to access data from (or save it to) a floppy drive as from a hard drive. Of course, if it's only a matter of a few seconds, it doesn't matter much. Still, most people back up their work to floppies only once a day. In the size department, a 3.5-inch floppy holds 1.4 megabytes of information. Compared to a 1-gig (1,000-MB) hard drive, that's rather small. For this reason, floppies are used for backing up small working files, not entire programs.

OTHER STORAGE DRIVES

Backup drive technology continues to evolve. Because enormous hard drives are now common, the issue of backing up larger files has become urgent. As more people use computers to make music and other art, they increasingly outgrow the limitations of small and slow floppy drives for saving their work. A few options have been introduced to deal with this problem:

■ **Tape backup drives.** These devices use magnetic tape, just like that used for recording music. The formats differ (like the differences between cassette tape and multitrack recording tape), but the principle is the same. Tape can hold a lot of data, depending on how wide and long it is. Tape backup drives can be purchased (they don't often come built into the computer) in either internal or external versions. The internals operate much like floppy devices, and are usually positioned just above or below the floppy drive. Externals sit outside the computer, connected to the back of the machine with a cable. Typically, tape drives can hold between 125 and several hundred megabytes of data; they offer a good way to back up entire hard drives, or at least large portions of them. They are somewhat slow, though. A massive backup session can take hours, and is often initiated just before bed.

■ **External disk drives.** Some companies have developed special disk formats for backup purposes. They are external units that plug into the back of the computer, and they enable you to copy files from your hard drive to a disk. These disks hold much more than a floppy, but usually less than a hard drive. One popular model, the Zip drive (made by Iomega), holds 100 MB of information. This is a convenient middle ground, especially considering the disks are removable. You can buy several disks for saving large amounts of work.

■ **New floppy drives.** Most recently, some companies have announced emerging floppy technology that would dramatically increase the capacity of 3.5-inch disks. The trick is to make a drive that can use the new high-capacity disks, but also read from and write to the lower-capacity floppies.

■ **Reusable CDs.** Until recently, CD-ROMs could be used only to deliver complex multimedia programs. They could not be used to save original data, like a floppy disk. But technology marches on, and the writable CD has been developed. Early models are expensive, but will soon become more common and less expensive as more models are developed.

■ THE MARRIAGE OF CDS AND COMPUTERS

If you don't own a computer but have seen advertisements for them, you might wonder about the CD drives that are increasingly standard equipment. Can you put a music CD in a computer, and if so, what is the point? Well, you *can* play music disks through a multimedia computer, but that is not the main function of a CD drive. Nor is it used in the same way as a hard drive, floppy drive, or other storage device.

CDs can store digital information, and lots of it. (Even music

CDs contain nothing more than data.) Accordingly, they are ideal for packaging large software programs. In earlier years, any computer program could be packaged on a single floppy disk. Those days are definitely over, as software has become more complex and swollen with multimedia features that take large blocks of memory. Just before computer CDs were developed, software packages were typically requiring three to five floppy disks. Now, a single CD houses huge programs that include colorful graphics, animations, videos, and sound.

The disks that fit into computer CD drives are called CD-ROMs. *ROM* stands for read-only memory, and implies that the disk cannot be used as a storage platter for your work. In other words, you can read from the CD, but you can't write (save) to it.

CD drives are becoming standard, and it may soon be difficult to find software packaged any other way. Currently, most popular programs offer both floppy and CD choices. The larger, CD versions generally provide more multimedia glitz, sometimes even including animated Help features, complete with explanatory videos.

BELLS AND WHISTLES: COMPUTER SOUND

A trip to a large computer store will convince you that these machines are talkative, musical creatures. Showroom models are usually busy running video self-presentations, complete with soundtracks and special effects. Not every computer can put on such an impressive show, but multimedia machines have become the norm.

The one computer part that defines a machine, more than anything else, as a multimedia computer is the sound card. A **sound card** is a circuit board with a small control panel that is visible on the back of the machine. This panel contains audio input and output jacks, a microphone jack, and a headphone jack. When speakers are plugged into the outputs, the computer is wired for sound. Furthermore, the sound card incorporates a miniature MIDI synthesizer (without a keyboard, of course), and as such is ready to respond to a MIDI sequencer. Finally, and surprisingly, the sound card is usually where game-players plug in their joysticks.

Sound cards deal with all sorts of sound files that the computer encounters. If a fancy software program includes the sound of wind chimes whenever a window is opened, for example, it is the sound card that processes the sound and plays it through the speakers. If an audio file is found during an online surfing session, the sound card plays it. Same with MIDI files.

There is some variety in the quality and fidelity of sound cards, as with any other audio component. The standard of 16-bit cards has become universal (*16-bit* refers to the amount of data used to define the digitization of sound; anything less than 16 bits isn't enough to convince our ears that the sound is real). Some of the cards provide better MIDI sounds; typically, the high-end models use digitally recorded instrument samples in addition to synthesized tones.

Sound cards can be added to mute computers, but they are useless without speakers. The most popular way to upgrade a computer's multimedia capabilities is with a multimedia upgrade kit; these one-stop solutions include a sound card, speakers, and CD-ROM drive. (Usually some CDs are thrown in, too.)

TYPING, POINTING, CLICKING, SEEING

Now for the obvious. You won't make much music with your computer if you can't communicate with it. The keyboard, mouse, and monitor provide the interface components between you and the computer.

- **Keyboard.** Based on a typewriter, the **keyboard** allows you to type words and numbers into the computer. There are also specialized function keys that perform particular tasks, depending on the program you're using. For the most part, keyboards are interchangeable and upgradable. They are like violin bows: If you don't like the feel of the one that came with your computer, you can replace it with a more agreeable model. Some revolutionary models attempt to cater to the unique shape and position of our hands when typing by splitting the keyboard and angling the two halves. Others include built-in pointing devices to replace the standalone mouse.

- **Mouse.** The **mouse** is a device that fits under your hand, and stands ready to roll around the desk (usually on a mouse pad). If you watch the screen while doing this, you'll see a small object moving in tandem with the mouse movements; this is the cursor, and is used to point the computer's attention to a certain spot on the screen. Once the cursor is positioned where you want, pressing the mouse's button tells the computer that the next words you type (or notes you enter, or lines you draw, depending on the program) should begin there. The mouse is a shortcut pointing device. Many models are available with several designs. Some remain stationary while you rotate a trackball, some are cordless, and some are built into the keyboard and require you to drag your finger across a small pad.

■ **Monitor.** The **monitor** is the computer's screen, on which you can see what's going on. Like televisions, they come in different sizes and degrees of resolution. (In other words, some look better than others.) The size is a diagonal measurement of the entire picture tube; the actual viewing size may be somewhat smaller than the advertised number of inches. Fourteen inches is the smallest screen generally available now; they range up to 21 inches, and these large monitors are very expensive. Laptop monitors are smaller, of course, because they are limited by the size of the laptop computer to which they are attached. The largest laptop monitor is about 12.5 inches diagonally. Like keyboards, monitors are interchangeable as long as you buy one for the same type of computer. (Don't buy a Windows monitor for a Macintosh computer.) They are simply plugged into the back of the computer.

PRINTERS

A modern computer is really a collection of components. It may look like an integrated whole, and certainly (at least ideally) it functions that way. But when it comes to upgrades and options, the computer can be approached as a collection of parts. All kinds of features can be added, upgraded, and tacked onto the exterior.

The **printer** is the most common peripheral component. Printers can be used for creating paper versions of manuscripts (words and music) and artwork.

Types of Printers

Nothing in the computer world is always simple, and that goes for choosing a printer. Here are the three main types:

- Dot-matrix printers work by placing tiny dots in familiar shapes on the paper. The earliest versions could draw only nine dots per inch; later models increased this barely adequate number to 24. Dot-matrix printers are not being manufactured anymore, and can be found only as very cheap used equipment.

- Inkjet and bubble-jet printers are closely related, and offer a great improvement in quality over dot-matrix. The early versions of this printer technology had the drawback of smearing on the page if you touched the ink too soon after printing. This has been corrected in most cases, but even the best inkjets don't create letters, notes, and images as sharply as laser printers. However, color inkjets have become quite popular and affordable, and a few models create very impressive color documents.

- Laser printers used to be priced for the corporate market primarily, but have become a feasible alternative for the masses. The prices for color lasers are still in orbit, but black-and-white desktop models have plummeted in price, and are now being used extensively in homes. They are faster, and provide crisper lines, than other types of printing. Most people, when shopping for a new printer, find themselves choosing between a color inkjet and a black-and-white laser.

MODEMS

Modems are the computer's key to global networking. Available in either external or internal models, they connect the computer to a phone line, enabling you to log into the Internet, online services, and specialized music bulletin boards. The advantages and delights of using a modem are described in more detail in Part Three of this book.

ADD-ON CARDS

The motherboard of most computers contains empty slots for plugging in new circuit boards. As such, most computers are built to be expanded and upgraded. It may seem impossibly technical to add a circuit board to your computer, but it is not difficult; even so, the intimidating task of taking the case off your computer and inserting a new board can be left for a service technician.

These add-on circuit boards are usually called **expansion cards.** Sound cards are typical; you can also upgrade the machine's video card, giving you faster screen movements and smoother video playback. Radio and TV cards allow your computer to receive broadcast signals. (Yes, you can watch a television program in the corner of your monitor while composing your latest piece or watch a video of a recording session while rescoring sections of the work.)

MEMORY

Adding extra **memory** is popular. The more random access memory (**RAM**) your computer has, the quicker it will operate, and the more programs you can run simultaneously. Memory comes in long, narrow chips that plug into slots on the motherboard. Again, you need to open up the computer to do this, or let the store do it for you.

3

MUSIC COMPUTERS AND SOFTWARE

The intersection of personal computers and music followed closely on the heels of the introduction of the personal computer itself. The early 1980s saw a growing interest in computing as a home activity, first as a hobby, then for productivity. As the technology developed, specific models and operating systems waxed and waned in popularity. The available music software largely determines the usefulness of any computer to musicians, and this factor as much as the machines themselves influences the fortunes of different machines.

EVOLUTION OF MUSIC COMPUTERS

The first music computers rode the coattails of the MIDI phenomenon in the early and mid-1980s. Today's music machines perform many varied musical tasks, but in the early days of music computing, MIDI was the only digital game in town. Sampling was not yet popular, hard disk recording was not yet a gleam in a producer's eye, multimedia was more than ten years away, and most musicians didn't have a clue that online networking was a possibility. However, MIDI began taking the music world by storm on all levels, from professional to hobbyist, and personal computers began moving into the first primitive home music studios.

REAL WORDS

Without computers, 98% of the music that comes out of this studio would be impossible. But that's not a bad thing: People have a bias against music that has anything to do with a computer, but the test is really in the music and the musician. Some musicians make music with computers that shouldn't be made. But that doesn't make the computers bad—it makes the composer bad.

Craig Patterson
midigod@aol.com

Looking back over the years 1982 to 1997, we can see a chronology of trends that has led us to the current state of computers in music.

THE EARLY YEARS

Pioneers of the personal computer age remember with fondness one of the first machines to enjoy widespread popularity: Amiga's Commodore 64. The *64* referred to the number of kilobytes of memory available, a pitiful amount by modern standards. Still, by the benchmarks of the day it provided abundant computational power and speed, and C-64s found their way into musical households almost as much as they infiltrated the bookkeeping and game-playing habits of nonmusical enthusiasts.

Equipped with a MIDI–computer interface, a MIDI keyboard, and appropriate software, a C-64 owner could record MIDI music into the computer, enjoying much more control in editing, altering, and otherwise manipulating the resulting musical data than was possible before.

AMIGA AND ATARI

During the 1980s, two computer companies were designing and building innovative machines that affected the course of MIDI and the lives of plugged-in musicians.

Amiga, beginning with the Commodore 64 and continuing with more advanced models, was developing an operating system that lent itself to two important computing functions: graphics and multitasking. (Multitasking is a computer's ability to run more than one software program at a time.) Although neither of these two features relates specifically to music, they helped build a following among all kinds of users, which encouraged software developers to write programs for the machine in various fields, including music. The emphasis on graphic manipulation served to establish Amigas as artistic computers, enhancing their appeal to musicians. A system that could multitask a few programs simultaneously made it a more convenient computer to use.

In the meantime, the well-known game manufacturer Atari was diving into the personal computer market with a machine that was designed specifically with musicians in mind: the Atari ST. It might not have been easy to overcome a corporate image as a builder of high-tech toys, but the ST was taken seriously by musicians right from the beginning because of a feature that has remained unique to the Atari brand up to the present: MIDI ports on the back of the computer. This eliminated the need to buy a MIDI interface to connect the computer with a keyboard, and more importantly, it scored big points in the musical community by recognizing the importance of MIDI applications in a computer. Many home producers, and professional studio-owners as well, felt that the Atari was the perfect music machine, and it appeared that the ST was on its way to becoming enthroned as the reigning music studio computer for both hobbyists and pros.

Both Amiga and Atari machines were encumbered by the typical drawbacks of early computers. Many of the features now long taken for granted, such as hard drives and plenty of working memory, were not yet standard equipment. It seems hard to believe that serious music was being produced on computers that didn't have hard drives, but the primitive technology was more than compensated for by the new-found power of home computing with MIDI. Software developers were beginning to write music programs of considerable sophistication, and the personal computer was well on its way to becoming a musician's power tool. Sequencers, the programs that make MIDI recordings, remained the cornerstones of a home producer's software edifice, but other applications began appearing, such as sound editors and patch librarians.

Sequencers are discussed further beginning on page 126.

THE MAC

As the Atari ST began gaining dominance over the Amiga because of its music-specific configuration and friendly operating system, the outlook seemed rosy for the game company. But Atari loyalists who were hoping for universal acceptance of the ST in music studios were disappointed as the Apple Macintosh rose to its position as the personal computer of the 1980s. The Mac was easy to use, well promoted, and established in almost every school that had computers, and became hugely popular in homes for balancing checkbooks, writing letters, keeping records, playing games, and all sorts of other tasks.

As legions of new computer users embraced the Mac, an economy of scale affected the music world. True, the Apple computers were more expensive than Atari STs, but the range of software was greater and more easily available, and soon more people had Macs than Ataris, making it easier to share music files if they came from a Mac. For a long time the ST held its own against the Mac as a music standard, but in the end two factors spelled its demise: deft marketing on Apple's part, combined with great music software being turned out by independent developers for the Mac. As the decade proceeded, it became clear that the Mac, not the ST, was becoming the industry standard. Most studios, especially professional and semiprofessional, housed a MIDI-equipped Mac. Atari continued to develop its product line, introducing new computer models pre-equipped with MIDI interfaces, and to this day Atari fans are keeping the platform alive through underground distribution of software and support, particularly in Europe. It is now very difficult (indeed, it was never easy) to find Atari music software in a store, and the company is no longer promoting or developing the computer end of its business.

The Mac brought maturity to music computing, as it did to general computing. Potent machines were running extremely powerful programs for recording and manipulating music in studios and homes all over the world. Although Apple never addressed the needs of musicians directly in its hardware design, and everyone still had to buy separate MIDI interfaces to connect a Mac to a keyboard, the Mac was as popular in the world of music as it was in other segments of the computing population.

IBMS, CLONES, AND WINDOWS

The final stage of this odyssey took place as the 1980s gave way to the 1990s, and continues to the present day. IBM computers played second fiddle to Macs through the mid-1980s, thanks to a thorny operating system, DOS, which requires users to issue text-based commands to run programs. By comparison, the graphic, mouse-driven, point-and-click operating system of the Macintosh was friendlier and more intuitive to new users than DOS. However, the balance shifted as a result of two factors: IBM clones and the Windows operating system.

Clones are computers made by different manufacturers, using the same operating system. They may have different hardware features, such as the number and type of storage drives, amount of memory, size of monitor, speed of the main processing chip, and so forth, but because the underlying software system is the same they are considered essentially the same computer. IBM licensed its personal computing system to other companies, thereby creating a marketplace filled with competing computer products. One sure result of such competition is lower prices, and suddenly the Macintosh was being drastically undersold on all sides. (Apple was not licensing its system to other companies.) This was not a problem for the Mac at the beginning because it was a much easier computer to use, and enjoyed the cachet of being the upscale, superior platform for many types of computing, certainly for music. Although MIDI and music programs were being written for the IBM and its clones, they were barely making a peep in the music community.

Then came the second development: Windows. The Windows operating system, developed by the Microsoft Corporation, created a Mac-like computing environment for IBM clones. This system, combined with lower, competition-driven prices, began making a difference in people's choices on a massive scale. This trend continued for several years, until the Mac's popularity lagged drastically. On the music scene, it has remained a productive and favored studio computer, thanks to great software and widespread use among studios that share files. A home producer who wants to create the background tracks of an album project at home and take the files to a professional studio for completion will have an easier job if the home computer matches the studio computer. The predominance of Macs in pro studios makes them a good choice in the home, if only for that reason.

Windows and its successor, Windows 95, have become so dominant in the world computing marketplace that it would be impossible for any industry, including music, to remain unaffected. People getting into music production as a hobby or avocation, and already owning a Windows computer, tend to prefer using that machine to buying another just for music. And the music software situation has changed dramatically, with excellent Windows programs rivaling the highly evolved Mac music creations now common. Although devoted Mac users have no reason to switch computer brands, new users no longer have such a compelling reason to choose Mac over Windows for their music computing platform.

MUSIC COMPUTERS TODAY

Where does this leave musicians who want to go digital today? There are several operating systems to choose from, but only two to consider seriously: Windows and Macintosh. The Amiga and Atari operating systems represent a choice not only of software, but of hardware—the operating system is owned exclusively by the computer manufacturer and is included with the machine. Macintosh OS runs on Macintosh computers and their clones. DOS and Windows run on IBM computers and their clones. (Windows does not run without DOS, which serves as a subplatform.)

Lots of Computer Choices

■ **Amiga.** Primarily a used-marketplace item now, the Amiga still runs music programs, if they can be found. You won't find the hardware or the software in most stores. If you acquire a used Amiga, you'll need to network with other owners and scour the online systems (such as the Internet) for music software.

■ **Atari.** The once-proud music machine is still in fairly wide use, and used computers can be found, very inexpensively. They are no longer considered powerful machines by any standards, but can still be productive. With their built-in MIDI capability, they make good introductory computers, especially if dedicated to a home music studio. They are easy to use; kids can learn them without much trouble. You might have to buy an external hard drive (that is compatible with this machine) if you get an older ST lacking this basic feature. Good software exists if you can find it; online networking is helpful.

■ **DOS.** DOS is the underlying operating system for IBM-clone computers. It exists as a foundation to the Windows operating system, but can also run on its own without Windows, and leaves available considerably more memory and disk space on the computer. Some people who have been using computers for many years still prefer the plain DOS interface, without the more graphic, menu-enhanced screen environment that Windows provides. There is plenty of older software for DOS, but little new software is being written. New programs generally can be run only in Windows, making the DOS choice something of a dead end.

■ **Windows.** This category includes Windows 95. Most older Windows programs can run under both systems, but new Windows 95 programs must use that operating system. Windows users can share files easily. There is also a tremendous amount of available software in all venues, from retail stores to downloadable **freeware** stored online. Although music software developers were slow to embrace the Windows platform, they have made up for lost time. Plenty of great software exists. You will need to purchase a MIDI interface to run a MIDI studio with a Windows computer.

■ **OS/2.** The operating system invented by IBM is not recognized as having any particular musical advantage over Windows, but you can run Windows software in the OS/2 operating system. OS/2 enjoys a loyal band of followers who insist on its superiority over Windows and Windows 95.

■ **Macintosh.** As a preeminent digital music tool, the Mac still stands strong. Excellent software and widespread use in all kinds of studios make this a good choice, even as the once-reigning company falters in the modern computer marketplace. Apple has finally begun licensing its systems to other manufacturers, which will result in broader selections and better prices. Also, Macs are being introduced that can run Windows programs, a substantial incentive for musicians who intend to run business software.

TYPES OF MUSIC SOFTWARE

A computer, even loaded with the latest operating system, is nothing without software. It is software programs, called **applications,** that enable computers to do things. Each application program essentially turns the computer into a new machine, although they all have similarities. Run one program (word processing) and your computer is a sophisticated typewriter; run another and the machine is suddenly a CD playback deck; a third application turns your computer into a video arcade game.

Music software is an application category in itself, comprising a range of program types that turn computers into specialized music machines. Here are the main music software types:

■ Sequencing (for recording MIDI tracks)

■ Hard disk recording (for making live tracks)

■ Sound programming (for creating new sounds from keyboards and tone modules)

■ Sampling (for creating new digitized examples of real sounds)

■ Notation (for turning compositions into written music)

REAL WORDS

While software has grown in ability by leaps and bounds over the last decade, look for much more to happen in the next decade. There's still a long way to go before musical software runs out of opportunities to help the composer, and much of the technology has a long way to go before it will be as useful as we would all like.

Craig Patterson
midigod@aol.com

SEQUENCING

Sequencing is a strange word for *recording,* and many newcomers to the digital scene are bewildered by it. Why not just call sequencing programs recording programs? The difference between (analog) sound recording and (digital) sequencing lies in what is being recorded. A tape machine records sound waves. Sequencers read MIDI data.

MIDI data is created when you play a note on a MIDI instrument, and it is that data that the sequencer records and then feeds back into the instrument to play the note back.

Because each note of MIDI data is a separate entity, called an event, existing autonomously from surrounding MIDI notes, the sequencer is recording a sequence of MIDI events. Sequencing programs keep track of the note values and intervals, organizing them into tracks representing different instrumental or vocal parts.

The difference between normal sound recording and sequencing lies in what is being recorded. A tape machine records sound waves. Sequencers record only MIDI data, which, when played back, causes MIDI instruments to make sounds (musical ones, it is to be hoped).

Continuum of Music Technology

Sequencing software, a MIDI tool, has been around only since the early 1980s. But the principle of sequencing—a device that records the mechanics of a musical instrument, as opposed to the sounds of the instrument—has a surprisingly long history. Consider two devices that are not high-tech by modern standards but nevertheless contain the sequencing principle: music boxes and player pianos. Music boxes, dating from the 1700s, encode their musical performances by placing sequences of upraised pins on rotating cylinders. Each pin, like a MIDI event, represents a note. Player pianos, which came onto the scene in the nineteenth century, also use a rotating cylinder, around which is wrapped a scroll of paper with sequences of holes punched in it. The holes trip the piano's playing mechanism.

A century and a half of technology aside, the big advantage to computer sequencing over a player piano roll is that the average person can use sequencing to record, not just play back an already-made recording. The first rudimentary sequencers were built into electronic keyboards. Sequencing software made its appearance in the 1980s, and although they were a giant step forward from the limitations of hardware sequencers, the early programs were primitive compared to today's slick software tools.

Sequencers are explained in detail beginning on page 126.

There are many popular and powerful sequencing programs for Windows and Macintosh computers, as well as lingering powerhouses for dwindling numbers of Amiga and Atari users. Each program is different in design and approach, but there are universal similarities. Typical professional-quality programs provide the following screen environments (using a variety of names) for composing and recording music through MIDI data:

- **Track sheet.** Like the paper map of tape tracks filled out by the recording engineer of a traditional studio, the software track sheet lets you sort out what part is recorded on which track. This is especially important because software sequencers have dozens of available tracks. The track sheet is an on-screen list, on which you can determine whether the track is in Record, Playback, Mute, or Solo mode. The tracks can be named, often with enough room for details such as the **synthesizer patch** (sound program) used for that track's part, or other production details related to the part.

- **Transport window.** The window containing the transport controls (Play, Stop, Record, Rewind, Fast Forward) doesn't need to be big and is often incorporated into a large window environment, such as the track sheet.

- **Track editing window.** Sequencing programs include some graphic representation of entire tracks for editing operations that affect those entire tracks. This is where you can swap tracks, or perform some operation (such as **quantizing**, which corrects rhythmic irregularities) that alters every event on a track equally.

- **Event editing window.** Another screen representation is used for making adjustments and corrections to individual notes within a track, or even MIDI events (such as pedaling and pitch-bend wheel movements) that aren't notes. The MIDI events can

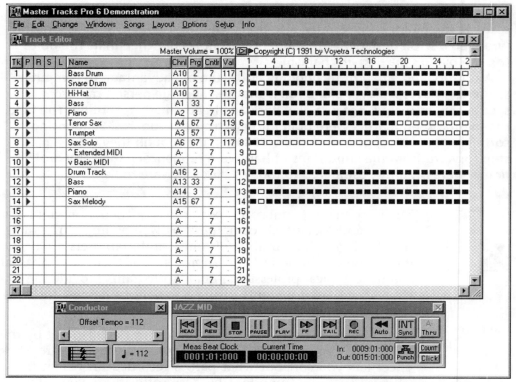

A typical sequencing software window, showing the track sheet and control panels. (Master Tracks Pro 6, Passport Software.)

be portrayed as a simple list, but this is considered the least intuitive and accessible way to view and address musical data.

■ **Piano-roll editing window.** You need to develop a real familiarity with music as a data sequence in order to make sense of an event list. A more friendly and very common software device presents MIDI events as black holes in an otherwise white player-piano roll that moves horizontally across the screen as the sequence plays back. A picture of a keyboard to one side acts as a pitch reference, and using this system is a painless way of finding mistakes in the recording and fixing them. This is a popular and effective way of presenting data to keyboard players who don't read music, and works pretty well for those who do, too.

■ **Notation editing window.** Best of all for musicians who read music, the sequence is displayed on the screen in standard notation. It can be comically confusing if the recorded track was played a bit inaccurately, as whole notes are turned into dotted half notes tied to a dotted eighth, with a sixteenth note rest to

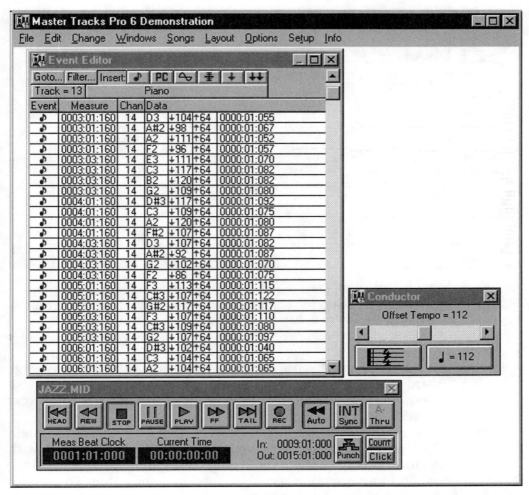

A MIDI event editing window in a sequencing program. Most programs let you edit individual MIDI events by presenting a list. (Master Tracks Pro 6, Passport Software.)

round out the measure. Such literalness must be expected from a computer, and the resulting fastidious clutter on the screen can make editing troublesome. Nevertheless, notation-based editing screens are a godsend for traditional musicians venturing into computer software, and are sometimes linked to a program's ability to print sheet music.

HARD DISK RECORDING

Hard disk recording software turns computers into digital recording decks. In theory, any computer with a hard drive will do, but

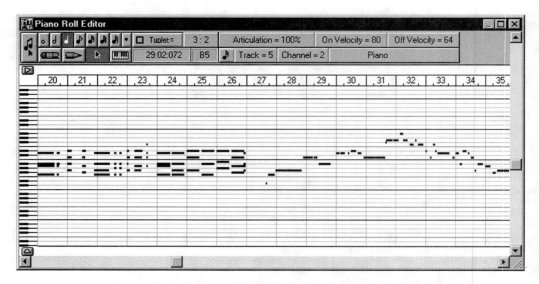

Piano-roll editing in a sequencing program. It takes some getting used to, but piano-roll editing of sequences is flexible and useful. (Master Tracks Pro 6, Passport Software.)

it makes practical sense only to use a machine with a very large hard drive and enough processing power to support the acquisition and manipulation of recorded sound files, which are very large, memory-hogging blocks of data.

Hard disk (HD) recording software must be attached to certain hardware additions to the computer, although computers with sound cards have the basic requirements already. Upgrading the audio input quality is usually a good idea for serious HD recording, and of course having a big hard drive is essential.

The software provides screens similar to those found in sequencing programs. However, because you're dealing with recorded sound, not MIDI data events, the editing screen looks different and has different capabilities. In most cases you can view and edit a graphic representation of the recorded sound waves. All the editing features of hard drive recording programs are geared to music as it exists in the real acoustic world, not as a series of discrete note-events. Here are some of the editing operations these programs can accomplish:

■ **Cut 'n' paste.** In a sense, hard drive recording software acts like a word processor for sound waves. Because sound waves cannot be taken apart as easily as the words of a sentence, such an analogy is limited. Still, you can select a portion of the recording (by clicking and dragging the mouse along part of the

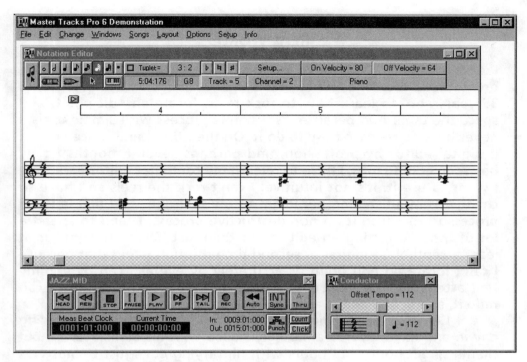

Notation software, integrated into a sequencer, shows you recorded parts as they would be written on a musical staff, ready for printing. The notation editor in a sequencing program lets you deal with written music. (Master Tracks Pro 6, Passport Software.)

sound wave graphic on the screen), cut it, copy it, and paste it somewhere else. This can be quite handy when recording pop songs that have repeated choruses, hooks, and vocal lines, as these elements can be copied and pasted into the song without your having to re-record them.

■ **Tempo alterations.** You must be very careful when altering the tempo of a sound wave recording because it changes the pitch. Accordingly, such operations are used delicately, and only in small increments.

■ **Volume changes.** Correct recorded volume is normally a function of setting the right input level, and altering the volume of an entire recording after the fact is usually not a good idea. However, software recording programs can create crescendos and decrescendos, which is very useful for creating a fadeout ending of a song, for instance, or **cross-fading** (merging one recorded part into another).

REAL WORDS

Progress is great, and we've made a lot. But there have been some great losses, too. One loss for me is time. It didn't take me very long, 35 years ago, to learn how to rock reels, locate an edit point, and splice the tape. And because it's a simple process with simple tools, I never have to re-learn how to do it. On the other hand, since I'm not a digital editor by profession, and perhaps several months go by between editing jobs, I have to relearn my computer editor each time I want to use it. It's not intuitive. I can't rock the reels so I have to change from a listening paradigm to a visual one. And (like a word processor), because it's a non-destructive process, I tend to spend a lot of time perfecting an edit rather than just having it right (or at least acceptable) the first or second time through. I find that because I can't locate an edit point as accurately by eye as I can by ear, my first attempt at a digital edit usually doesn't sound right, but I can redo it, again, and again, and again.

I have a friend who does digital editing and music mastering day in and day out. He's amazingly skilled with his Sonic System, but clients spend hours and hours with him trying edits just because it's possible. It's not always clear that the final product is better as a result.

Mike Rivers
mrivers@d-and-d.com

- **Inversions and looping.** Only rarely would a producer want to play a musical part backward. But such a device is common and quite useful when creating special effects for soundtrack production, and even some musical effects. (The reverse snare drum hit became a standard musical effect for a few years.) **Looping** is used to create rhythmic grooves and effects that last indefinitely.

- **Tonal alterations.** Some recording programs have built-in **EQ** features, enabling you to refine the tonal quality of a recorded part, or even an entire mix.

SOUND PROGRAMMING

Programs for programming? If the very thought makes you dizzy, think of them as programming assistants, or just programming software. This kind of music software is usually written to be used with a specific MIDI synthesizer, as well as a specific computer

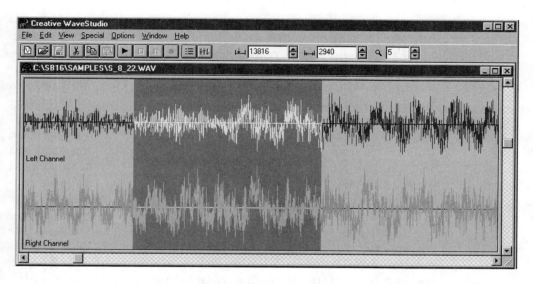

Hard disk recording programs let you manipulate recordings at the waveform level.

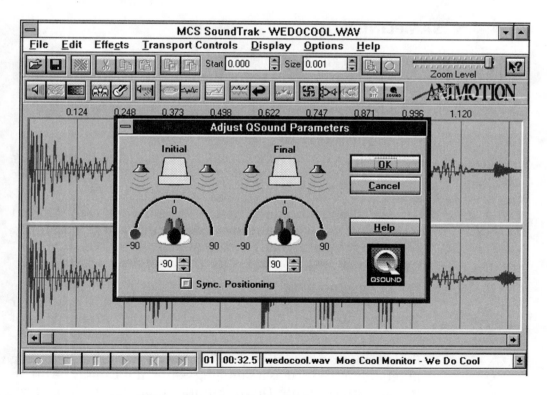

Hard disk recording software lets you adjust many aspects of a recording. This window is for changing the pan settings of the stereo image.

operating system. However, a couple of ambitious programs provide sound creation help for a wide range of popular synthesizers.

For those who enjoy creating their own synth patches, software assistance is invaluable, even if the synthesizer permits sound programming with its own front-panel buttons. Most synthesizers have a myriad of variables, categories, and selections for making up new timbres, and provide inadequate screens for seeing what you're doing. The larger computer monitor solves that problem. You can view **sound envelope** shapes (the graphic representations of a sound's changes over time) as you adjust them (and hear them), and view large numbers of variables at once. It makes programming more intelligible when you can get an overview of the sound you're creating.

A MIDI program wouldn't be very useful if it did not enable you to hear the changes you're making to a patch, so the computer is linked to the synthesizer being programmed. Using MIDI, you can hear almost immediately how your sound is progressing with every change you make to any variable.

SAMPLING

Samplers, with their unique ability to acquire sounds from the real world and play them across the range of a keyboard, always include the necessary hardware and internal software to acquire new sounds. Audio input jacks make up the hardware, and an internal operating system that allows you to manipulate the sampled sound makes up the software.

Computer sampling software makes a tricky job easier in the same way that synth programming software simplifies that difficult task. There are a few different kinds to know about:

■ **Sample editing programs.** These programs work with sampled waveforms that have already been acquired by the sampler. They cannot perform any recording functions themselves, but they can edit samples from within the sampler.

■ **Sampling programs.** These programs can record the sample and then manipulate it until it sounds best within a particular sampler instrument. The software works only with one kind of sampler.

■ **Basic computer recording programs.** Any hard disk recording program can be used as a sampling editor, if it can save work in the universal **Sample Dump Standard** (SDS). The **SDS** allows samples to be loaded into any sampler that understands that file format. Having a universal standard for sample files means that a generic recording program can record and refine a sample, then load it into one or more samplers.

Regardless of which type of software is used, sample editing performs looping, inverting, and cross-fading just like hard disk recording programs, but the emphasis is on much shorter sound wave recordings.

NOTATION

Notation software allows you to create sheet music on your computer screen and print it out. There are two kinds of notation program:

■ **Standalone.** These software notators are independent programs that translate MIDI sequences into music notation. They also let you notate music yourself, using the computer's mouse and keyboard. But they are not part of the MIDI creative process, and you cannot hear music they display.

■ **Notation/sequencing.** Some notation programs are adjuncts to sequencing software, so the entire creative process, from composing to recording to notating to printing, is tied together in a single computer environment. The notation screen in these programs often lets you perform editing operations such as correcting notes; conveniently, both the sequence and the notation file are corrected.

Notation programs took several years to get up to speed with the rest of the computer music tools. There are still inherent difficulties with translating recorded music to notation, and the literalness of a computer hinders as much as it helps. The slightest irregularity in playing style was perfectly reflected in the early programs, which often displayed gobs of tiny rests and fractioned notes to interpret the natural imprecision of musical performance. Intensive on-screen editing was required to get the scores in shape for printing. Modern programs have become more intelligent, and deliver better tools for cleaning up a manuscript file.

4

THE MUSICIAN'S SHOPPING GUIDE TO COMPUTERS*

A computer is the broadest leap into the digital age that a musician can make. With a computer in your home or studio, you're ready to dabble in MIDI, participate in the online music scene, experience multimedia, record digitally, and use musical software to learn and create music. Because of its versatility, and because it tends to become the center of digital life, you should choose your computer carefully. They are also fairly expensive machines, so it's worthwhile knowing their ins and outs, at least in a basic way, before taking the plunge.

WINDOWS OR MAC?

When shopping for any electronic device, from a VCR to a toaster, most people rarely choose based on the manufacturer. Instead, they look for certain features, then choose a model that delivers those features at a good price, preferably with a recognizable, generally trusted brand name. In some cases, buying a computer should reverse those priorities, focusing first on the computer brand, then on features. But in this case, *brand* refers mainly to the operating system, not to the hardware manufacturer. Because there are only two choices, this is a crucial decision.

Why is it so important to consider the computer's operating sys-

*Price ranges in this chapter are based on 1997 retail prices.

tem? Because each OS runs different software programs, although there is some overlap between different systems, and a computer is only as good as the software it's running. Music programs, like all software, are written for a particular operating system. These days, it boils down to two choices: Windows and Mac.

So one approach to a new computer is to work backward, starting with the software you want to use. Of course, it's hard to know what software is best without having a computer in the first place. But there are a few ways you can educate yourself in a general way about software and operating systems:

Computer Self-Education

- Talk to musical friends who have computers. If possible, have them give you tours of their OS and favorite programs. You can also discuss the question with computer-literate friends who aren't involved in music, as they might have opinions, observations, and warnings gleaned from their experience.

- Visit music stores that carry computers, as well as general computer stores. Try to find salespeople who will take the time to answer basic questions.

- Read computer magazines and music technology magazines. Browsing the newsstand in a large bookstore is more efficient than subscribing to several publications.

A Few Considerations

- **Platform.** Windows (including Windows 95) is by far the most common operating system, and this brings certain advantages. On the other hand, the Macintosh has been a preeminent music computer for much longer, resulting in a wide base of music software written for Macs. If a new computer is to be dedicated to music production, the Macintosh offers the advantage of experience.

- **Available software.** Many computers end up doing multiple duties beyond musical ones, including administrative tasks related to the artistic profession. Word processing, graphic design, and online networking are likely endeavors, so the choice of computer should take them into consideration. Music and art are very well represented in the world of Macintosh software, but business software and online programs are harder to find. Windows, the dominant computing platform, carries the bulk of general software. A trip to any computer store demonstrates the inequity between the two operating systems; shelf space is almost entirely taken with yard upon yard of Windows programs, with Mac titles off in a distant corner, if they are stocked at all. (In fact, many Mac users buy all their software by mail through Mac-oriented catalogs and magazines.) This need not be a problem for Mac users who remain loyal to the distinctive and elegant machines, and make use of a few basic, excellent programs to work with music and other creative media. However, owning a Mac can be a liability if you like choosing from a very wide selection of software. There is not nearly as much **shareware** (which is usually available in a free trial versions online) for the Mac as for Windows, so the Macintosh computer is drastically crippled in taking advantage of online services.

- **Educational software.** One area in which Macs are historically superior to Windows machines, and have remained strongly competitive, is education. There is a good deal of children's and education software available for the Mac, and many CD-ROM products of all types.

- **Collaborations.** If you will be sharing files with computer-savvy musical friends, or a local studio that uses either Mac or Windows, you can save yourself some future headaches by matching equipment. Bringing Mac files into a Windows studio for production work is a recipe for headaches. (However, modern Macs can read Windows files, and even run Windows software.) Also, if you get the same equipment as friends who are a few steps ahead of you on the learning curve, you can benefit from their experience when you run into the inevitable rough spots.

- **Workability.** There are fundamental differences in the workability of Mac and Windows machines. It's not important to know the technical details of how the chips and operating systems work together for the benefit of modern, powerful multimedia software. But one helpful image is to think of Macintosh machines as similar to an integrated stereo system, whereas a Windows computer is more like a collection of components made by different companies. In a Windows computer, the operating system, main processing chip, disk drives, multimedia chip boards, and monitor are usually made by different companies. There is an advantage and a disadvantage to this patchwork system.

The Windows Patchwork

- **The disadvantage:** Windows machines don't operate as reliably as Macs. (This is an opinion, but a widely held one.) They crash more, which is an inconvenient interruption that sometimes causes loss of work. Windows owners often must learn more about their computers in order to fix problems.

■ **The advantage:** You can upgrade individual computer components more easily because there are so many interchangeable alternatives among the chips, disk drives, and other items listed above.

Bottom Line

Windows and Macintosh Computers

New computers of both Windows and Macintosh persuasions have a wide price range, considering all the different models, levels of power, and added features. Broadly speaking, a new computer costs $1,000–$5,000. Practically speaking, a basic multimedia computer sufficient for MIDI production, online navigation, and basic computing tasks costs $1,200–$3,000. Less expensive machines within that range may not have a modem, sound card, or speakers. Features that add to the cost are a large hard drive, extra RAM (memory), a large monitor, and lots of preinstalled software.

Here are the bottom lines:

Basic desktop without multimedia components	$1,000–$1,500
Basic desktop with multimedia basics and modem	$1,500–$3,000
Basic laptop without multimedia components	$1,700–$2,500
Basic laptop with multimedia basics and modem	$2,200–$4,000

■ WHERE TO SHOP

THE USED SCENE: DESKTOPS AND LAPTOPS

There is a fantastic market for used computers. As with any other electronic equipment, there are risks in buying a machine from a private owner, but there is a brisk trade in used computers for a good reason: It's a fairly safe buy. Computers are reasonably sturdy machines without many delicate or moving parts. However, it

---

REAL WORDS

You don't need an expensive or advanced system to do tracking that sounds as professional as you make it. You can create a CD-quality tracking system using just a 16-bit sound card (such as the Sound Blaster 16 or Pro), a 486 computer with 4 MB RAM (minimum), and tracking software, of which many free packages exist. FastTracker II and Scream Tracker are a few, and there are many others that aren't as well known, but are just as powerful. It's up to you to find the one that suits you best. If you have Internet access, you can find these and many others online.

Todd Hendricks
ev@mcs.net

---

should be emphasized that used laptops are much more risky than desktops. If you are considering buying a used portable music computer (it is tempting because new laptops are more expensive than new desktops), remember that you have no way of knowing whether the machine was dropped from a MIDI rack during a gig.

Computer technology has developed so quickly that many worthy designs and configurations have been left in the dust as new models are relentlessly rolled out. This rapid obsolescence is especially true in the Windows market, where you can find used machines with older processing chips, less RAM, and smaller hard drives than contemporary models, machines that have only recently slipped into the gray area of non-chic but are still good computing tools, perfectly capable of holding their own in a MIDI studio. However, advanced computing such as multimedia online navigation requires more up-to-date features. Finally, it must be noted that the Windows 95 operating system doesn't work nearly as well on older computers.

WHERE TO GO

If possible, try to buy your computer in a music store, or at least do some shopping there. The best way to test a computer that will be used for music is to run some music software and talk with salespeople who understand the needs of musicians. Most music stores that carry computers stock both Windows and Macintosh machines. If no computer-equipped music store is within reach, it's off to one of these locations:

- **Dedicated computer store.** Computer stores, ramping up to support the digital revolution, have become supermarkets of computing equipment, from desktops to laptops, from software to accessories to furniture.

- **Consumer electronics store.** Most large electronics retail chains have computer sections with good selections of basic equipment and competitive prices. Don't expect to see music software demonstrated, though.

- **Office supply store.** Sales help is minimal, selection is slim, but prices are competitive.

- **Mail-order catalog.** With great prices and the chance to configure the computer exactly to the customer's specifications, mail-order is the purchasing avenue of choice for experienced buyers. Beginners can do well by this method as well, but a little research, either by reading the magazines whose ads you can order from or by soliciting advice from experienced friends, is well advised.

Essential Shopping Questions: Computers

Whether you're talking with a salesperson or reading computer ads in a magazine, it helps to know what questions to ask about a computer.

- What is the speed of the processing chip? This specification may seem arcane, but has a lot to do with the speed of the computer's functions, which is very important for more processing-intensive tasks such as hard disk recording, sampling, and graphic design. However, it has little effect on the speed with which a computer can navigate online. MIDI computing is also not affected much by low processing speed. Processing speed is measured in megahertz (MHz) and is sometimes known as cycle speed. The lowest cycle speed acceptable for high-end computing is 75 MHz, and current computers go as high as 300 MHz. Higher speeds show up in daily computing tasks such as faster boot-ups of programs, faster save times of files, and faster graphics on the screen.

- How much RAM is there? RAM (random access memory) is built-in memory that holds running programs and creative files in progress. It is cleared out every time you turn off the computer. The more RAM in a computer, the more programs can be running at the same time, and the more room the computer has for storing files while you are working on them. With low memory, the operating system must struggle to maneuver during basic computer operations, and crashes are more likely. RAM is measured in megabytes (MB, or megs); 8 MB is minimal, and 16 is required to run Windows 95. RAM is usually added 8 or 16 MB (depending on the computer) at a time. Thirty-two megs covers most computing situations with memory to spare.

- How big is the hard drive? Hard drives store everything added to the computer (programs and created files). Many music programs are not that large, but graphics, desktop publishing, and online browsing packages can take up a lot of room. Add a few CD-ROM games, and a hard drive can be full before you know it. Hard drives are measured in megabytes and gigabytes (GB, or gigs); 1 GB is 1,000 MB. Hard drives of 1 gig and over have become common, and are recommended if you will be using many programs. If the computer is to be used for hard disk recording, a large hard drive is essential.

- Does the computer include multimedia components? For multimedia, you'll need a sound card, speakers, and a CD-ROM drive. A high-speed video card (64-bit or higher) is also helpful.

- Is the case a desktop style or tower? There is no functional difference in the two designs, but the cosmetic differences are significant. Tower computers fit under a desk, clearing surface space. On the other hand, it's harder to reach the disk drives when you have to reach down for them. It's important to think about where the computer will be placed.

- Does the computer include a modem? If not, going online is impossible until one is added.

- Is a monitor included? Believe it or not, monitors are sometimes optional, so this is an important question. If the price seems too good to be true, it's likely that you'll have to add a monitor.

- Is there a toll-free, 24-hour phone number for technical support? You may be very glad for this feature.

SHOPPING FOR PERIPHERALS

A computer is more than the sum of its parts, and the variety of possible parts is almost endless. The attachments that get squeezed into a computer, and are attached to it from the outside, are called peripherals. Many of them relate directly to musical life in the digital world. With Windows computers more than with Macs, peripherals are interchangeable and upgradable by the owner. This section gives blow-by-blow shopping tips for the devices most relevant to musicians, with the exception of modems, which are covered in Part Three.

Before getting started, a word on peripheral installation and how it relates to the shopping experience is in order. Peripherals are of two types: external and internal. In some cases you have a choice, but sometimes not. Installing external devices is fairly straightforward, requiring a cable connection from the peripheral to the computer's main case, not unlike connecting a CD player to a stereo system or a guitar into an amplifier. (There is usually some accompanying software, but if it's well designed, installation is simple.) Internal peripherals require the possibly intimidating enterprise of opening the computer, plugging the device into a slot on the main circuit board, tightening a couple of screws, and putting the computer back together again. It is not difficult for gadget-minded folks, but some musicians understandably feel it is not their destiny to be quite that computer-friendly. Some stores will perform the installation for you, so if you don't feel comfortable doing it yourself, choose a store with a good service department.

Where to Shop for Peripherals

Computer add-ons are sold in pretty much the same stores as computers are, with one important difference: Music stores don't usually stock peripherals. The exception is sound cards, which are a music store specialty item. Some may carry multimedia upgrade kits, but printers, CD-ROM drives, and the rest are usually not found in music instrument stores unless they are already attached to a displayed computer system. If you find a music store that sells peripherals separately, become a customer! You'll get the best music-oriented advice there.

The market for used add-ons is erratic, and in many cases it isn't a good idea to buy used equipment anyway. Certainly, you shouldn't get a used hard drive, and printers are risky too, because you can't tell how much they have been used. Expansion cards such as sound cards are traded for in classified ads.

MULTIMEDIA UPGRADE KITS

If you already have a computer, or if you buy an inexpensive stripped-down model, the time may come when you want to take advantage of modern computing's audio elements, the CD-ROM marketplace, and the increasingly audible online experience. At that point, several companies come to your rescue with all-in-one, everything-you-need packages that turn your computer from a silent, CD-challenged machine to a screaming (or at least humming) multimedia workstation. Conversion kits include the following elements:

■ **CD-ROM drive.** It fits into your computer case, usually beneath the floppy drive.

■ **Sound card.** This small circuit board is plugged into the inside of the computer, and contains output jacks that stick out the back.

■ **Speakers.** Available in various sizes and levels of quality, stereo speakers are plugged into the sound card, and sit outside the computer.

Special note: Macintosh computers built within the last few years are all multimedia-ready off the shelf, and don't need to be upgraded.

Why Get Multimedia?

Having a multimedia computer rather than a nonmultimedia computer has these advantages to a musician or music lover:

• Access to CD-ROM multimedia programs such as music education titles. There is a large selection of music education material for kids and music appreciation for adults.

• The ability to play MIDI files through your computer.

• The ability to play sound files, such as those found all over the Internet.

• Access to other online audio, such as real-time concert broadcasts and album previews.

Some multimedia upgrade kits also contain a collection of CD-ROMs to get you started, but if you'd rather select your own titles, and if you look around hard enough, you can probably find a kit for a bit less money that doesn't force discs on you.

Of all the peripherals discussed here, multimedia upgrade kits involve the most grueling installation process. Putting in the CD-ROM drive is usually the hardest part, followed by the sound card. Connecting the speakers is no problem, as long as you haven't thrown the computer out the window by that time. Getting everything in place and working can be a fun project for the technically minded, but is not recommended for those who don't have a knack for taking things apart and wrestling with wires. Find a store that will perform the installation for you.

Essential Shopping Questions: Multimedia Upgrade Kits

When considering the selection of one-stop multimedia solutions, here are the important considerations to keep in mind:

- How fast is the CD-ROM drive? The faster the better. Double-speed (2x) is obsolete, quad-speed (4x) is minimal, 8x to 12x drives deliver excellent performance, and even higher ratings are emerging from the boiling cauldron of technological development.

- Is the sound card Sound Blaster compatible? The Sound Blaster brand has become the de facto standard. Most other brands now adhere to it.

- Does the sound card have built-in samples in addition to synthesizer patches? Sample-based sound generation is much better than synth-based sounds, but more expensive.

- How good are the speakers? You can pretty much tell by their size. Little 4-inch speaker cases are going to sound like little 4-inch speakers.

- Who are the manufacturers? In most cases, the components are made by different companies. If you don't recognize any of the brands, ask a salesperson for an opinion and the product's track record.

- Which CD-ROM titles are included? Chances are, there won't be music-specific discs in there, but the number and selection of titles might sway you toward one kit or another.

Bottom Line

Multimedia Upgrade Kits

All four main components of a multimedia upgrade (CD-ROM drive, sound card, speakers, and CD-ROM titles) can vary in quality, affecting the price of the kit. Overall, prices range from $150 dollars to about $500. The bottom lines:

Budget multimedia upgrade with 4x CD-ROM drive, 16-bit sound card, adequate speakers, and no titles	$150–$300
Basic multimedia upgrade with 6x–8x CD-ROM drive,16-bit sound card, medium-grade speakers, and a handful of starter titles	$200–$400
High-end multimedia upgrade with 12x or faster CD-ROM drive, sound card with samples, very good speakers, and an impressive array of titles	$300–$500

CD-ROM DRIVES

If you don't want to dive into a complete multimedia makeover, the centerpiece of multimedia upgrade kits—the CD-ROM drive— can be purchased separately. Although external CD-ROM drives can still be found, they are throwbacks to earlier days. Now, almost all drives are internal, and must be installed within the computer casing. It is one of the most difficult installations to accomplish, not so much because it's hard to understand as because the space into which it must fit is cramped, and completing the wiring can require manual dexterity normally only found in bagpipe players.

A computer equipped with a CD-ROM drive without the other multimedia peripherals (sound card and speakers) is only half the multimedia story. You won't be able to hear any sounds, either online or in multimedia programs, but you will be able to use programs packaged on CD, of which there are many.

Essential Shopping Questions: CD-ROM Drives

There are two main questions to consider when getting a CD-ROM:

- **How fast is the drive?** CD-ROM drives must spin more quickly than music CD players in order to display video effectively on a computer screen. The first advance in CD-ROM brought us double-speed drives (2x), and it's been *tempo più allegro* ever since. Quad-speed drives (4x) are currently standard, with 8x and 12x drives becoming much more common. Faster drives have two main benefits. First, they deliver smoother video playback, less jerky than slow drives. Second, large files stored on CD load into the computer faster.

- Can it be used in a tower-style computer case? Vertical computer tower cases sometimes have rotated drive bays, so an installed CD-ROM drive is vertical, not horizontal. If that is the case, be sure to buy a drive that has small clamps to hold the CD in place.

Bottom Line

CD-ROM Drives

CD-ROM drives have decreased in price very gratifyingly, to the point that there is little point in getting less than an 8x-speed drive for a desktop computer. Laptops, generally more expensive in every respect, can also be upgraded with a CD drive, but the upgrade is more pricey.

8x CD-ROM drive for a desktop computer	$125–$250
4x CD-ROM drive for a desktop computer	$80–$150
8x CD-ROM drive for a laptop computer	$400–$500
4x CD-ROM drive for a laptop computer	$300–$400

SPEAKERS

Adding speakers to a computer is one of the coolest ways for a musician to upgrade. The benefits are obvious. As long as a sound card is present in the machine, speakers enable you to hear sound files on the Internet, play MIDI files through your computer, and even play music CDs through the CD-ROM drive. (The CD-ROM drive is not necessary on the Internet or for MIDI playback.)

In theory, any speakers can be used, as long as you can find a way to plug them into the mini-jacks of the computer's sound card. But take note: Neither the computer nor the sound card provides an amplifier for the speakers, so the amp must be in the speakers themselves. (You could also connect a separate amp between the sound card and the speakers, but this is getting needlessly complex.) All speakers made specifically for computers are powered speakers, with on/off switches and sometimes other controls.

There is a pretty wide range of quality, from weak, small, adequate speakers to monstrous self-contained sound systems complete with sub-woofers. The first question to ask yourself when buying speakers as a separate component (not part of a multimedia upgrade kit) is how good you need them to sound.

What to Buy?

- Do you merely want to hear the Internet? Because of data compression, bandwidth, and other technical problems, the Internet doesn't sound too good yet anyway, so there's no point in approaching it aggressively with high-fidelity speakers. Get a cost-efficient pair.

- Do you want to enjoy multimedia CD-ROM presentations? Some of them are quite good, especially (as you might expect from an audio viewpoint) those devoted to musical subjects. This is an entertainment and educational opportunity worthy of better equipment. Remember, though, that the audio portion of many music-oriented CD-ROMs can be played over a regular CD deck. So this goal warrants medium-fidelity speakers.

- Do you want your computer to be your main sound system for music discs, in addition to handling multimedia chores? In that case, go for the gold with a high-fidelity speaker system.

Speaker installation is a breeze, and nobody asks for store help. It's as easy as connecting speakers to a stereo, with no bare wires. It's truly a plug-and-play situation.

Essential Shopping Questions: Speakers

- **What do they sound like? OK, this is painfully obvious. The point is, try to buy your speakers at a store that displays working models of the choices, so your ears can compare.**

- **Will they fit in your space? Don't forget, these things have to be put somewhere, so don't buy large bookshelf models if you have to put them on the floor.**

- **Is there a sub-woofer? You've never heard a computer sound so good.**

- Are there tone controls? Minimal speakers can be tweaked into respectability if there is a bass boost feature or some kind of rudimentary equalization.

Bottom Line

Speakers

Low-end speakers	$30–$75
Mid-fidelity speakers with basic tone controls	$50–$125
High-end speakers with separate sub-woofer	$100–$250

SOUND CARDS

Sound cards are the computer musician's best friend. Remember, a sound card by itself, without speakers attached, is almost useless. (Some of them have headphone mini-jacks, but that's an inconvenient option to rely on.) At the beginning of sound card development, there were many different brands and a few standards, not all of which were compatible. This made life hard for game and CD-ROM developers, who had to account for differing computer systems. Over time, though, a single standard (Sound Blaster) emerged as fairly universal. Any card you buy should be Sound Blaster compatible, and they almost all are.

Sound cards are complete little digital instruments, featuring a complete **General MIDI** set of synthesizer or sample patches burned into the card's circuitry. Unlike those on a keyboard synthesizer, you cannot program, delete, save, or otherwise manipulate the built-in sounds. It is primarily a playback device. You also cannot count on a MIDI interface being included, although many cards are so equipped.

Installation of a sound card is of medium difficulty, between a CD-ROM (most difficult) and speakers, which are easy. The computer must be opened, the card inserted into the main circuit board and screwed in place, and the computer case closed again. Some stores will do this for you; if you're a do-it-yourself type, literature is available that describes the process pictorially.

The sound card (with speakers) is necessary for enjoying the musical Internet, CD-ROMs, General MIDI files over the computer, and all other sound file sharing. Curiously, the sound card is also where you plug in a joystick for playing simulation games. Furthermore, if the card has a microphone input, you can record directly to your computer.

Essential Shopping Questions: Sound Cards

- **Which company makes the card?** This is a more significant question with sound cards than with some other peripherals, for an esoteric but important reason. All peripheral computer cards require small specialized pieces of software called drivers in order to work. Sometimes the drivers must be updated when other aspects of the computer are changed. For example, when many people upgraded from the Windows operating system to Windows 95, there was (and continues to be) a scramble for new drivers to run expansion cards. If you buy a sound card from a small, unknown company, there is the risk of the company not being around in the future when you need a new driver. A few of the most prominent music companies manufacturing sound cards are Creative Labs, Turtle Beach, and Ensoniq.

- **Is there a microphone input?** A sound card that accepts audio input gives you sampling capability. How sophisticated that capability is depends on the audio specifications of the card, the accompanying software, and the cleanliness of the input circuitry. But at the very least, being able to record into your computer can be a fun and easy way to create digitized sound files of music you have produced on other systems.

- **Is it a wavetable card?** Wavetable synthesis is a higher-level, better-sounding system than FM synthesis, which is the system included on most 16-bit cards. Wavetable cards are generally 32-bit (representing better fidelity), and the built-in sampled waveforms elevate the overall sound of the card.

- **What kind of accompanying software is included?** Some cards bundle a few audio utility (single-function) programs together into a software suite, enabling you to record with the card, play sound files, and play MIDI files. In the best case, recording software allows for multitrack recording, although you need a large hard drive to fully take advantage of it.

- **Does the card contain on-board memory?** Some upgrade sound cards can be upgraded with memory chips that plug right into the card. This enhances the card's features and its ability to sample more effectively.

Bottom Line

Sound Cards

Basic 16-bit FM-synthesis sound card	$80–$150
Basic wavetable card	$150–$300
Enhanced, high-end 32-bit wavetable card with rich accompanying software and great sounds	$300–$500

HARD DRIVES

Hard drive upgrades are tempting any time the old drive gets cramped for space, which happens quite a bit with older computers. New multimedia software and files have grown beyond the capacities of once-ample storage drives, and have made new demands on the hard drive industry. Fortunately, the industry has responded by producing high-capacity drives and continually (so far) lowering prices.

Upgrading the hard drive is necessary for musicians who decide to use the computer as the main recording deck, through hard drive recording technology. Combined with the necessary space for standard software needs, such a computer should be equipped with a single hard drive of at least a couple of gigabytes, or even two hard drives.

In earlier years, hard drives came in external (SCSI) and internal (IDE) models. That is still true, although externals are getting less popular, and most computer owners are reluctant to use a valuable connection port on a device that could go inside more efficiently. Furthermore, internal peripherals are usually less expensive.

Installing a hard drive is slightly easier than putting in a CD-ROM drive and harder than adding a sound card. Part of the challenge lies before the installation, and part of it waits until afterward. First, you need to consider how to transfer the files from the old hard drive to the new one (at least, the files you want to keep, which will probably be most of them, or you would have made room on the old drive by deleting them). After you've solved that problem and installed the device, it must be formatted, possibly defragmented, and loaded with your operating system.

The first challenge—transferring your files—can be done with a backup device such as an archival tape drive, or a store may perform the transfer for you. The second challenge, formatting and defragmenting, is accomplished with accompanying software.

Essential Shopping Questions: Hard Drives

There are two crucial questions to ask when considering hard drives:

- **How big is the drive?** Hard drive capacity is measured in megabytes (1,000 MB) and gigabytes (1,000 GB). Five hundred megabytes used to be a big drive, but now is considered inadequate. Although you can have a wonderfully creative digital life with some basic programs stored on a hard drive of that size, over time the multimedia age will probably tempt you into expanding your computer's storage capacity. Certainly, if you are working with large digitized sound files, and most definitely if you are involved in hard disk recording, you need a hard drive at least twice that big, which is 1 GB. Drives are now available with over 3 GB of capacity, which should be ample—for a little while.

- **How fast is the access speed?** This measurement gauges the amount of time needed to locate and begin loading a requested file from the hard drive. It is measured in milliseconds (ms), and the smaller the number is, the better. For standard computing tasks such as MIDI recording, word processing, and graphics, the access speed isn't a crucial specification. But it definitely comes into play with hard disk recording computers because musical timing can be thrown off when a hard drive takes too long to access a track on playback. Twelve milliseconds and under is a specification to shoot for.

Bottom Line

Hard Drives

Hard drive prices depend primarily on capacity, with some consideration for the access speed.

Small hard drive (850 MB–1.2 GB) with fast access (10–14 ms)	$100–$175
Medium hard drive (1.2–2.0 GB) with fast access (11–14 ms)	$170–$250
Large hard drive (2.0–4.0 GB) with fast access (10–14 ms)	$200–$400

PRINTERS

Musicians use printers in conjunction with notation software to make hard copies of music, and also use them to print text and graphics files. New printer technology has brought fairly high-quality color printing within reach of home computer systems.

Dot-matrix printers, the standby technology of earlier years that printed tiny dots in configurations of letters, numerals, and lines, have given way to a more modern age. Now, you have two basic choices: inkjet and laser. Laser printers produce the sharpest output and are quicker, and inkjets offer affordable color.

Installing a printer is usually easy on the hardware side: simply plug it into the **parallel** port (or the printer port on a Macintosh). Sometimes, software installation must accompany this simple procedure.

New printers are purchased in computer, office supply, and consumer electronics stores. There is a used market, but a used printer is a risky investment. There are many moving parts, and printers are fairly portable, which means droppable.

Essential Shopping Questions: Printers

- **Laser or inkjet?** This question really boils down to whether you want color output as an option. Color is irrelevant for music scores and text manuscripts such as letters. It is very nice, though, when designing an album cover. Color printers also perform black-and-white printing, but inkjet printers, which are commonly chosen for low-cost color, do not do B&W as darkly or sharply as lasers. Lasers tend to be quicker, but more expensive. Another consideration involves maintenance cost. Inkjets use ink cartridges that must be replaced from time to time. Lasers require replacement toners. You should find out how long the replacement parts last in each case, as measured in number of pages printed.

- **How many dots per inch?** Printer resolution—the precision with which graphic details can be portrayed on paper—is measured by the number of dots squeezed into an inch of paper. (This measurement is used in all printers, and does not imply that the printer is a dot-matrix model.) The more dots per inch (DPI), the more finely resolved the print output will be; 300 DPI means very good text printing. Some color printers resolve as highly as 360 DPI, but the best affordable models go as high as 720 DPI.

- **How fast is the printer?** Printers vary in how quickly they print, and the specification is measured in pages per minute (PPM).

Beware of the PPM you're told by salespeople and read in ads! Like miles per gallon when shopping for a car, the PPM spec is useful for comparison only. It's based on a certain (low) amount of ink on the page, so the actual speed is lower in many situations, as when printing a musical score. Furthermore, color printing on an inkjet can slow things down profoundly, especially when the resolution is 720 DPI. Keeping all this in mind, a printer speed of 4 PPM is acceptable on the low end for black-and-white, and 6 PPM or more is good.

- Is special paper required/available? Some inkjet printers, especially color models, create their best results on special coated paper that is, as you might guess, more expensive than regular paper. The results are sometimes excellent, however, so the question may be not whether the paper is necessary so much as whether it is available.

- In color inkjets, are the ink cartridges divided? Some models contain one cartridge with the three colors that get blended into a full-color document. Other models allot a small cartridge to each color. Why does it matter? In the first case, the (more expensive) cartridge must be replaced whenever a single color runs out, whereas in the latter, you can replace specific colors as needed. It is likewise important that the black ink be held in an independent cartridge.

Bottom Line

Printers

Inkjet color/B&W	$275–$400
Laser B&W	$350–$600

Part One
GLOSSARY

There are a lot of computer terms. The goal of this glossary is not so much comprehensiveness as usefulness. Only essential terms are included here, but even so, it's a big list. To make things easier to find, the list is divided into three sections:

- General terms that refer to functions, features, and other aspects of computers

- Hardware terms having to do with the machine and its components

- Software terms that relate to programs, files, and other non-machine attributes of computing

GENERAL TERMS

CD-ROM CD-ROM is a technology developed in the 1990s for storing and playing back multimedia. CD-ROM technology has two parts: the CD-ROM disc and the CD-ROM drive. The discs are just like music compact discs (CDs) and can be used to hold software, multimedia files, movies, and of course music. CD-ROM drives are computer accessories, usually built into new computers, that access the files on a CD-ROM disc. The relationship between CD-ROM drives and discs is exactly like that of floppy drives and floppy disks, except that CD-ROMs hold over five hundred times as much information. CD-ROM drives must operate (spin) faster than music CD drives in order to deliver data to the computer at a fast enough speed. Double-speed drives have been bypassed by quad-speed (4x) units, and even those are being surpassed by 8x and 12x machines.

The large storage capacity of CD-ROMs is what makes them valuable. Software programs packaged on CD-ROMs can be many times larger than older programs, and may contain more graphic elements, sounds, pictures, and even video clips. As an entertainment medium, the CD-ROM affords new opportunities for electronic musicians by creating a need for CD-ROM soundtracks for multimedia packages such as games and educational programs.

Clone Clones are computers based on the original design of Macintosh or IBM personal computers. Clones all can use the same operating system as the original computer, even though they are made by many different companies. The operating system used on most IBM clones is DOS. Since the late 1980s the DOS operating system has been used in conjunction with the Windows operating system, and more recently Windows 95. (Other operating systems can be used with clones also.) IBM clones are sometimes known as DOS/Windows computers.

Cross-fading A software feature by which one sound fragment is faded down while another is faded up, connecting the two seamlessly. Cross-fading is found in hard disk recording software, sample editing programs, and the internal software of digital samplers.

Desktop Desktop computers, as opposed to laptops, sit on a desk. Desktop models are not portable, but have the advantage of bigger screens and greater expandability through peripherals. Many people prefer desktop keyboards to the laptop variety. Despite their larger size, desktops are substantially less expensive than laptops.

DOS DOS is the underlying operating system beneath the popular Windows screen environment on personal computers. DOS is used only in IBM clone computers; the Macintosh (and other computer platforms) uses a different operating system. Some computer programs are written for use in DOS, without the Windows shell, but such programs are increasingly hard to find as more people switch to Windows. However, existing DOS programs can still be used, even within Windows. Operating a computer from DOS (without Windows) is difficult for newcomers to computing because it doesn't provide a graphical interface with drop-down menus, icons, and other navigational aids. It is a command-based operating system with a fairly steep learning curve. Fortunately for musicians just diving into the world of computers, there is little need to learn DOS.

File All software is in the form of files: program files, application files, MIDI files, sound files, graphics files, and multimedia files. A file is any coherent arrangement of data that has its own integrity and can be transferred or saved as an individual unit. For example, many programs consist of several files: the main program file and secondary support files that help the program do things when it's running. In a word processor, a typical support file is the dictionary or spellchecker. When musicians create music on computers, they are creating files that can be played back, edited (altered in some way), shared, and played on other systems. File sharing is one of the most important advantages of going digital. Creating music in the digital format makes it portable.

General General MIDI is a subset of MIDI, with particular assignments
MIDI between instrument sounds and program numbers. One big problem with the MIDI standard is that a musical sequence that sounds great when played in one studio sounds completely different in another studio. The disparity is caused by the different equipment between the two studios, and—even more importantly—by the different voice assignments within that equipment. A piano sound might be assigned to sound program number 1 in the first studio's synthesizer, whereas the second studio's synthesizer has a MIDI drum kit assigned to that program number. (Great way to ruin a piano solo.) General MIDI solves this incompatibility by assigning certain sounds to program numbers in MIDI instruments. All General MIDI instruments keep the same lineup of sounds in the correct order, so that sequences recorded with General MIDI sound roughly the same when played through all General MIDI instruments.

Gigabyte A unit of memory capacity, a gigabyte (sometimes called a gig and abbreviated as GB) equals one thousand megabytes. A megabyte is one thousand kilobytes, or one million bytes. Gigabytes are mostly used in the measurement of hard drives, which are commonly at least 1 GB in size. A hard drive listed as 1.6 GB has a storage capacity of 1,600 megabytes.

Hard disk Hard disk recording represents the marriage of music production
recording and computers. With the help of specialized software, it's possible to record music directly to a computer's hard drive, instead of to a tape deck. Because the recorded sounds are in a digitized form, they can be manipulated and edited much more easily than if they were on tape. However, this process should not be confused

with MIDI recording, in which MIDI events (such as note-on and note-off signals from a keyboard) are memorized and played back by a sequencer. Editing maneuvers possible with hard disk recording include stretching and compressing a track in time and cleaning a track by removing unwanted frequencies. The software associated with hard disk recording lets you view and manipulate the sound waves that have been recorded. Serious hard drive recording, in which entire songs are produced tapelessly, requires a great deal of hard drive memory. It's not unusual to dedicate an entire computer to the task. Another choice is one of the several specialized hardware devices that offer self-contained tapeless digital recording. These machines have their own hard drives, and come with all the software you need.

Hardware Hardware is the machinery that processes, displays, and prints data. (The data itself is software.) The computers that you see on the shelves of computer stores are hardware, although they contain software. The basic hardware for a single computer includes the case (which could be a desktop or tower model), monitor, keyboard, and mouse. If you were to open up the case, you would find other pieces of hardware, perhaps including a sound card, video card, modem, and RAM chips. A computer's performance and effectiveness depend on the smooth interaction of hardware and software. Every computer comprises a blend of the two because each is useless without the other.

Language A system of symbols including rules for the formation of expressions that perform computer functions.

Laptop Laptops are portable computers, so named because they sit conveniently on one's knees in traveling situations. Over the last several years, laptops have gained in power and usefulness, to the point of rivaling desktops as a preferred computer format. Modern laptop computers feature multimedia perks such as speakers, a CD-ROM player, and large, high-resolution screens.

Looping Looping is the repetition of a sound or group of sounds without a break. Such repetition is accomplished in software programs that edit samples, transforming brief sounds into sounds that extend indefinitely. This way, a 4-second sample of a violin sound can be played as if it were being bowed continuously. Looping also proves useful with rhythmic fragments, which can be repeated endlessly for an ongoing percussive groove. Looping, as a software feature, is found in MIDI sequencers, hard disk recording programs, and the internal operating systems of digital samplers.

Macintosh The Apple Macintosh computer, also called the Mac. Macs became the preeminent music computer in the late 1980s and early 1990s.

Although they are still used far and wide in professional and amateur music studios, the computer's general popularity has slipped, and DOS/Windows PCs far outnumber Macs. Accordingly, it is harder to find a large variety of software for the Macintosh. However, Mac users tend to be fiercely loyal, and a good deal of music is produced on those excellent computers.

Megabyte A megabyte (sometimes abbreviated MB) is a measurement of digital storage capacity. Memory devices such as hard drives, floppy disks, CD-ROMs, and a computer's internal RAM are measured in megabytes. A megabyte equals roughly one million bytes, or one thousand kilobytes. A single byte is made of a cluster of bits, which are the smallest unit of data.

Mega-hertz The measurement of the processing speed of a computer chip (abbreviated MHz).

Memory Memory is an aspect of all digital equipment, whether it be a computer, synthesizer, sampler, digital effects box, or drum machine. Memory comes in two forms: the type you can put things in and erase things from (called random access memory, or RAM), and the type you can access but not alter (called read-only memory, or ROM). In computers, the main repositories of RAM memory are the hard drive and the RAM chips that store running programs. In digital music instruments, RAM is used to store sound patches created by the user, samples that have been recorded into a sampler, sequences recorded by onboard MIDI sequencers, and other digital creations that are to be stored semipermanently. Truly permanent storage happens on ROM chips, and digital instruments come from the factory with the ROM chips stocked with material never to be erased. This material includes sound waveforms (synthetic and sampled) for use as building blocks of new sound patches, and the instrument's operating system (the software that governs the internal processing functions of the instrument). Computers are more RAM-based than digital music instruments, and contain very little data that can't be erased or replaced.

Multi-media *Multimedia* refers to computer processes, displays, or products that engage more than one sense. Multimedia computer programs feature not only text, but pictures, sound, animation, and movies in some combination. Multimedia is the most important development in personal computing, affecting the way computers look, sound, and are operated; the online experience; and the opportunities for the digitally wired musician. Multimedia is not a new technology: Television, for example, provides a multimedia entertainment experience, as does a movie. Computers are interactive, though, accepting input from the user that determines the course of events, and it is that difference that has captured the imagination and enthusiasm of so many people.

Operating system Operating systems are fundamental software programs that tell computers how to accomplish tasks such as storing files, displaying programs, organizing the hard drive, and installing new components. Often abbreviated OS, the operating system is built into every new computer, but can be changed or upgraded. Macintosh computers must use the Macintosh OS, which undergoes periodic improvements and updates. IBM-clone computers have more variety in operating systems, although most of them run DOS as their basic OS. Because DOS is difficult to operate and uses an unattractive, obsolete interface, other systems have been developed to provide a friendlier interface, or shell, for DOS. These other systems have such a profound effect on the computer's operation as to be considered complete operating systems in their own right, although they are useless without the underlying DOS system. (Some old-timers still use DOS in its raw form, without a Windows shell, but this is unnecessary and not recommended for beginners.) Microsoft Windows (and its variations) is the most popular; an IBM creation called OS/2 is another system that has a fairly large base of loyalists. Operating systems define how computers look and behave. Software programs usually work only with one OS, and are authored specifically for that system. Accordingly, computer users shop for Mac programs, Windows programs, or, occasionally, DOS programs.

OS See *Operating system*.

PC Although generically it stands for *personal computer, PC* is usually used to indicate a personal computer running the DOS/Windows operating systems. In other words, an IBM or IBM-clone computer, as opposed to a Macintosh, Amiga, or Atari personal computer. These days, the computer choice for most musicians has boiled down to two types, so the question you hear when someone has bought a machine is, "Mac or PC?"

Pentium The Pentium is a central processing chip manufactured by Intel that powers most new IBM-clone computers. Although it is not the latest-generation chip, it is still considered cutting-edge for productivity applications. Pentiums are not used in Apple Macintosh computers. PCs with Pentium chips are usually called Pentiums.

Platform Computer platforms are defined by the operating system they use. The two main platforms currently are DOS/Windows and Macintosh. Platforms shouldn't be confused with computer brands.

Many companies make DOS/Windows computers, contributing to the broad-based popularity of that platform. More recently, the Apple Macintosh has also been cloned, but by many fewer companies. Other musically useful computer platforms developed since the early 1980s include Atari, which gained support among musicians because of its MIDI-savvy design, including built-in MIDI ports, and Amiga, which was good for multitasking and graphics as well as music programs.

Program   Programs are pieces of software that make a computer do specific tasks. Application programs allow their users to create, save, and share files such as music, MIDI, text, picture, sound, and database files. Programs reside on a computer's hard drive, and can be used at any time. Computers come with a certain number of programs installed, and others can be purchased separately and added later.

Quan- **tizing**   Quantizing is the process of correcting rhythmic irregularities in a sequencer. Of course, in many cases small rhythmic inconsistencies are desirable in music, but sometimes a piece calls for precision above all else, and in those cases quantizing is invaluable. Sequencers avoid sounding too robotic when quantizing by offering a range of quantizing settings. You can make every note align with any fraction of a whole note, from half notes to 64th notes, or even finer rhythmic resolution in some cases. Also, most sequencers can take the edge off rigid quantizing by introducing tiny irregularities in the rhythmic accuracy, keeping the notes mostly in line but giving a more "real" feeling to the track.

RAM   An acronym for *random access memory*. RAM is where programs and files are stored in a computer as you are using them. When you open (boot up) a program, the computer transfers the necessary operating files from the hard drive to RAM memory. Similarly, when you are working on a file, such as a musical composition in a sequencer program, the work in progress resides in RAM memory until you save it, at which point it is stored on the hard drive. RAM is the working memory of a computer, where material is stored for the short term. New computers come with a certain amount of RAM included, measured in megabytes. Most new computers are equipped with at least 8 MB, often 16, but rarely more at the beginning. You can add RAM at any time by buying the chips, opening the computer case (or having someone at the computer store open it for you), and plugging them into sockets that attach the chips to the main circuit board. Adding RAM chips increases the number of programs you can run simultaneously and speeds up the operations of your operating system and applications. Computers that process high-memory files such as sound samples and graphics work better with lots of RAM.

RAM is also found in synthesizers, samplers, tone modules, and any digital musical instrument that stores information created in that instrument. RAM memory is where sound patches are stored in a keyboard, and where samples are stored as you record and edit them in a sampler.

ROM An acronym for *read only memory.* ROM chips hold a computer's fundamental data that should never be erased. Information stored on ROM chips can be accessed (read) but not changed, erased, or replaced with other data. Such information includes instructions crucial to the operation of the computer. In keyboards, samplers, and tone modules, the ROM portion of memory holds the instrument's operating system and the onboard waveforms, both of which must be present at all times and can never be erased or changed.

Sample The Sample Dump Standard is a standard for dumping samples, of
Dump course! Samples—digital recordings, usually of instrument tones—
Standard are created by instruments called samplers, and generally cannot be shared among samplers of different brands. In other words, a sample recorded in Sampler A cannot be played back by Sampler B. The Sample Dump Standard comes to the rescue by providing a universal format for sharing samples. Any sampler equipped with the Sample Dump Standard can play back samples from similarly equipped samplers.

Software Software is data organized into a meaningful arrangement. That can mean several things. A program that lets you compose music is a software program. Likewise, the piece of music you create is software. Programs can be used again and again to make new pieces, but each individual piece composed with that program can only be enjoyed as a creation, not used to make other creations. However, the most common use of the word *software* refers to programs that do something. A computer's operating system is software, and like any other program it can be bought separately and upgraded. Most software is added to a computer after being bought separately. For example, you might get a MIDI sequencer, a word processor for creating flyers and press releases, a graphics program for designing album jackets, a Web browser for cruising the Internet, and a few specialized utilities for optimizing the performance of your computer. These would make up the basic software tools of your computer. Some computer users have dozens (even hundreds in cases of drastic addiction) of software programs, whereas other people have just a few that they use every day.

Sound A sound's envelope is what happens to the sound over time. If it gets
envelope softer or louder, if it varies or warbles in pitch, if the tone changes

during the course of the sound—any change helps define the sound's envelope. Sound envelopes are important parts of a synthesizer's sound programming features. When you create a new synthesizer sound patch, changing aspects of the envelope (volume, pitch, and tone) profoundly alters the character of the sound.

Synthe- Synthesizers come with sounds built in, and for some reason
sizer those sounds are called patches. Synthesizers are equipped with
patch dozens, sometimes hundreds of patches. Additional patches can be created by the user or bought from companies that specialize in custom-designed patches.

Tower Computer cases, which hold all the main circuitry and the disk drives, come in two configurations: desktop and tower. Tower cases are vertical units that can be placed on the floor, and are tall enough to provide access to the disk drives even when under the desk. There is no difference in computer functionality between the two case styles; choosing between them is mostly a matter of convenience and office or studio layout.

Windows *Windows* is a generic term for an operating system created and marketed by the Microsoft Corporation, used in IBM-clone PCs. The two main Windows incarnations (version 3.1 and Windows 95) are by far the most prevalent operating system in the world; accordingly, there is more software written for Windows than for any other system. Most programs written for version 3.1 can be used in Windows 95, but the reverse is not true. Windows was not a popular choice among musicians when it was first released because the Macintosh computer was already well established in digital studios. Windows is becoming more popular among musicians, but there is still plenty of cutting-edge music software for the Mac and for alternative platforms such as the Atari.

▨▨▨ HARDWARE

CPU The central processing unit (CPU) is the computer's main internal chip. It handles most of the computations performed by the machine. CPU specifications are sprinkled through computer advertisements like pepper on a salad (but are not nearly as agreeable to the palate). CPUs are identified by three variables: manufacturer, model, and speed. So when you see an ad about the Intel Pentium 133 CPU, you know you're being tempted to buy a computer whose data processing is powered by a Pentium (model) chip made by Intel (manufacturer), running at 133 MHz (speed). Macintosh owners don't have as many variables to cope with. It's not important for musicians to know a great deal about CPUs, but when you're buying a computer, it is important to know what they are.

Expansion card Expansion cards are used to upgrade a computer's features. The word *card* may suggest a flimsy cardboard item, but in fact these cards are small circuit boards that are plugged into the main circuit board inside the computer, augmenting its capabilities. Expansion cards are also known as expansion boards. There are several different types, with different specific uses, including sound cards, video cards, modem cards, and TV and radio cards. The cards are purchased from computer stores and can be installed fairly easily at home, although technophobic people can also find stores that will perform that operation for a small charge. Each card has controls and jacks (plugs of various types) at one end, which sticks out the back of the computer. This method allows you to plug in speakers to a sound card, for example, or a phone line to a modem card. Expansion cards take advantage of a PC's modularity, and are an easy, inexpensive way to upgrade the multimedia or telecommunication properties of a computer.

Hard drive A computer's hard drive is an internal device that stores all the computer's programs and files. Every piece of software you own, and everything you create with that software, is stored on the hard drive. Naturally, they are pretty big! Hard drives really expanded in size when two things happened at roughly the same time: Multimedia computing, with its enormous memory requirements, emerged into the mainstream; and the price of hard drives fell drastically. Hard drives can be replaced when they are outgrown. They can also be archived (usually called backing up the hard drive) with secondary storage devices using tape or CD-ROMs.

Keyboard The computer keyboard is a separate component that can be replaced. Until recently that didn't mean much, but in the last few years keyboards have sprouted multiple varieties of the basic typewriter design. They arrangement of letters is still the same, but you can now choose among different feels, according to how stiff or light you prefer the touch to be. Furthermore, some models are split in the middle, with the resulting two halves allowing a more natural placement of the hands. Keyboards are connected to a plug in the back of the computer's case by a flexible cable, permitting you to place the keyboard wherever it is most comfortable.

Modem The modem is a computer peripheral that connects the computer to a phone line. Modems are used to log onto the Internet and online services. External and internal models are available in different speeds. External modems plug into the serial port on the back of the computer, whereas internal models are expansion cards that plug directly into the internal circuit board, revealing a phone line jack protruding from the computer's rear panel. Currently, the most common speeds available are 14,000 bps (bits per second) and 28,000 bps. The faster models are more expensive, but worth it for enjoying the musical and multimedia aspects of cyberspace.

Monitor The monitor is the computer's screen. Monitors are independent computer components, and can be purchased separately or upgraded. New computers are sold either with or without a monitor. Typical monitor sizes range from 13 to 21 inches in diagonal screen size, but buyers should be aware that there is often a difference between the advertised size and the viewable size. Multimedia monitors include speakers that can be plugged in to the computer's sound card.

Mouse Computer mice are sliding, hand-guided devices that control a screen pointer. The pointer (known as the cursor) selects certain displayed items, and clicking buttons on the mouse activates that item. Users of Macintosh, Atari, and Windows computers use the mouse as their primary navigation tool when working on the computer. Pointing and clicking is the way drop-down menus are unfurled, screen buttons are pushed, menu items are selected, and portions of a file are highlighted, copied, and pasted. Variations on the mouse design abound, including stationary ball devices, touch-sensitive pads, wireless mice, and pointing instruments integrated onto the computer keyboard.

Multi-media computer Computers qualify as multimedia machines if they are equipped with a sound card and speakers; most multimedia computers also contain a CD-ROM drive and a video card that can handle high-speed graphics. Most Macintosh computers are multimedia machines right off the shelf, and many IBM clones also are. You can upgrade PCs by adding multimedia kits that contain an integrated set of peripherals or by purchasing the components separately and installing them. Multimedia computers are necessary to enjoy the graphic and sound elements of the online experience, but are not necessary to accomplish MIDI sequencing or other MIDI studio work.

Parallel cable/port Parallel interfaces are one of the two main ways of connecting an external device to a computer. Such devices are attached to the computer by means of a cable plugged into a port (jack). The parallel interface is used to connect printers, networking cables, and some other peripherals, but usually not modems, MIDI interfaces, or mice. See also *Serial cable/port.*

Printer Printers are external computer peripherals that produce paper replicas of files. Printouts are sometimes called hard copy. The first personal computer printers were of a type known as dot matrix, and delivered readable but unprofessional results. Currently, black-and-white inkjet and laser printers are standard, and color printers are available. Musicians use printers in conjunction with notation programs to print copies of scores and charts. Printers don't often come with computers, and must usually be purchased separately.

Serial cable/port Serial interfaces are one of the two main ways of connecting an external device to a computer. Such devices are attached to the computer by means of a cable, plugged into a port (jack). The serial interface is used to connect mice, modems, MIDI interfaces, and occasionally printers. See also *Parallel cable/port.*

Sound Blaster A popular brand of sound card for computers. It has become so popular that sound cards in general are sometimes called sound blasters.

Sound card A type of computer expansion circuit board, sound cards are plugged into the motherboard (main circuit board of the computer), thereby upgrading the audio properties of the computer. They are an important part of a multimedia upgrade. Once installed, the card reveals audio inputs and outputs at the back of the computer case. They give the computer basic audio capabilities, although you have to add speakers or headphones in order to hear anything. They are also MIDI instruments, and make audible MIDI files played through the computer. If you have a music keyboard attached to the computer by means of a MIDI interface (included on some sound cards), the built-in MIDI sounds can be accessed and played from the music keyboard. High-end sound cards feature sampled waveforms in addition to the synthetic waveforms on the lower-end models, and generally offer better fidelity.

Standard Computer instructions that are built into the computer and apply to a specific type of operation.

Video card A type of computer expansion circuit board, video cards are plugged into the motherboard (main circuit board of the computer), thereby upgrading the visual properties of the computer. Every computer has a video card, whether from the factory or added later, which acts as the liaison between the circuit board and the monitor. Instructions from the internal circuits pass through the video card and are translated optimally for display on the monitor. Upgrading the video card usually adds memory for speeding up the display process, or internal bandwidth (a measure of how much information can pass through at once), which also quickens video performance. Video cards have a jack on one end, which remains visible at the back of the computer after installation, into which you plug the monitor.

SOFTWARE

Application
An application (or "app") is a software program that creates something that can be saved, such as a letter, musical composition, synthesizer patch, retouched photograph, album liner notes, or any number of other creations, musical and nonmusical. The application "applies" itself to a task, at the direction of the user, and ends up with a file that can be saved on the computer's hard drive, reviewed at a later date, changed, and saved again. Application programs differ from software that operates automatically, without human input, such as on-screen clocks or screen savers. Such automatic utility programs, although they do affect the operation of the computer, don't create new files as applications do.

Digitization
The process by which a real-world phenomenon is translated into computer data. For musicians, the essential digital translation process applies to sound and music. (Other multimedia digitization applies to pictures and video.) Sound is digitized by hardware converters that make numeric representations of the shape of sound waves. The resulting mass of numbers constitutes a sound file. When the file's numbers are played back, other converters perform the opposite task, reshaping the sound wave from the numeric description. The digitization process varies in accuracy and fidelity, depending on a few factors including the equipment used. Under the best conditions and equipment, digitized sound (as heard on CDs, for example) is quite accurate to most ears. Sound digitization is used in music studios to create instrument samples, record a performance to a computer's hard drive, and create a computer sound file for sharing online.

File extension
Every computer file is named according to a certain format, in which the name is followed by a period, which in turn can be followed by one, two, or (usually) three characters. An example is FILENAME.XXX. The file extension is .XXX, and it indicates what type of file it is. Every type of application program uses a specific file extension for saving its files. MIDI files, for example, usually

have the .MID file extension, and digitized sound files often have the .WAV extension. Graphic files have many different recognizable file extensions.

Freeware Freeware is free software, usually available from online sources. When you download freeware programs, keep in mind that you get what you pay for. However, many amateur and professional programmers create helpful utilities for their own computers and distribute them as freeware, with no interest in earning revenue from the product. See also *Shareware*.

Graphic file A graphic file is a digitized picture. Some common graphic digitizations include scanned photographs and artworks created with computer paint programs. Most graphic files are recognizable by one of the graphic file extensions (.GIF, .JPG, .TIF, .BMP, .PIC, and .PCX).

MIDI file MIDI sequences that have been saved as computer files are called MIDI files, and they can be stored, uploaded online, distributed on a floppy disk, shared with other musicians, and played through any MIDI studio. Because MIDI files contain simple data commands from digital instruments, not digitizations of sound waves, they are much smaller and easier to share than sound files. Because they save so much memory, they are often used in multimedia game soundtracks, where memory is at a premium. (Of course, they don't sound as realistic or rich as sound files.)

Multimedia file A multimedia file is any graphic, sound, movie, animation, or other nontext file that can be used on a computer. The word *multimedia* also refers to a program that uses pictures, sounds, and videos.

Music software There are many types of music software, and hundreds of titles within each type. Music programs are similar to other types of software, except that they have a specifically musical purpose. The main types of music applications for musicians are MIDI programs (sequencers, synthesizer programmers, sound librarians, samplers), educational programs (instrument tutorials, music theory learning), notation programs (scoring and printing of music), and hard disk recording programs (multitrack digital recording and editing).

Sequencer A sequencer is a MIDI data recorder, used in MIDI production as the main recording device. Sequencers do not record sound, and do not take input from microphones. They record data events such as note-on and note-off commands from keyboards (generated when you press a key), as well as all other events associated with a performance on a MIDI instrument, such as pedalings and manipulations of the pitch-bend wheel. When the recording (sequence of data events) is played back, the MIDI instrument receives the data and re-creates the performance. Most sequencers are software packages used on personal computers, but standalone hardware models are also available.

Share-ware Shareware is a software distribution system that relies on the honesty of its customers. Shareware programs are acquired from online sources by means of downloading, and can be used free of charge for a trial period. If you keep the program beyond the trial period, you must register and pay for it. Using an honor system eliminates the retail link of the distribution chain, making shareware products less expensive than their store-bought counterparts. Some shareware programs automatically become disabled when the trial period expires, so you have to register the software to continue using it. Other programs pester you with notices flashing on the screen until you register them. Music shareware includes sequencers, synthesizer editor/librarians, and all kinds of tutorial programs.

Sound file Sound files contain digitized sound, and can be played on a multimedia computer with the proper software. They are created through an audio digitizing process accomplished either on a PC with sound recording software, or a dedicated hardware sampler. Sound files can be found and shared online on the Internet and other online sources. In most cases they must be downloaded to be played, which is often a time-consuming process, and sound files can be large. New Internet technology also makes available audio streaming, which plays a sound file immediately, bypassing the download process. Sound files, whether streamed or not, are a high-tech method of promoting and introducing music online. Some commercial music stars release singles on the Internet, in the form of a sound file, before making them available to radio stations or stores.

Utility Computer utilities are small programs that serve a specific purpose. Unlike applications, which tend to be larger, more complex programs offering a variety of features and uses, utilities are geared toward doing a single thing very well, such as decompressing files, putting a clock on your screen, or displaying a certain type of graphic file. There are thousands of utility types, many of them available for downloading as shareware.

WAV file A WAV file is a type of sound file, distinguished by the .WAV file extension. This type of file is often found on the Internet. They should not be confused with MIDI files. WAV files are digitized versions of acoustic sounds; MIDI files are sequences of MIDI data.

Word processor Word processors create text documents, sometimes enabling you to include graphics in the file. Musicians use them to write press releases, promotional copy, album liner notes, and other relevant text documents. There is great variety in user-friendliness and power among word processors. Almost all new computers come with a basic text program included, from which users can upgrade to a more powerful program if desired. The best word processors are available only in computer software stores, not online.

PART TWO
MIDI

The Musical Instrument Digital Interface (MIDI) begins to affect Penelope Envelope's professional life in two ways. First, she buys a portable digital piano so she can play gigs in rooms that don't have an acoustic piano. Over the last few years she has turned down such jobs, and now figures it's time to exercise her back muscles by hauling around her own rig. Soon after, in a studio session, the producer asks her to lay down a simple synthesizer part—just a few chords. It dawns on Penny that if she had a similar synth at home, she could enhance her arrangements, and possibly get some work recording other people's arrangements. She talks to the producer and gets some hints. Soon after, Penny has a basic setup clustered around her computer. She buys a software sequencing program for MIDI recording, and uses her digital piano and new synthesizer tone module for all the sounds she needs to start.

Pat Chedit, meanwhile, has started experimenting with MIDI in his band. A fair keyboardist in his own right (though not nearly as facile as Penny), Pat bought a workstation: an all-in-one instrument that can record an 8-track composition using its own instrument and drum sounds. At first, Pat used it primarily to sketch new tunes, and it helped the band learn them much faster than the old, haphazard method of trying to play and sing all the parts at once. Eventually, Pat started incorporating MIDI sequences into the band's performances, fattening their sound and spicing up their textures. Getting hooked, Pat put more and more effort into his MIDI arrangements as he acquired new tone modules, hooking everything up to his computer at home and using the workstation by itself at gigs.

5

HOW MIDI WORKS

You may have heard of MIDI and know that it plays a part in the digitization of music, and is something that can be used at home by any musician or music-lover; perhaps you have even seen a MIDI studio. But what is it exactly, what does it do, how does it work, and where do you get it?

THE UNIVERSAL LANGUAGE

MIDI is an acronym for an intimidating string of words: Musical Instrument Digital Interface. That phrase alone can put off a digitally tentative musician. But when you break the phrase down to its components, it begins to show its essentially friendly and useful nature. Right away you know it's about musical instruments. Then there's the digital part: You know it belongs to the digital revolution.

Finally, MIDI is an interface, which simply means a go-between. All interfaces stand between two or more things, making it easier to bring those things together. As an interface, MIDI acts as a bridge between musical instruments (such as keyboards and electric pianos) of the digital persuasion. It acts as a translator by providing a common language for digital instruments. What is the point of this?

Electronic instruments have been around for decades. Organs,

REAL WORDS

MIDI has done more to change the face of all music, from popular to filmscores, than any other innovation since the pencil. But it's only a tool: It won't make you a better composer, but it may make it easier for you to get whatever composition is in your head onto tape or paper. People often overlook the possibilities of using MIDI for automatic transcription of your pieces, ear training, musical and vocal practice, and experimentation with various sounds and techniques. Musique concrète, for example, can also be accomplished with MIDI.

Craig Patterson
midigod@aol.com

guitars, and pianos have had electronic counterparts since the 1960s and earlier. For a long time it never occurred to anyone to force them to communicate with each other. What would be the point of hooking together a guitar and an organ, even if it were possible?

Such a conception began with the advent of digital instruments. A digital instrument is one whose operation is based on printed circuits and computer processing. At some point between pressing a key (or plucking a string, drawing a bow, or tapping a stick) and hearing a sound, digital data is generated. The big real-

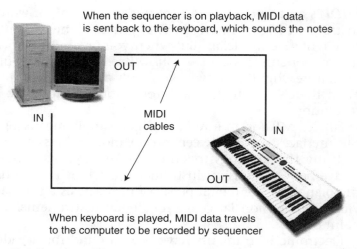

When the sequencer is on playback, MIDI data is sent back to the keyboard, which sounds the notes

OUT

IN

MIDI cables

IN

OUT

When keyboard is played, MIDI data travels to the computer to be recorded by sequencer

The simplest MIDI sequencing setup, using a computer and a keyboard.

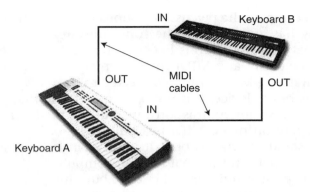

A simple MIDI connection between two keyboards. The most basic
two-keyboard MIDI setup is connected like an endless loop. The MIDI
Out jack of Keyboard A is plugged into the MIDI In jack of Keyboard
B, and the MIDI Out jack of Keyboard B is connected to the MIDI In
jack of Keyboard A. In other words, each MIDI In and Out jack is connected to the opposite jack in the other keyboard. This setup lets you
control the other instrument's sounds from either keyboard, or
merge the output of both keyboards.

ization among instrument manufacturers at the beginning of the
computer revolution was that the functions common to all digital
instruments could be digitized in a single language. Those functions consist primarily of beginning a note, ending a note, and
controlling the force (loudness) with which a note is played and
the pitch of a note. A note's pitch, volume, and duration could be
translated into digital terms understandable by any instrument or
by a computer.

The value of this translation lies in MIDI's ability to control a
digital instrument from either a computer or another instrument.
So with everyone speaking the same language through a translator, any one participant can call the shots and bring the rest along
in a unified activity.

One of the extraordinary features of MIDI's ability to link
instruments together is the equality it brings to different *types* of
MIDI instruments. From the neutral digital viewpoint of MIDI, a
violin is equal to a keyboard, and a drum set is equal to a digital
piano. Any musical instrument equipped at the factory to generate **MIDI data** can be linked to any other such instrument
through MIDI, regardless of whether the instruments are struck,
bowed, plucked, or blown through in their acoustic form. A digital drum set (yes, there are such things!) equipped with MIDI
capability can therefore be used to play the sounds of a keyboard,
as long as the two instruments are connected together. Likewise, a

Tone modules are described beginning on page 122.

Computer operating systems are discussed beginning on page 15.

keyboard can play the percussion sounds of a drum machine. This flexibility has given rise to the **tone module**, a common MIDI device that contains sounds like a keyboard, but no keyboard. It can be played by any MIDI instrument (such as a keyboard, a MIDI guitar, or a MIDI violin) connected to it.

MIDI is not a device, it is not a separate thing that you buy to apply to an instrument. It is software, but not the kind of software that you buy on disks. MIDI is a built-in agreed-upon language (called a standard) that is built into MIDI instruments and computers and MIDI software that runs on computers.

Like the programming number code built into some VCRs, or a computer's operating system, the MIDI spec is not something you need to worry about, purchase, install, or even understand in detail. When you buy a MIDI keyboard instrument, MIDI software package, or MIDI computer, you have MIDI, ready to be used.

Just about all keyboards made today are MIDI-equipped, but if you have an older instrument, or if there is ever any doubt about whether a keyboard is MIDI, just look at the back panel. Among the plugs for audio output cables are jacks labeled with the word *MIDI*.

If such jacks are not present anywhere on the back panel, it's not a MIDI instrument, and cannot be connected to other MIDI instruments or to a computer. In the case of nonkeyboard instruments such as guitars and violins, the MIDI versions always come with accompanying hardware, so there's no mistaking whether it is MIDI or non-MIDI.

Note: Although we can speak of "MIDI computers," it's worth noting again that most computers are not manufactured with MIDI capability. With the exception of Atari computers, which are no longer available in new-equipment stores, that capability must be added either in the store by the dealer, or in the home by the user. The necessary addition is called a MIDI interface, one of the peripherals discussed below. If a MIDI interface is added in the store (only high-tech music stores make such an addition), customers can buy, off the shelf, what is effectively a MIDI computer.

Using MIDI requires a few accessories:

Sequencers are explained beginning on page 126.

■ **MIDI jacks.** On the back of all MIDI devices are **MIDI ports** or MIDI plugs, which have five holes in a face-down semicircle, and come in three types: In, Out, and Thru. The In jack receives MIDI data from MIDI instruments and recording devices. The Out jack sends MIDI data from the instrument's own keyboard to other instruments and sequencers. The Thru jack takes MIDI data arriving at the In jack and passes it on to any instruments or computer connected to it.

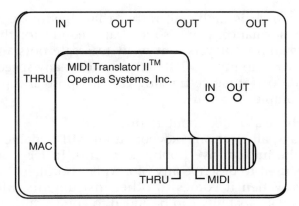

A computer MIDI interface.

■ **MIDI cables.** Insulated wires similar to those found in the back of a home stereo system, **MIDI cables** connect MIDI devices at their MIDI ports. At each end of a MIDI cable is a plug with five small pins that correspond to the five holes in a MIDI jack. MIDI cables are completely interchangeable, and can be used with equal effectiveness when connecting to MIDI In, Out, or Thru jacks.

■ **MIDI interface.** A little box equipped with MIDI jacks connecting via cable to the jacks on a computer, the **MIDI interface** enables the computer to understand and process MIDI note data coming from MIDI instruments.

Aside from the hardware peripherals discussed above, the primary components of a MIDI studio are the instruments, of course. You need at least one of these to make MIDI music—as well as a sequencer, and, generally speaking, a computer. Read on to see what MIDI instruments consist of and what types are available.

Q & A: STARTING WITH MIDI

Q What can you do with MIDI?

A MIDI instruments are used for both performance and recording, just like acoustic instruments. As a performance tool, the advantage to MIDI is that it can coordinate the playing of many different instruments as though one player had 4 or 40 pairs of hands to play all the instruments, all heard through a single speaker. As a recording tool, its advantage lies in the control you have over what you've recorded: You can correct mistakes in a MIDI performance, which is digitized, rather than having to re-record an entire performance. It is also a great medium for those who are not outstanding players, but want to create outstanding music. Because you can input MIDI data (music) at any speed, even those with little performance training can compose and produce wonderful, complex recordings.

Q Do you have a choice about getting MIDI?

A These days, all electronic keyboards are MIDI-enabled (the exception is the inexpensive hobby keyboard). In fact, the word *keyboard* is used to describe any of a wide assortment of MIDI components. When it comes to other instruments, MIDI must be added. MIDI capability can be added to guitars fairly easily, and to pianos with great difficulty.

Q Are there different types of MIDI?

A There are two types. General MIDI, described later in this chapter, is an important variant of MIDI (MIDI upgrades are not produced, as with computer software). However, MIDI is the same in every brand of MIDI instrument. There is no such thing as a brand of MIDI, although there certainly are brands (manufacturers) of MIDI instruments. The key features of MIDI (receiving and emitting digital and sound data, recording and manipulating the data) and its key components (instruments, sequencers, computers, interface boxes) work exactly the same way in all MIDI instruments, regardless of brand.

Q Why doesn't MIDI evolve through upgrades like other software and computer operating systems?

A That is one of the great unresolved issues of MIDI. Many people have proposed a second version of the MIDI specifications, which would create MIDI 2.0, just like software programs that issue more advanced, progressively numbered versions. Because MIDI is a standard agreed upon by many instrument manufacturing companies, not a product created by a single company, developing successive versions and agreeing on improvements, is more complicated than with typical computer software or operating systems. It's a miracle that MIDI was ever implemented in the first place, and it looks like MIDI musicians must be content with what they have for the foreseeable future. Aside from General MIDI, no variations have been introduced in MIDI's lifetime.

Q Is MIDI expensive?

A It depends very much on how enthusiastic you become with it. MIDI production can be a fairly expensive hobby or business, and one with great rewards. On the other hand, the expense can end after an initial modest purchase if you remain satisfied with the

LINK

For complete price information, see Chapter 8, "The Musician's Shopping Guide to MIDI."

sounds and features of your components. In the early years of MIDI, the technology was developing and improving so rapidly that many musicians were replacing equipment at a furious pace and spending large amounts of money to remain current. It was worthwhile in those days, because the improvements in sound quality and power features were significant. Now that the technology is more mature, the improvements are more subtle and perhaps less worth trading in components for.

Q Is MIDI difficult to use and master?

A Getting comfortable with MIDI, especially when recording (sequencing), requires thinking about music in a different way, in different terms. Once you gain a basic fluency, though, MIDI is easier in some ways than mastering an acoustic instrument. Because it enables you to construct music bit by bit if you choose, MIDI supports a more analytical approach than real-time music performance does. Hooking up MIDI connections is no more challenging than setting up a multicomponent home stereo system.

MIDI brings other unique skills into play. Sequencing software is as powerful, and mastering it requires about the same dedication, as a state-of-the-art word processing program. Synthesizer programming is a specialized skill that yields to experimentation, but requires a fairly steep learning curve; however, it's not a necessary skill. Creating original samples with a sampler is perhaps the most difficult MIDI task, but it is likewise an optional skill. The upshot: MIDI delivers results no matter what your level of dedication, and becomes more rewarding the more you apply yourself to its mastery.

THIS IS AN INSTRUMENT?

MIDI instruments look like traditional musical instruments, but if you were to open one up, you might have trouble relating to the insides. MIDI instruments consist of these components:

- **The keyboard.** MIDI keyboards have the look and feel of their older electronic keyboard cousins.

- **The circuit board.** Like a computer, MIDI instruments are digital devices. The circuit board, like a computer's processor chip, handles tasks such as receiving input from the built-in keyboard when you press the keys and passing that input on to other parts of the instrument.

- **Oscillators.** Oscillators in a musical instrument? That may evoke images of round, flickering screens in the laboratories of

B-movies, but sound oscillators are the components that make the sounds emitted by MIDI instruments.

- **Input and output jacks.** The back panel of a MIDI instrument, like a computer, contains various jacks for emitting and receiving electronic signals. The MIDI jacks are usually placed a threesome: In, Out, and Thru.

- **Separate audio output jacks.** Cables are plugged into these jacks, which take the keyboard's sound to a mixer or amplifier. Audio inputs are found on digital samplers, which are described later in this chapter. Advanced MIDI keyboards may also have other interface jacks, such as a Small Computer Systems Interface (SCSI, pronounced SCUZZY) connection with a computer or a video connection for an external monitor.

- **Disk drives.** Not all MIDI instruments have a disk drive, but it has been an increasingly common feature since the late 1980s, and solidifies the connection between MIDI instruments and computers.

So, a MIDI instrument is basically a specialized computer. The circuit board receives input from its own piano-style keyboard, processes that input, sends it to the oscillators and from there to the output jacks.

MASTERS, SLAVES, AND OTHER CLASS DISTINCTIONS

MIDI devices are divided into three classes:

- **Masters.** Commonly called **MIDI controllers**, masters are devices that control other devices. MIDI is the common lan-

---

REAL WORDS

I have built a home studio around an Atari and have worked with MIDI for years. MIDI and digital audio recording allow me to get my creativity out of my head and into something tangible that I can share, not to mention allowing me to work at my own pace without studio fees and costs. I have used MIDI to do a graphics show, timed in conjunction with my songs, at live shows. Using digital tools, time and space are mine to manipulate.

Paul Luscher, Insanity Void
lenkel@ultra1.inconnect.com

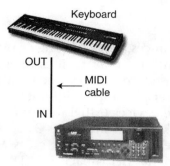

Keyboard

OUT

MIDI
cable

IN

Tone module (slave)

Connecting a keyboard master to a tone module slave with a
MIDI cable. Connecting a keyboard to a tone module is the simplest possible MIDI setup because only the keyboard can be a
master and only the tone module can be a slave. Because of the
defined roles of the two instruments, only one MIDI cable is
needed, linking the MIDI Out jack of the keyboard to the MIDI In
jack of the tone module. With this connection, you can play the
tone module from the keyboard as if they were a single instrument, even combining the outputs of the two instruments.

guage by which they exert their control. An example of a controller is a MIDI instrument that controls a tone module or
drum machine. Keyboard controllers are the most common
type, but any MIDI instrument can control any other.

■ **Slaves.** When a MIDI device is being played by another MIDI
device, it is said to be a **MIDI slave.** This may violate the civil
liberties of machines, but it is one of the most useful aspects of
MIDI. A slave receives input not from its own keyboard (in
fact, it may not have a keyboard), but from some other source.
That source could be another instrument "MIDI'd up" to the
slave, or it could be a sequencer playing back a recorded part.

LINK

Using MIDI In
and Out jacks
is explained
beginning on
page 102.

■ **Recorders.** MIDI **sequencers** fall into their own category
because when they are in record mode they are neither controllers nor slaves. While recording, they are simply keeping
track of the MIDI input arriving through the MIDI In jack.
When playing back, on the other hand, they become controllers, as the MIDI data leaving the sequencer through the
MIDI Out jack controls any instruments hooked up to the
sequencer. Because sequencers most often reside in computers
as software (although hardware sequencing devices also exist),
the computer becomes a MIDI device when running the
sequencer.

MIDI CHANNELS

In most technological advances, there are one or two features that distinguish the new invention from previous ones, and drive the effectiveness of devices based on the new technology. The critical feature of MIDI is its universal compatibility; it is a standard, and as such connects disparate devices (MIDI instruments, computers) into a coherent network (**MIDI studio**). Once that has been accomplished, the compelling feature that gives MIDI its power and flexibility is its multichannel capacity. MIDI channels drive the usefulness of MIDI as a recording and performance standard, and are, more than any other single aspect of the standard, responsible for the digital revolution in music.

WHAT ARE MIDI CHANNELS?

The 16 **MIDI channels** have nothing to do with broadcasting (as TV channels do), but they do relate to transmitting MIDI data and distributing it through a MIDI studio. Every sound **patch** used in a MIDI recording is assigned to, or tagged with, a MIDI channel, with the result that the virtual instruments performing a MIDI sequence are kept separate and distinct by their channel assignments. MIDI channel assignments are recorded along with other MIDI data, as part of each **MIDI event.** For example, when you record a note played on a MIDI keyboard into a sequencer, you are recording not only the pitch (key assignment), volume (force with which the key is struck), and duration (how long you hold the key down), but also the MIDI channel currently set to transmit from the keyboard. When that recorded part (which probably contains more than one note) is played back, the receiving keyboard responds by sounding the patch assigned to the recorded MIDI channel. If you change the patch assigned to that MIDI channel in the instrument between recording the part and playing it back, you hear the new sound on playback. In this way, you can record a part and plug in different sound patches as you repeatedly play it back, until you find the perfect virtual instrument for the part.

In recording situations, MIDI channels are associated with MIDI tracks, but they are not the same thing. Musicians with a recording background might find the concept of MIDI channels particularly perplexing if they are accustomed to thinking of a channel as an input slot on a mixing board. Mixing channels are definitely connected in a one-to-one relationship with recorded tracks. MIDI channels are more independent, and may or may not correspond directly with **virtual tracks** (tracks of MIDI events rather than sounds) recorded in a sequencer. If you haven't spent time in a recording studio, and this metaphor is meaningless, you only need to remember one thing: MIDI channels are the numbers to which you assign the patches (sound programs) you want to use in your sequence. The channels keep all the parts of your sequence straight.

MIDI channels are used in performance as well as recording. In fact, they are used anytime one MIDI device communicates with another. Typical MIDI performance setups use one or more controllers (usually keyboards) and one or more slaves. The slaves can be rack-mounted **sound modules** or other keyboards. On stage a keyboardist needs to switch from one sound to another very quickly, either between songs or during a song. By assigning sound patches (and stacks of patches) to different MIDI channels, the keyboardist can access those sounds from a keyboard controller by changing the MIDI channel of that controller, which takes only a second. MIDI channels are used in three modes: Receive, Transmit, and Omni.

Sound modules, also called tone modules, are described beginning on page 122.

MIDI Channel Modes

■ Receive mode is used by MIDI slaves to determine which MIDI channel they will respond to. For example, if a sound module is set to Receive MIDI channel 5, then data coming in the MIDI In jack tagged with other MIDI channels will be ignored, and no

Sequencer Track	Sample or Synth Patch	MIDI Channel	Sound Source: MIDI Component	Mixer Channel
1	piano	1	digital piano	9
2	bass	9	tone module	10
3	synth strings	13	tone module	11
4	kick drum	5	drum machine	12
5	snare drum	5	drum machine	13
6	high-hats	5	drum machine	14
7	congas	5	drum machine	15

MIDI channels. This table shows how the instrument sounds used in a MIDI sequence might be distributed among sequencer tracks, MIDI channels, and mixer channels. The point is that MIDI channels don't need to match sequencer tracks, and neither category needs to match mixer channel assignments. All these factors are distributed differently depending on the piece's requirements; the alignment in this table is just an example. The MIDI studio in this setup contains a digital piano, a tone module, and a drum machine. Note that all the drum tracks, though separated on different sequencer tracks and mixer channels, are assigned to the same MIDI channel in the drum machine.

sound will result. Receive mode can be set to only one channel at a time.

■ Transmit mode is used by controllers to access sound patches assigned to a certain MIDI channel in sound modules and other slaves. When a keyboard controller is set to Transmit MIDI channel 5, MIDI data tagged with that channel is transmitted through the MIDI OUT jack and circulated through the MIDI studio; sound modules and other slaves set to receive MIDI channel 5 will generate tones in response to that data. Transmit mode can be set to only one channel at a time.

■ Omni mode is a specialized Receive setting that is most commonly used in MIDI recording studios. Omni mode enables a MIDI **multitimbral** instrument (an instrument capable of playing more than one part simultaneously when connected to a sequencer) to respond to all MIDI channels that come streaming through the MIDI In jack. The Omni setting is used when a sequencer is playing back a multitrack, multichannel MIDI composition through a single keyboard or sound module. The sound module receives all the parts, each recorded with its own MIDI channel, and simultaneously plays the correct parts with the correct sounds. You must assign the correct patches to the desired MIDI channels within the sound module, then set it to Omni channel reception.

Q & A: MIDI CHANNELS

Q Can more than 16 MIDI channels be used?

A The answer is *yes,* even though the official MIDI specification only allows for 16 channels. Software and hardware manufacturers have gotten around the 16-channel limitation in response to demand by MIDI musicians. Sixteen channels may seem like a lot at first, but when you think about it, and especially when you begin producing MIDI music, it's an uncomfortable constraint. If you were creating an orchestral MIDI texture, for example, 16 parts would be barely enough to represent a symphonic range of instrumentation. Even pop songs can require more than 16 parts if several of the drum and percussion instruments originate in different sound modules and are assigned to different MIDI channels. Expanded MIDI channel capacity requires an addition of both hardware and software, usually connected to the sequencing program. It is the sequencer that must recognize higher-numbered MIDI channels and be able to play them back. The extra hardware generally consists of a MIDI port expander that multiplies the studio's channel capacity in increments of 16.

Q Are MIDI channels the same as MIDI tracks?

A No, but they are related. A MIDI channel is often associated with a single MIDI recorded track. For example, the bass part of your song may be sounded by an electric bass sample from a particular tone module, assigned to MIDI channel 9. To help keep things straight in your mind, you might decide to record the part on track 9 in your sequencer, labeling it "electric bass ch. 9." But it's not necessary to be that organized, or even desirable in some cases. Many MIDI sequences use far more tracks than channels, for one thing, and it's impossible to stay organized so easily. MIDI channels separate your sound patches so they play only when they're supposed to; MIDI tracks separate your recorded parts, regardless of the sounds you're using. You might record a piano solo seven times, for instance, with each recording on a different track, but the MIDI channel (and the sound sample assigned to that channel) would be the same in each case. (Of course, you would play back only one at a time, using the track muting feature of your sequencer on the other takes.)

Q Can more than one sound patch be assigned to a single MIDI channel?

A Yes. This is known as sound layering, and is an efficient way of thickening the musical texture. Say you have a piano sample assigned to channel 1, and it's the main solo instrument part of your MIDI composition. After you record the main parts, the piano part seems a bit thin—it doesn't cut through the mix with a high enough sonic profile. You might assign a hard-edged electric piano patch from another sound module to channel 1, and when you play back the sequence the added patch will automatically play the part in unison with the original piano sample. Lush orchestra parts and orchestral hits can be synthesized the same way, by layering wads of sound onto the same MIDI channel. Layering is a popular technique in performance, where the keyboardist has fewer options than the studio artist. Layering onto one MIDI channel is a useful live way of getting a fat sound, and stage players often create complex layers in advance, selecting them quickly in performance by switching from one MIDI Transmit channel to another on their master keyboard controllers.

Q Can different MIDI devices be set to the same MIDI channel?

A Yes, but this is a less economical way of accomplishing sound layering. Rather than thinking in terms of a device's MIDI Receive channel setting, it's usually better to consider each sound patch's channel assignment. Doing it that way, you would set all the participating sound modules to the Omni receive setting.

Q Do I really have to worry about MIDI channels?

A Not at first. With a one-keyboard setup, organizing sounds by MIDI channel doesn't usually come into play. Then again, if that single keyboard happens to be a recording workstation, you might want to get acquainted with MIDI channels to create some multilayered music. Even so, workstations often equate channels with the tracks of their internal sequencers, to a greater degree than when the sequencer is a separate component. It's when a MIDI studio adds a separate sequencer that MIDI channels really become important, and at that point the best education is to learn by doing.

BASIC MIDI CONNECTIONS

Getting started with MIDI requires very little, although it can easily expand in complexity. A single MIDI instrument makes up a studio of sorts, but things get more interesting as other instruments and devices are added. With two (or more) MIDI devices and two (or more) MIDI cables, you're ready to make MIDI music. As mentioned before, MIDI jacks are located on the back of digital instruments, and are either In, Out, or Thru jacks. Here are the principles of MIDI connectivity:

■ **In to Out and Out to In.** Never connect a MIDI cable from one

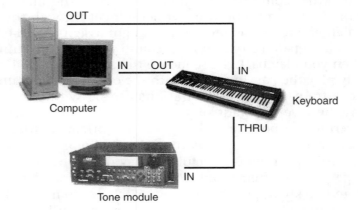

A basic MIDI setup with a computer, using the keyboard's MIDI In, Out, and Thru jacks. The MIDI Thru jack enables several instruments to be daisy-chained. In this diagram only two instruments are connected to a computer, but you can extend the chain to include any number of MIDI keyboards and tone modules. The MIDI Thru jack takes MIDI information coming into the keyboard from the computer and passes it unchanged to the tone module. It happens so fast that the keyboard and tone module process the information at virtually the same time.

MIDI jack to another of the same persuasion (In to In, for example). The cables are meant to carry MIDI data from a controller through the Out jack to a slave through the In jack.

■ **Thru to In.** The MIDI Thru jack replicates data arriving at the In jack, and automatically sends it out again by means of the Thru jack. Thru differs from Out in that the host instrument doesn't need to be generating any data for the Thru jack to be active. The Out jack carries only information produced by the host machine, whereas the Thru jack takes everything coming through the In jack and passes it on indiscriminately. Why? Because not all data is meant for all instruments. If a sequencer is playing back a multitrack composition to a studio of several keyboards and sound modules, the multiple parts will be tagged (by MIDI channel) for different machines. The Thru jack ensures that each instrument in the MIDI loop gets the playback data.

With the simple principles of MIDI connectivity, you can expand a simple studio setup without limit. With just two devices (either two instruments or one instrument and a computer/sequencer), you need only make the In to Out and Out to In connections between the two machines. When you add a third device, the Thru jack is used to create a chain of MIDI data. This chain can be extended to as large a circle of instruments as you like (or can afford).

Q & A: MIDI CONNECTIONS

Q Are there different types of MIDI cable for incoming and outgoing MIDI data?

A No, all MIDI cables are the same. MIDI cables come in different lengths, but each one is interchangeable in function with every other one. Don't be confused by colored cables; that's just for convenience, and doesn't affect how the cable should be used.

Q Is there ever a delay in sending or receiving MIDI data?

A Some people are afraid of building up long MIDI instrument chains, in which every bit of data travels sequentially from one instrument to another until it completes the circuit of the entire studio. The fear is that the last instrument will receive the data a bit later than the first, and the resulting sounds will be slightly out of synch. The fear is unfounded. Delays can exist in some situations, but they are so minuscule as to be unnoticeable. Practically speaking, MIDI data reception delays are not a concern.

Q Is there any danger of plugging MIDI cables into the wrong jacks?

A In a word, no. It's impossible to plug a MIDI cable into a jack other than a MIDI jack. It is possible to plug it into the wrong MIDI jack, such as mistakenly running a cable from one MIDI In jack to another MIDI In jack. In that case, and in all other examples of confused connections, the result will be an unfortunate silence when you are expecting sound, but there is nothing damaging (except perhaps to your dignity) about making wrong connections. Simply correct the mistake and get back to the music.

GENERAL MIDI

One of the hallmarks of MIDI is compatibility. In fact, that's the whole purpose of the MIDI standard. MIDI instruments are by definition compatible with each other. By extension, MIDI studios are compatible with each other—to a point. A MIDI sequence recorded on one computer, loaded into another computer's sequencing program, will play back and control any MIDI instruments that are connected to the second studio setup.

MIDI sequencing software is described on page 42, and sequencers are explained on page 126.

However, if those MIDI instruments are different from the synths, samplers, and modules of the first studio, the sequence will have quite a different sound. So, although the sequence plays back normally, and the MIDI event data is perfectly understood by the second studio, it's not always an easy task to make a sequence sound the same as in the original studio. All the same notes, tracks, and timings are there, but the sounds may differ drastically.

The General MIDI (GM) standard deals with the variations of studio instrumentation by instituting a basic sound-type palette that is identical from one GM setup to another. This is a good moment to make note of the difference between a sound-type palette and a sound palette. General MIDI doesn't deal with sounds at all. Instead, it assigns sound types—such as piano, electric piano, flute, electric bass, string section, and snare drum—to specific slots in the GM lineup of sounds. There are 128 slots, and therefore 128 sound types. Some overlap is built in to accommodate variations within a sound type. Any manufacturer of a General MIDI device, such as a sound module or computer sound card, places proprietary versions of these sound types in each appropriate slot. So one GM device might have a great piano patch but lousy percussion sounds, while another contains beautiful electric pianos but unrealistic strings. In each case, regardless of the device's sound quality, the arrangement of sound types conforms to the General MIDI alignment.

General MIDI ensures that a sequence created in one studio will sound roughly the same in another studio. But the results are always approximations because the sound patches differ among GM instruments. It is a low-level way of ensuring **MIDI file** compatibility between studios because it doesn't allow for any original sound programming or sampling. Accordingly, GM devices tend to represent the lower end of the spectrum of MIDI instruments. Few professional-level synthesizers, for example, bother with the General MIDI sound-type alignment because their power is centered on creating new sounds, not using factory presets.

Q & A: GENERAL MIDI

Q Are all MIDI instruments General MIDI instruments?

A No. General MIDI is a certain lineup of MIDI sound types, useful in certain studio applications. Many synthesizers, and all samplers, are non-GM instruments.

Q How can you tell a GM instrument?

A When an instrument fulfills the General MIDI standards, it is usually advertised on the packaging and advertising brochures. Look for the words *GM-capable* and a GM logo. All computer sound cards comply with General MIDI, as do many portable sound modules. Most professional synthesizers do not contain the GM lineup of sound patch types.

Q Should non-GM instruments be avoided?

A Not necessarily. In fact, some people take the opposite approach, avoiding GM instruments if General MIDI compatibility with other studios is not important. There are two main questions to ask yourself when deciding whether you need General MIDI. First, do you want to listen to downloaded files in your studio, and not just on your computer's sound card? Second, do you need to share your own MIDI files with other studios, and upload them to the online world? If the answer is *yes* to either question, then GM is a standard you want to look for, but not necessarily exclusively.

Q Does General MIDI sound as good as regular MIDI?

A General MIDI is limited to a certain range of sound types, and as such is bound to suffer in comparison to the unlimited sound creation properties of non-GM instruments. In light of this, it's no surprise that a GM-only studio may not have the depth of realism, or the sonic imagination, of a studio that is not bound by GM limitations. General MIDI is a standard of convenience, based on the need for highly portable files and compatible playback setups. It sacrifices fidelity to realize that convenience. On the bright side, General MIDI instruments are often less expensive than their professional counterparts.

6

THE MIDI ORCHESTRA

MIDI orchestras, sometimes called virtual orchestras, contain innumerable virtual instruments. An infinite number, actually, when you consider that through sound programming and original sampling, an endless number of timbres can be created and used in a composition. The MIDI composer is absolutely unfettered by traditional limitations of instrumentation. (The MIDI composer has other limitations unique to the digital realm, however.) One of the great appeals of MIDI composition, in fact, is that the composer can be both arranger and *creator* of sounds; the creative process extends to the sounds themselves, and is not constrained to making up melodies, harmonies, and rhythms. To those three traditional building blocks, the MIDI studio adds creative control over the sounds themselves.

Although the virtual MIDI orchestra cannot be inventoried like a classical orchestra, the instruments that produce all the myriad sounds of virtual instruments can be categorized fairly easily. There are several types of MIDI instruments, each fulfilling a definite purpose in a MIDI studio.

SYNTHESIZERS

Strictly speaking, a **synthesizer** is any instrument capable of making new sounds. Synthesizers synthesize sound. These instruments come in many shapes and sizes: They can look like pianos, guitars, computers, or featureless boxes. But typically a synthesizer is a keyboard—in most cases, when someone refers to a synthesizer, they mean a keyboard. Likewise, when you say *keyboard,* you are implying a synthesizer. Most portable performance keyboards used by stage bands are synthesizers of one kind or another. Not all keyboards are synthesizers, and not all synths are keyboards, but that's usually the case.

However, several other kinds of keyboard fit into the galaxy of MIDI instruments. Some have rudimentary synthesis abilities, but more as an afterthought than as a main feature. Others, most notably digital pianos, forsake synthesizer engines completely in favor of other performance or studio resources. More on this shortly.

Synthesizers can be powerful computing devices, capable of bending sounds completely out of shape and twisting them back again. As compositional tools, their home is in the studio. As performance instruments, they require specific playing techniques,

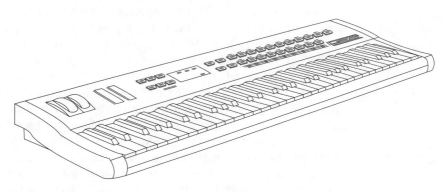

A keyboard synthesizer.

and pianists are often shocked by the adjustment to their technique that these modern keyboards demand. This adjustment is made necessary by the following crucial differences between synths and performance-oriented pianos:

■ For one thing, the keyboards are usually shorter in range than the traditional 88-key piano. Some contain 76 keys, but most are limited to 60 keys (an even five octaves). So right away you know they're not adequate for playing Liszt etudes.

■ The action is very different from that of a piano. The piano is a mechanical instrument, and its action—the internal mechanism that transfers the motion of a key to a struck string—is a complex piece of machinery full of levers, springs, straps, and other finely balanced implements that combine to give the instrument a certain feel under the fingers. Each piano is unique, but a distinctive similarity among them gives the instrument its characteristic playing sensation.

■ A synth, on the other hand, is a plastic keyboard with sensors under the keys, attached to a circuit board. Not exactly a hand-crafted old-world artifact! Plastic keys don't weigh as much as the wooden keys of a piano, and synthesizer keys are not pushing a mechanical action with each key-press. Accordingly, the action is light, and playing on one is disconcerting at first for most pianists. The keys respond more easily, and the lack of resistance makes it all too easy to commit playing errors. Some keyboards address this problem with artificially weighted actions and wood keys, but most synthesizers don't.

■ Synth keyboards are designed to be played in the styles for which they were developed, specifically, rock 'n' roll and rock-influenced modern jazz. Keyboard playing styles in those modern genres feature a good deal of single-note soloing, as opposed to the traditional melody-and-accompaniment style the classical piano was built to accommodate. A peculiar feature of the single-note style is the use of pitch-bend and vibrato. The pitch-bend swoops a note up or down by a controlled degree, and the vibrato adds a certain expressivity to an elongated note, rescuing it from the static sound of a sustained, unwavering tone. Both features enliven the unavoidably artificial sound of a synthesizer by emulating the inaccuracies we take for granted in natural acoustic instruments. Vibrato and pitch-bend are controlled by devices (usually wheels, but sometimes joysticks) located beside the keyboard. Becoming facile with these wheels involves a unique left-hand technique of jumping back and forth between the keyboard and the wheels.

In the studio, synthesizers needn't be performance-friendly to fulfill their potential. As composition and recording tools, they're designed to sound good when playing back sequencer tracks. Recording those tracks is a forgiving experience, and even players uncomfortable with light actions, short keyboards, and the odd challenges of pitch-bend wheels can construct their parts slowly, even one note at a time if necessary. The studio environment brings out the computerish quality of synthesizers, emphasizing their ability to create sounds and process large amounts of MIDI data simultaneously when controlled by a sequencer.

Synths come preloaded with sounds (called patches), divided into banks. There is no standard number of factory sounds to expect in a new keyboard, but most modern models give you over a hundred right off the shelf. When you first unpack and plug in a synthesizer, it sets itself up to play the first sound, probably located in the A-01 slot (bank A, sound 1). Buttons on the top of the keyboard case let you switch among the sounds; in this way you can explore all the instrument sonorities loaded into the synth at the factory. To this sonic palette you can add your own variations by manipulating the tone quality of existing patches, or buy additional sounds from either the manufacturer or a third-party vendor. Typically, the synth provides a couple of empty banks of slots for inserting new sounds; those new sounds are then available through button-pushes, just like the factory sounds. You add newly purchased sounds to a synth by loading them from a floppy disk if the keyboard has a floppy disk drive built in, or by using a small memory card that plugs into a special slot in the synth.

Synthesizers create sounds by means of an internal program called the **synthesis engine.** It sounds more propulsive than it is: The synthesis engine is a number of variables that can be set in fine increments, each influencing the sound in a particular way. The settings available to the user vary from one synthesizer to another, but some broad categories of settings are common to most synth models:

■ **Envelopes.** There is no good reason why one of the most important elements of sound synthesis should be called an envelope, but there's nothing to be done about it. A sound **envelope** is defined by what happens to a sound over time. Does it start with a percussive smack, like a piano hammer hitting the string? Does it have the scratchy beginning of a violin bow? How quickly does the tone decay? Does the tonal quality change during the sustained portion of the note, like a saxophone player changing from a gruff squawk to a sultry tone? Is there vibrato? These are all characteristics of a sound's envelope. Anything that happens to a note, not matter how short

	A			B
01	piano 1		01	orchestral strings
02	piano 2		02	low orchestral strings
03	piano 3		03	thin orchestral strings
04	honky-tonk		04	octave orchestral strings
05	electric pno 1		05	pizzicatto
06	electric pno 2		06	orchestral hit
07	electric pno 3		07	synth strings 1
08	Fender Rhodes		08	synth strings 2
09	rock organ 1		09	synth strings 3
.			.	
.			.	
.			.	

Built-in synthesizer sounds are arranged in banks of programs called patches. Like instruments tend to be grouped together, as illustrated in this example. Most synths contain at least a hundred preloaded sounds, plus some empty bank slots for storing new and altered sounds created by the user.

or long it is, even the brief slap of a woodblock, defines its envelope. Every sound, from a tenor's high C to a gust of wind blowing through a grove of trees, has an envelope. In a synthesizer engine, the envelope is a group of sound characteristics that defines what will happen to the sound. Each synthesizer patch has its own envelope. Some of the envelope settings in synthesizers can be heroically complex, taking the user along a steep learning curve before he or she can work with them comfortably, much less masterfully. Common to all envelopes are three variables: the sound's attack (the very beginning), sustain (the duration of a note), and decay (how the note ends). Most instruments allow you to alter attack, sustain, and decay for three separate aspects of a sound: pitch, tone, and loudness. These three envelopes, in all their individual settings, combine to define how the notes of a patch behave from the moment a key is pressed until the note ends (the envelope completes its cycle) or the key is released (closing out the envelope).

Filters. Like a coffee filter, synth **filters** stop grunge from creeping into a sound. Or, if your prefer, they can create a sound full of grunge. Filters work with sound frequencies (the many different pitches that combine in most sounds). When we listen to a flute playing the C above middle C, for example, we hear primarily the fundamental note (C above middle C), but the human ear also registers other inconspicuous frequencies (pitches) that wouldn't be consciously noticeable unless they were removed. Overtones may be present, and the player is probably contributing a high-frequency sound of breath whistling quietly over the mouthpiece. A synth filter can take a representative flute patch and eliminate the breathy sound by filtering out all frequencies above a certain limit. Or it can emphasize the breath sound by clamping a filter on lower frequencies. Filters work in all sorts of ways; some (high-pass filters) specialize in allowing frequencies above the cutoff point, and others (you guessed it: low-pass filters) open the gate to lower frequencies.

■ **Modulation routings.** The nerdy sound of this parameter makes some musicians run screaming from the room. But modulation routings are easy to define, and result in fun patch behavior. They allow a sound to be modulated (changed in some way) when you move a physical controller (such as the pitch-bend wheel) to which it is routed. So you can make a tone change from smooth to rough by moving the vibrato wheel, give a note vibrato by pressing the volume pedal, or increase its volume by pressing harder on the key. Modulation routings give a patch greater expressive potential.

■ **Waveform substitution.** Switching one waveform, the primary building block of a patch, for another is one of the basic ways of altering a sound, and one of the easiest. Synthesizers are stocked with waveforms (some synthetically created, and some sampled from acoustic instruments) to build new patch creations. In many synths, any patch may contain two or more waveforms simultaneously. Substituting a different waveform in one of those slots can change the sound dramatically. Imagine, for example, a sound patch built on two waveforms: a flute sample and a synthetic waveform that adds a slightly raspy quality to the pure, soft sound of the flute. If you substitute a trumpet sampled waveform for the flute sampled waveform, the result will be drastically sharper and more cutting sound.

To the above basic synth engine parameters, each instrument adds a host of specialized settings that give that model of synthesizer its unique sound characteristics. Creating new sounds in synthesizers is called programming, and slightly adjusting existing sounds by resetting a couple of patch settings is affectionately called tweaking. Many players do not care to delve into the craft, artistry, and science of sound programming; others tweak patch settings here and there to tailor a sound to their playing style. A few enjoy the adventure of creating new sounds, and these few sonic explorers usually invest in computer patch-editing software that is written specifically for their model synthesizer. Most synthesizers can be programmed from their own front panels, using buttons and a small display screen, but dedicated software makes the job much easier. On a computer's larger screen, the complex shapes of sound envelopes can be represented graphically, and all the other (sometimes hundreds) of settings can be consolidated more efficiently.

A Brief History of Sound Synthesis

The history of synthesizers roughly approximates the history of computers. In both cases, they started as large, institutional machines and proceeded through the miniaturizing trend of technology to become smaller, more powerful, and destined for personal use. Early synthesizers of the 1950s and 1960s were unwieldy machines that vaguely resembled telephone switchboards. Changing aspects of the sound (what we now call patch parameters) was accomplished by cabling together various sound-generating modules in different configurations. Though electronic, these machines were analog (not digital), relying on fluctuating voltage currents to produce a basic range of sounds. They could produce only one sound at a time (monotimbral) and, in the early years, only one note at a time (monophonic). The now-antique *Switched-On Bach* recording demonstrated the glittery potential of synthesized sound being put to use with serious cultural intent, but constructing that recording was a complex job encumbered by the limitations of the era. Such an album would be a breeze now, produced with the help of computer-based multitrack sequencing.

Still in the analog age, synthesizers became more compact, eventually being packaged in keyboard forms that could be brought into the home (or professional music studio), and sound creation became an avocation for the hobbyist. Constraints still existed, to be sure: Multitimbrality (the capacity to sound more than one patch at a time) was still to come, and the early keyboard synths, though polyphonic (able to play more than one note at a time) in some cases, had a polyphony ceiling (a limit on the number of notes able to sound simultaneously) too low for complex performances.

As musical instruments moved into the digital age, printed circuits opened the capacities of modern synths. Multitimbrality and polyphony became standard. The first ground-breaking, mass-market keyboard synthesizer was the Yamaha DX-7, which produced a sparkling, glittery, identifiable sound featured on almost every pop recording made in the mid-1980s. The DX-7 was a standard part of every performing keyboardist's rig during this period. Yamaha had innovated and popularized a type of synthesis called frequency modulation (FM) synthesis, with a synth engine that introduced electronic musicians to the trials and rewards of complex envelopes and filters. An entire programming industry was started by the DX-7, comprising hundreds of grass-roots companies creating literally millions of new patches for a musical marketplace hungry for the novelty of original sounds. The DX-7 didn't sound like "real" instruments; the building blocks of its sound were synthesized waveforms, and it had an artificial but not displeasing sound.

The ball was rolling, and innovations came fast and furious. Synth engines developed in complexity. As computers got into the act software was developed to make programming synths easier, sampled waveforms were introduced to make keyboards sound more like the real world, and as digital technology evolved, manufacturers were able to incorporate higher-quality components and more memory, all of which led to deeper, more interesting, more varied sounds. These days, several major manufacturers keep the marketplace alive with new models almost continuously, and although the growth curve has leveled, delivering innovations in smaller increments, there is a synth out there for every taste and budget.

DIGITAL PIANOS

Pianists looking for MIDI instruments on which they can play without altering their style too much are attracted to **digital pianos** for their weighted action and realistic sound. They are not as portable as lightweight keyboard synthesizers, for a good reason: The weighted action adds a lot of weight! Digital piano keys are often made of wood, not plastic, and the keyboards comprise the entire 88-key range of pianos or an abbreviated 76-key design—still more than the 60 keys normally found on portable keyboards. Making the most of their solid design, digital pianos sometimes go further in the direction of inertia by incorporating elaborate casings and stands, making them nothing short of living room–style console instruments for the digital age. Why buy a digital piano instead of an acoustic instrument, then, if you can't carry it around? Because it is a MIDI-capable instrument, and can be connected to a computer or other MIDI devices as part of a home studio. Digital pianos are for home performance and electronic recording. They have built-in speakers, and can also be plugged into a mixer or amplifier.

Great strides have been made since the late 1980s in the sound quality of digital pianos. Obviously, the acoustic version provides the standard against which they are measured. More than that, acoustic pianos provide the waveforms that reside in their digital cousin's memory chips. Real piano samples—digital recordings of individual notes—are recorded and stored in memory, then played back when you press the keys. (The keys are touch-sensitive, too, so pianists can control the volume of the notes naturally in the course of their playing.) Many digital pianos contain note-by-note recordings (samples) of a few different pianos, so you have a choice of playing a Bösendorfer concert grand, for example, or a Steinway nine-footer, or a honky-tonk bar piano.

The sonic experience, as might be expected, falls somewhat short of the ideal, depending on the model you're playing (and your expectations). There are a couple of reasons why digital pianos fall short of their acoustic forebears. First, although sampling technology is wondrous and convenient, it doesn't quite capture the complex timbre of even a single note played on a concert grand piano. Additionally, in order to conserve memory, the entire duration of the note cannot be preserved, and the recording (sample) is cut short before being stored in memory. Then the full decay of the notes is added artificially, by elongating the envelope. Second, when you play more than one note at a time, the illusion falls apart for discerning ears. The acoustics of the piano, when it is playing complex music with chords, melodies, and pedal movements, is incredibly dense; it cannot easily be reduced to a formula, analyzed, or reproduced by rote. Vibrating strings affect each other in a thick tangle of sonic intricacy that is conspicuous in its absence when a digital piano combines its individual note samples into a chord.

Nevertheless—not to paint too bleak a picture—anyone who first sits down to a digital piano will probably be amazed at the sounds it produces. There is no mistaking the pianolike quality of the instrument, and even discriminating ears can be fooled when listening to an ensemble recording featuring a digital grand in the mix. No solo artist would cut a CD on a digital piano, and the digital grand's purpose is not to replace acoustic grands, but to serve as an alternative with special functions and advantages. Digital grands provide good, serviceable piano sound plus the interfacing capability to fit into a MIDI setup.

Digital pianos are not synthesizers, and usually don't offer much in the way of sound editing functions, much less sound creation features. They usually do provide tone controls, a number of piano settings, other related instrument settings, and pedals. Some models include the middle sostenuto pedal. The weighted action is not as complex as that of a grand piano (long-time players will miss the slight bump that precedes the hammer's impact with the string), but it's a huge improvement over the plastic, weightless feel of portable keyboards.

Q & A: DIGITAL PIANOS

Q Do digital pianos come in grand and upright models?

A Yes, but the difference is only cosmetic. The keyboard and circuitry of the instrument might be housed in a case resembling an upright, or a larger package similar to a baby grand, but the sound quality is completely dependent on the piano samples stored on the internal memory chips. Those samples are usually taken from fine (and large) concert grand pianos. In truth, most digital pianos don't look like either grands or uprights—they resemble nothing more than electronic keyboards sitting on very sturdy stands, with pedal assemblies built into the construction. Some manufacturers make an effort to create an appearance of an acoustic instrument by building the electronics into wood cabinets.

Q Are digital pianos the same as electric pianos?

A No, although they are, of course, electronic instruments. Electric pianos have become established over the years, beginning in the 1970s, as a distinct type of musical instrument with a particular sound. The Fender Rhodes is the best known make of electric piano, and its metallic sound, almost like a vibraphone, graces pop and jazz records even today. Digital pianos have a different intent, which is to emulate the sound of an acoustic piano. They also have a different keyboard feel than an electric piano. It should be noted, however, that many models of digital piano contain at least one electric piano selection in addition to the grand piano settings.

Q Do digital pianos have a full range of sound selections?

A No, they are on the slim side when it comes to instrumental variety. Because high-quality piano samples take so much memory, there isn't enough left for samples from many other instruments. Generally, the best digital pianos contain a few different grand piano selections, an electric piano or two, perhaps a vibraphone, maybe a harpsichord, a Fender Rhodes piano, and occasionally a smattering of other instruments. They don't contain synthetic waveforms, synthesizer sounds, or the capacity to program new sounds.

Q Given a choice, why would anyone choose a digital piano instead of an acoustic?

A Price is one important reason: Digital pianos are not cheap, but they are much less expensive than acoustic pianos. Second, they are portable (if not easily so, then at least feasibly). They can certainly be moved across a room with much less vertebrae-popping effort than a grand piano.

Also, because they are quite a bit smaller, they ease into tight living situations better. Digital pianos also require no maintenance, never go out of tune, and are invulnerable to most climate conditions. The ability to play the instrument through headphones undoubtedly attracts the interest of apartment-dwellers and roommates. Add to this list of advantages the extra sounds most models offer and, of course, their MIDI capability when connected to a sequencer, computer, or another digital device. All in all, digital pianos are an attractive alternative, though not a piano replacement, for musicians who have a piano background, perhaps even a classical history.

HOME KEYBOARDS

At the other end of the spectrum from digital pianos are a vast array of **home keyboards** or hobby keyboards. They are small and lightweight, and their sound might colloquially be described as cheap. Home keyboards are distinguished from pro-level synthesizers by their built-in speakers. Besides that crucial characteristic, there is a considerable overlap in features. In fact, during the 1990s, more sonic power, synthesis features, and general bang for the buck has been crammed into home keyboards, blurring the lines between amateur and pro keyboards.

Home keyboards are similar to their professional brethren in design: They arrive out of the box equipped with banks of factory-installed sounds, and sometimes offer synthesis engines for tweaking the presets or creating new sounds from scratch. Banks of empty sound slots might be provided to store your creations. (Intense frustration may ensue if those empty banks are missing.) Home keyboards are much more button-intensive than the sleek design of pro models. This can be a confusing nuisance or a godsend, depending on personal preferences. Sparse front panel designs look mysterious and chic, but invariably require the few buttons that do exist to perform double or triple duty, each with more than one function. That means a steep learning curve. A front panel bristling with controls gives away a manufacturing lineage of hobbyist keyboards, but provides the convenience of a dedicated button for every function. On the back panel, home keyboards have the essentials: MIDI ports and audio outputs, at least. (Even though hobby keyboards have speakers and don't need audio outputs to send the sound to an amplifier, such outputs are often included as an option for louder playing.) They usually don't contain multiple outputs (more than the basic left–right pair), as are often seen on professional synths.

Some features are typically found on home keyboards that help sell them in stores but don't contribute much value once the instrument is taken home. In particular, the inclusion of preset sequences (songs) allows store sales personnel to show off the general sound of the instrument, but have little use later. More practical is the presence of an onboard recorder (sequencer). These invite the owner to try some composing, although memory constraints usually limit such creative enterprises to short, thinly scored pieces. If a disk drive is included in the keyboard (as they typically are in higher-priced models), original pieces can be stored to disk; otherwise, they must be saved to the instrument's generally inadequate internal memory. This is not to say that a good home keyboard cannot be part of an ambitious MIDI studio, but it's best to connect it to a more generous sequencing resource, such as a computer.

WORKSTATIONS

In the marketplace of MIDI gear, **workstations** attempt to do it all in a single package. Like fully integrated home stereo systems that include a receiver, tape deck, CD player, and speakers in one package, workstations combine several crucial MIDI components, allowing for fairly complete music production right out of the box. Best of all, they sometimes don't cost more than a single keyboard synth. Their inadequacies are predictable; specialized components do a particular job especially well, and combining several components usually involves cutting corners.

REAL WORDS

I guess one of the most important things that digital sampling and MIDI has done for me is to allow me to simulate orchestras, bands, or any instrument class (including electronic). When I do a soundtrack for a low-budget video and the producers want to sound expensive, a pseudo-orchestra can get the job done! SMPTE timecode has been invaluable in terms of syncing to picture with little hassle. I also like having a MIDI band for playing gigs where I can do the music I want without having to worry about my bandmates! Sometimes, I just want to do a song they haven't learned and so I go ahead with a sequence. They can play along a bit, so it comes across okay. And they don't mind!

Ellsworth Hall, Cyber Composer
Affinity Music
ehall@mail.bcpl.lib.md.us
http://www.bcpl.lib.md.us/~ehall/aml.html

Workstations usually combine these functions into a single keyboard package:

- **Sequencing.** Onboard workstation sequencers don't hold a candle to dedicated computer sequencing software, but they don't slouch, either. They are multitrack MIDI recorders with editing capability. Some models have powerful features, but all models are limited by the small screen on the keyboard's front panel. Workstation sequencers tend to assume that the user will be composing pop song stylings or creating arrangements of current hits. Indeed, that is a large part of the marketplace for workstation instruments. Accordingly, the sequencer might implement features that are conducive to such work, enabling you to manage song portions such as verses, choruses, and bridges as units that can be moved and manipulated in various ways. This differs from free-form sequencers that deal with individual notes and tracks, without assuming or encouraging any particular structure. However, it should be noted that not all workstation sequencers operate this way, and even the ones that do can usually be persuaded to record more freely.

- **Drum tracking.** Workstations have built-in **drum machines**, but without the pads found on standalone drum machine boxes. They have drum samples built in as part of their preset arsenal of sounds, and the drum sounds are treated, accessed, and recorded just like any other onboard sound. You play the drums by means of the keyboard. Furthermore, like drum machines, the workstation might provide a selection of preprogrammed rhythms and grooves from which full-fledged drum tracks can be constructed. However, the presence of factory percussion tracks is not de rigeur in a workstation as it is in a specialized drum machine.

- **Synthesis.** Manufacturers often spin workstation products out of synthesizer keyboards that are already being built and sold. It makes sense, then, that the synth would be the heart of the workstation, complete with a high-powered synthesis engine and the capacity to create and store new sounds. Like dedicated synths, workstations vary in the quality with which they design sounds and the preset quality of their sound. Sound programming from the workstation's front panel is hardly a day at the beach, but they can be connected via MIDI to a computer running specialized sound editing software.

Following the theme of trying to provide everything in a single package, workstations usually are equipped with standard conveniences such as a floppy disk drive (almost always), a hard drive (sometimes), and a back-panel jack for connecting an external hard drive (rarely). Some offer, as an option, a weighted-key action for piano-style performance. MIDI ports are always there, and multiple audio outputs, for connecting to a multichannel mixer, are typical.

KEYBOARD CONTROLLERS

One peculiar type of keyboard doesn't create any sound at all, and is used only to control other MIDI instruments that are sound-enabled. Keyboard controllers are equipped with features that suit them particularly well to playing the ringleader role of dictating data to the other members of the MIDI orchestra:

- **Full-sized keyboards.** Like pianos, keyboard controllers feature the full 88 keys; no skimping with 76 or stumbling with an octave-challenged 60 notes.

- **Weighted keys.** Keyboard players who cut their teeth on synthesizers prefer lighter action, so weighted keys are not desirable for them. Accordingly, some keyboard controller models offer a choice of weights: fully weighted or partially so. Piano players are in heaven with heavier controller actions, but a strong back is required to haul these devices on the road.

MIDI channels are discussed beginning on page 98.

- **MIDI channel flexibility.** With MIDI, a player can have many different sounds available at once, and they are quickly selected by changing from one MIDI channel to another. The sounds are assigned to these channels, one sound per channel, and keyboard controllers are especially facile at making these switches convenient. Complex keyboard-splitting features are used to spread channel ranges across the keyboard. This way, the lower octaves might be used to play an electric bass sound from a MIDI instrument on one channel, the middle range could be used to play a piano patch from a different MIDI instrument on a second channel, and the upper notes might be assigned to a third channel, delivering a synth patch from yet another MIDI component.

- **Multiple MIDI ports.** Expanding on the typical In, Out, Thru triad of MIDI jacks can be a way of controlling the flow of MIDI data in a complex system.

Are dedicated keyboard controllers for use in the studio, or on stage? Both, pretty equally. Although they're not easy to carry around, many players favor them for live performance because of their substantial actions and pianolike feel, as well as the easy MIDI management of a complicated stage rig. In the studio, where performance considerations may not be paramount (but are still important for some kinds of production), they are excellent central processors of MIDI data, sometimes eliminating the need for certain peripheral MIDI components. Home-based MIDI composers like to create studios that operate, as much as possible, like complex, integrated instruments. Keyboard controllers manage MIDI data flow with ease, letting the musician concentrate on music.

SOLOING KEYBOARDS

On stage, guitarists have all the glamor. With their instrument strapped on, they are free to strut, gyrate, and otherwise express their angst or flaunt their untamed hormones in the service of the music's sublimity. Keyboardists, contrarily, are traditionally trapped behind a rack of 'boards and related equipment. Even when handed the musical spotlight in the form of a solo, the keyboardist appears encaged by the machines he or she has presumably mastered. Keyboard players who hanker for the grungy flair of wearing their instrument on their hips can resort to a soloing keyboard that straps on, guitarlike, around the shoulders. Naturally, it's not a full-size keyboard, or the hapless player would probably smack other band members every time he or she performed a raunchily choreographed movement. But keyboard solos don't generally need to roam over a range of more than four octaves, the typical size of a soloing keyboard. These little instruments are equipped with pitch-bend wheels and, usually, touch-sensitive keys. In some cases, the pitch-bends are accomplished by means of a sensitized strip at the end of an extended neck; such models carry the guitar emulation to the limit.

SAMPLERS

A specialized breed of MIDI instrument can record sounds then play them back. When a sound is recorded digitally, it is called a **sample.** No surprise, then, that these recording instruments are called **samplers.** Samplers are peculiar in that certain models may not contain any sounds when they are new: They won't make a peep until a sample is loaded into them. The value of a sampler lies in the infinite variety of new sounds that can be acquired and played. Synthesizers are equipped with preloaded waveforms (the building blocks of sound patches), both synthesized and sampled. Sampled waveforms are usually notes played by acoustic instruments, such as flutes, violins, and pianos. Whether a waveform is synthetic or sampled, it can be used by that synthesizer as the basis of a new patch.

Samplers, on the other hand, have the distinct value of being able to acquire new waveforms at any time, from any source, then play the new sound back from their own keyboards. When sampling they use an audio input jack, to which a microphone can be connected, as the primary way of acquiring original waveforms. Sing into the connected mic with the sampler in Record mode, or make your dog bark into it, and a new waveform is at your disposal. Turn the microphone on during a storm, and you can be playing thunder on the keyboard within minutes.

Most samplers are built with some ability to edit sounds—in other words, some kind of synthesis engine. How powerful that engine is differs widely among sampler models. Most sampling machines are built to be samplers first and synthesizers second, so the sound-editing features might be rather simple compared to those of a dedicated synthesizer. At the very least, you should be able to change the envelope and filter characteristics of any sound you record, tailoring it to be as playable as possible in a keyboard format. Furthermore, good samplers let you adjust the recorded sound to play well in different ranges. Optimally, instrument samples are recorded several times over the range of the instrument being sampled, making the final sample sound more faithful to the instrument source. But when memory shortages preclude this technique, called **multisampling**, sound editing can make a single sample sound more realistic when played.

Sampled waveforms are much larger (in terms of data) than synthetic waveforms. Because they require so much more memory, samplers have more memory storage features than plain synthesizers. In addition to a floppy disk drive (also found on synthesizers), samplers often contain a built-in hard disk. Certain models also contain a large RAM area.

The Art and Craft of Sampling

Sampling seems easy on the face of it. Plug in a microphone, record a sound, and play it back across the range of the keyboard. A quick way to turn your keyboard into any instrument you can record, or a library of sound effects sampled from the natural world. There is truth to such a simple view, but the harder truth for serious MIDI producers is that sampling is a finicky craft requiring specialized skills and, sometimes, equipment. As with other endeavors, you get as much out of it as you put in. The ingredients are time, care, equipment, and knowledge.

The first stage of effective sampling is recording. Whether you record directly into the sampler or onto tape (later to be fed into the sampler's audio input jack), the better the recording, the better the result. Recording instruments is ideally done in a silent space, unless you specifically want the sound of cars from the street rumbling through your instrument sample. (Not likely.) Some musicians record samples in a professional sound studio if their personal space isn't conducive. Wherever the sampled instrument is recorded, many MIDI producers prefer pure tonal samples without vibrato or other inflections, figuring they can be added artificially later. But the reverse philosophy holds sway in some quarters; it's really a matter of preference, experience, and what the sampler's features allow in the way of postsampling alteration. Considering the intimidating (and often costly) complexity of live instrument recording, it's not surprising that many musicians avail themselves of commercially produced sample collections, usually packaged on CDs. Such collections offer samples of many instruments (often in groups, such as orchestral stringed instruments), sampled one note at a time throughout their range, both with and without expressive inflections. These CDs make it easy to cue up a sample and record it through the silence of cables directly into the sampler.

In recording an instrument sample, whether live or from a CD, a balance must be struck between the ideal and the reality of the sampler's memory restrictions. Ideally, every note of an instrument is sampled, from the bottom of its playable range to the top. Realistically, it's not always possible to devote so much memory to one patch. In that case, memory must be allocated, and a decision made about how many notes will be used. It is this consideration that makes demands on the mythical mathematical ability with which musicians are supposed to be so richly endowed.

The second stage of effective sampling involves making the raw, unedited sample playable. This requires such esoteric functions as looping (enabling the short sample to sustain indefinitely when a key is held down), filtering the individually sampled notes to conform to each other tonally, and setting decay envelopes so the sample fades naturally when the key is released. Each of these and other tasks requires a range of skills, experience, and understanding of the machine's particular features. Editing the raw sample is just as important as obtaining a good raw sample: Without some tweaking, the sound won't play realistically when controlled by a keyboard.

In a nutshell, sampling is hard but rewarding. Some musicians enjoy the challenge of original sampling, and others avoid the whole process by purchasing samples that have been prerecorded and pre-edited to sound good in their particular instrument. These are available from the manufacturer in some cases, and from third-party companies.

TONE MODULES

The connective beauty of MIDI allows one instrument to control another. If you prefer the action of a favorite keyboard, you can restrict your playing to that keyboard and use it to hear the sounds contained in other keyboards, as long as all the instruments are MIDI'd together. After doing that for a while, anybody would begin to wonder why they had so many keyboards in the first place. They just take space, and if only the internal features (the sounds) of those keyboards are being used, there must be a way to reduce their size.

There is. Tone modules are MIDI instruments that must be played by an external MIDI controller. They are simple boxes without keyboards, usually attached to racks of a standard size that can hold several modules, each containing all the sounds and other internal features of a synthesizer or sampler, but lacking the ability to play themselves. Typically, a manufacturer builds two versions of a synth: the keyboard version and the tone module version. This way, MIDI enthusiasts can reduce studio clutter by settling on a single keyboard that controls a series of tone modules. Generally, the features of the two versions are identical—same sounds, same synthesis engine, and same operating system—but one is a keyboard and one is a simple box.

Tone modules carry the usual complement of MIDI In, Out, and Thru jacks. They are used by connecting a keyboard's MIDI Out jack to the module's MIDI In jack. Once that connection is made, the keyboard can play the tone module as if the module's sounds resided inside the keyboard. Modules can also be hooked into computers just like keyboards, and can be programmed using the same sound editing software available for the keyboard version.

DRUM MACHINES

There are a few good reasons why drum machines—specialized MIDI instruments that produce drum and percussion sounds—appeared on the scene early in the MIDI revolution.

■ Drum kits, as musical instruments, consist of many different instruments: snare, tom, and kick drums; ride, crash, and hi-hat cymbals; and often miscellaneous percussion implements such as woodblock, triangle, chimes, shakers, and the rims of

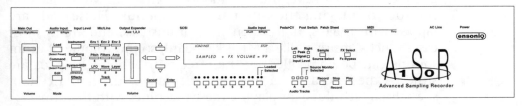

A rack-mount MIDI tone module.

the drums. For this reason, representing the sound of a drum kit in a MIDI instrument requires many different sounds. So many sounds need to be represented that dedicated devices have been developed with that specialty.

■ Drum parts play a huge role in pop music. When producing a pop-style song, a great deal of attention must be devoted to the drum tracks alone, sometimes disproportionate to the other tracks. It makes sense that specific MIDI tools would be useful in creating rhythm tracks as pop music production is seriously influenced by the digital revolution.

■ Performers have found drum machines extremely useful in a variety of public settings, from piano-bar lounges in which a solo pianist is accompanied by electronic rhythms, to huge stage productions of superstars who use prerecorded drum sequences, occasionally, to set tempos or fill in arrangements.

■ Drum and percussion sounds make the digital translation with remarkable effectiveness, much better than some other instruments. This is simply because most of them are short (with the notable exception of cymbals, which are unusually difficult to digitize effectively). Sampling a drum hit requires less memory than a sustained sound, such as a piano tone, and it plays back well when controlled by a keyboard device or drum machine pad. Making drum samples sound realistic, as if they were being played by a real drummer on real drums, is not nearly as difficult to accomplish as with more sonorous orchestral instruments, or highly expressive pop instruments such as electric guitar and saxophone. Accordingly, drum machines appeal to MIDI production enthusiasts.

Drum machines are nonkeyboard MIDI devices (although many keyboard synths have drum sounds) that enable users to access drum and percussion samples and arrange the sounds into full-fledged drum tracks. Composing rhythm parts can be accomplished either with the built-in sequencer or by hooking the drum machine with MIDI cables to a general-purpose sequencer used by all the other MIDI devices in the studio. Drum machines are box-like pieces of hardware, usually studded with small **MIDI pads** on the top for playing the internal drum sounds. These pads are tapped with fingers, not beaten with drumsticks, and are in most cases touch-sensitive, like a MIDI keyboard, so the volume of drum sounds can be controlled by the force with which the pads are struck. Experienced drum machine aficionados develop a certain specialized technique for playing these machines with their fingers.

In popular music, rhythm tracks traditionally consist of drums and bass. Other instruments, such as guitar and piano, also may contribute to the ongoing rhythm bed, but drums and bass are the two indispensable elements. Many drum machines, aspiring to provide production elements for an entire rhythm part, also have bass samples on board. The range of percussion samples included varies widely among machines. Bread-and-butter machines do a great job of covering the basics: all the standard drum kit sounds, with alternative samples of each type of instrument. The emphasis is on high-quality samples, and a deep variety is preferred to a broad variety; exotic percussion instruments are bypassed in favor of sounds useful to pop-music styles. Owning such a drum machine is like having ten different drum kits at your disposal, but not a single carob-bean rattle imported from South America. Some drum machines take the opposite approach, covering the basics more briefly and devoting substantial machine memory to esoteric percussion samples.

There is a distinction to be made between drum machines and drum modules. Here are the differences:

- Drum machines are standalone units that can be set on top of a production desk, keyboard, or piano. Their controls are on top. Drum modules, or **percussion modules**, are rack-mounted boxes that take a place in a rack of tone modules in a MIDI studio. Their controls are on the front panel.

- Drum machines can be played from their top panels, thanks to a couple of rows of raised pads to which you can assign the internal sounds. Typically, a different type of drum is assigned to each pad for a complete kit. They are not meant to played as a performance instrument; rather, the pads are useful in recording drum patterns and song tracks. Drum modules lack the pads, and are controlled by an external device such as a keyboard. In that case, drum sounds are assigned to keys on the external board, which obviously gives you a potentially much larger drum set.

- Drum machines almost always come equipped with a rhythm-track sequencer. These specialized sequencers behave a little differently from normal sequencers, enabling such tricks as looping an eight-bar percussion segment and allowing you to add new instrument parts to it, layer upon layer, without stopping the machine or using different tracks. Usually, drum machine sequencers treat recordings as fragmented patterns that can be cut, pasted, and interchanged freely—all very helpful for constructing the next chart-busting hit. Drum modules, on the other hand, generally have no sequencers, depending instead on the studio's generic sequencer. Like all the other tone modules in the setup, the drum module is played by a keyboard controller, and the data is recorded by the same sequencer that is recording the song's other parts (usually a computer software sequencer).

■ Drum machines sometimes have built-in speakers, letting you hear the sounds without an amplifier or headphones. Drum modules never stoop so low as to give away their sound in such a fashion.

■ Finally, but not least importantly, drum machines are less expensive. Part of the price difference can be accounted for by sheer volume of samples: Drum modules usually carry more sounds. Drum machines are also smaller and not built to the rocklike standards of modules.

SEQUENCERS

Sequencers are the conductors of the MIDI orchestra. Of course, they can only do what a human tells them to, so it is always a person who directs the musical action. Sequencers keep track of every instruction that goes into a MIDI composition (and there are a mind-boggling number of them), and replicates them in perfect order with each playback. During the composition and production process, a good sequencer makes available sophisticated and helpful (as well as needlessly complex and questionably useful) tools and tricks to fine-tune the piece to perfection.

Sequencers were first constructed as hardware, later evolving into computer software. Hardware sequencers are now rare in advanced MIDI studios, but simple sequencing devices can still be bought for less than a high-end software package (never mind the cost of a computer). Sequencers come in three basic incarnations:

■ Hardware boxes that accomplish MIDI recording when hooked up to at least one MIDI instrument.

■ Software programs that record MIDI data when the computer is interfaced to at least one MIDI instrument.

■ Sequencers that exist as part of an instrument, such as a workstation or drum machine.

The word *sequencer* may seem to imply a hardware device, and it can be confusing when the word is used to describe a software program running in a computer. By definition, a sequencer is a MIDI data recorder, whether it is hardware or software. Thus,

REAL WORDS

It is often secretly thought that if one only had a sequencer it would make one a composer. Another thing often and secretly thought by composers is that if one only had a sequencer, composing would be a much faster process. These thoughts originate from salesmen, naturally, and are both false. Composing takes the time and talent, regardless of the tools. If you have a Ferrari that can go 100 mph, it won't take you through New York City at rush hour any faster than an old Buick. And anyway, what's the hurry? If you know where you're going and you know the way, you'll get there. One sign of a person who doesn't know where he or she is going is hurry. I think MIDI helps a lot trying out arrangements and as a musical notepad. I don't use MIDI in my musical representation but there are some good musicians who use it. I think one should, as with every new and complex tool, read and study the advantages and disadvantages before buying.

Miikkali Leppihalme
Miikkali.Leppihalme@opev.hki.hki.elisa.fi
Sound Engineer, Cozmik Lama Soundworks, Finland

when a computer is running sequencing software it can be called a sequencer, even though it's the software that really is the sequencer. Throughout this book, I use the word *sequencer* to refer to any MIDI data recorder in a MIDI studio, whether it's a hardware device, a computer program, or the sequencing portion of a workstation. No other features are required, but additional abilities are usually included.

Sequencer Features

■ **Multitrack.** The many-timbred quality of MIDI dictates that MIDI recorders be multitrack recorders. They are modeled on multitrack tape machines, long standard equipment in sound recording studios. You can record one MIDI part (say the piano patch of your synthesizer) on the first track, then record another track (with another sound) while the first track plays back. Multitrack recording allows you to layer parts into a complex orchestration, no matter what genre of music you're working with. The most rudimentary hardware sequencers were track-impoverished devices, sometimes offering as few as two but allowing the user to merge track one into track two an infinite number of times, so a track is always left empty for recording. More tracks dispense with the need for such merging, and permit more editing control over each recorded track. Drum machine sequencers often only have a single track, but let you merge parts ad percusseum.

▪ **Tape-style transport controls.** There is nothing to transport in a digital sequencer because there are no moving parts. But recording industry tradition holds sway, and the Record, Play, Stop, Rewind, and Fast-Forward sequencer commands are still called transport controls. They work the same, too, but much faster, unencumbered as they are by physical tape and reels. You can zip to any spot in the recording instantly, and when using Rewind and Fast-Forward controls you can hear the piece whiz by without a corresponding chipmunk-change in pitch.

▪ **Editing control.** Because sequencers record bits of MIDI data, not sound, the result is a list of events, each event representing a minuscule occurrence in the played performance, such as a key being pressed down, a pedal being stepped on, a pitch-bend wheel being moved, or a key being released. As you can imagine, a huge number of MIDI events can pile up in even a short recorded passage. In a good sequencer, virtually all those events can be altered in some way. Editing control can be as fundamental as moving an entire track to a different location in the piece, or it can be as detailed as changing the timing of the beginning of a single note by one 256th of a quarter note. The obvious and most useful edits entail correcting wrong notes, changing tempos, transposing to new keys, and other alterations that have always been so frustratingly impossible with tape recording. Software sequencers are generally more powerful editors than their hardware counterparts.

▪ **Playback.** Once you have recorded and edited your parts, the sequencer would be useless if it couldn't play them back. Actually, playback of MIDI data happens throughout the production process, as recorded tracks are played while you record a new track. (Selective track muting is a standard feature.) The sequencer keeps track not only of played data, but also of MIDI channel assignments; when the sequence is played back, all the instruments in the studio respond appropriately to the recorded tracks as per their channel assignments, the result being a multipart, perfectly synchronized performance of the piece.

What a Sequencer Can Do to Music

Sequencers record MIDI data, but their real power lies in editing that data in various ways. What exactly does it mean to edit musical data? Following is a list of basic sequencer editing functions and the effect they can have on music.

- *Quantize.* Quantizing is the name for smoothing out rhythmic irregularities. Sequencers allow you to correct inaccuracies in timing by aligning recorded notes to the nearest fraction of a beat. For example, you can quantize a snare drum part by quarter note, so the drum hits fall exactly on the backbeats. Or an instrumental part consisting of 32nd-note runs can be made exact. It is the quantizing capacity of sequencers that has given MIDI a reputation for producing mechanical-sounding music. The truth is, in many sequencers you can adjust the degree to which the quantization works, introducing a random factor in the operation. Of course, sequencers can produce any type of music, mechanical or free-flowing. It's all in the hands of the producer; the sequencer is just a tool.

- *Correct note attributes.* Sequencers have a big advantage over tape recorders in their ability to correct individual wrong notes. That's not all they can do with a note, however. A sequencer can also lengthen or shorten a note, increase or decrease its volume, adjust its pitch, and move it to a different place in the measure.

- *Change instruments.* Because the sequencer is not recording or playing back sounds, but is merely controlling a digital instrument that contains many sounds, it's easy to substitute one virtual instrument for another when playing back a track. In this way composers can try out different instrument parts on the fly, finding the perfect sound for the recorded part.

- *Alter tempo.* With a tape recorder, changing the speed of a recording invariably alters the pitch: Going faster raises pitch, and slowing down lowers it. Not so with a sequencer, which is only playing back data events. Insert new tempi during a piece, and experiment with accelerandos; the pitch and key remain constant.

- *Transpose.* In a sequencer, transposing recorded music is easy, and doesn't require altering the tempo in any way.

The sequencer is the centerpiece of the MIDI recording studio. Every bit of MIDI performance data travels through the sequencer during production.

▦▦▦▦▦ **ALTERNATIVE CONTROLLERS**

In addition to the instruments that actually make the sounds of a MIDI piece, other devices may be essential. There are so many utilitarian MIDI components that a complete survey would be tiresome to read. Happily, this section just covers the most-used tools.

Keyboard controllers are discussed earlier in this chapter. Although keyboards are by far the predominant controller format (MIDI has always been biased in favor of keyboardists), plenty of controller formats have been developed to accommodate other instrumentalists. (Never mind for now that sequencers are also MIDI controllers, because they activate the sounds in instruments during playback; this section is concerned only with instrument controllers.)

Almost any instrument can be turned into a MIDI controller, and impressive ingenuity has been applied to that task. But the most common alternative controllers can be counted on one hand:

▣ **Guitar.** Guitar controllers can be added to regular guitars (acoustic or electronic), and are also available as specialized instruments. Prebuilt MIDI guitars make no sound of their own; they are controllers only, and must be hooked up, with a MIDI cable, to a tone module in order to play. Add-on controllers consist of a pickup device that absorbs the sound of the vibrating strings and transforms each note to a MIDI equivalent, plus a tone module that stores the MIDI sounds. This process turns it into a hybrid instrument because it is making its own sound while controlling a MIDI sound with the same played notes. (An electric guitar can be turned off to hear only the MIDI sound.) The early guitar controller devices introduced a noticeable delay between a played note and the MIDI response. It was disconcerting and problematic, especially with fast playing. Response times have quickened with design improvements in the meantime.

▣ **Wind.** Wind controllers are modeled after clarinets, saxophones, trumpets, and other blown instruments. Add-on controller mechanisms have been attempted, but it is much harder to accomplish on a wind instrument than on a guitar or piano. Most wind controllers are specialized instruments that make no sound unless connected to a MIDI tone module. They can be used with any module, but it's best to use the module that comes with the instrument, if there is one, or a recommended module. Some enterprising people have made a business of creating sound patches for specific modules that respond especially well to wind control. Wind controllers should not be confused with breath controllers. A breath controller is a small device that plugs into a keyboard (if a breath control input jack is present) and fits in the player's mouth; while playing a single-line solo on the keyboard, the musician uses the breath controller to add expressive articulations. The idea is to emulate the soulful eloquence of a sax, for example, when playing a sax sample on the keyboard. Breath controllers are for keyboard players, and require quite a bit of practice to use effectively. Wind controllers are for wind players.

- **Drum.** Drum samples are effectively played from a keyboard or drum machine pads—at least, that's what keyboard players think. Drummers are not satisfied. Catering to drummers' longing to participate more naturally in the MIDI creation process, manufacturers have developed MIDI drum pads that can be configured as surrogate drum kits, complete with foot-controlled kick drum, ersatz hi-hats, and variously sized pads for snare and tom-toms. Other pads can be assigned to any sound at all, from a-go-go to a sampled orchestral flourish. The drummer sits before this synthetic drum kit, which is MIDI'd to a drum machine or drum module (or any MIDI device containing drum samples), and plays fairly normally. The drum module must be connected to an amplifier, or the drummer must wear headphones, in order for sound to be part of the experience.

- **Piano.** Wait a minute—isn't the piano a keyboard? Yes, but it's not (in its natural state) an electronic keyboard. Real pianos can be transformed into MIDI controllers by means of a gut-wrenching (if you subscribe to the notion that pianos are living beings), wood-splitting, wallet-draining operation to insert a massive system of sensors and circuitry into the piano's action. Avoiding all that, you can also get new MIDI pianos with sensors already added. They are only for those with a symphonic budget.

ALTERNATIVE SLAVES

Just as there are alternative controllers, so there are in the spirit of fair distribution of labor, alternative MIDI slaves. Standard MIDI slaves include instruments such as keyboard synths, samplers, drum machines, and tone modules. Other, noninstrumental devices can be pushed around by a MIDI controller. They include

---

REAL WORDS

I originally played a Tama seven-piece Swingstar acoustic set with Zildjian cymbals. I added to that set a five-piece electronic set from Yamaha, which multiplied the variety of sounds I got, but the acoustic set was always a problem. We could never get the right bass drum sound (tried lots of different mics and dampening methods) and the snare drum and cymbals were often too much for the other band members, although they were about right to the audience. With the purchase of a better sound module for the drum kit, I disbanded the acoustic set and used them just for practicing at home. By then I was using electronic drums with normal Zildjian symbols (truly weird if the speakers weren't on). My father fashioned a set of four little tube triggers that we mounted on the cymbal stand, for use as a cowbell, woodblock, whatever the song needed. Although I'm not currently playing professionally (still looking for the right band), I know from experience that this type of setup can be far superior to a traditional acoustic set. There are no problems with dampening or the microphones, it's not nearly as hard on the ears of the rest of the band members, it's easier to set up and tear down, and it'll even transport in my little two-door sportscar. In addition, the parts aren't nearly as expensive to upkeep. (Replacing a $250 crash cymbal when it breaks can be a real downer.) And drumsticks don't wear out playing it. On the bright side, it can still be a good workout!

Eric M. Wilson
emw@sprynet.com

- **MIDI mixers.** Mixers have sliders and other controls with which you can control the volume and tone quality of every instrument connected to them. **MIDI mixers** operate on the same principle, but they also respond to specialized MIDI commands that make their faders move up and down, changing the volume of the instruments connected to them.

- **Effects boxes.** Digital effects boxes (also known as digital signal processors, or DSPs) add ambiance to a sound in the form of reverb, digital delay, flanging, distortion, and other exotic-sounding transformations that give electronic instruments unusual sonic personalities. **MIDI effects** boxes were invented to give MIDI command control over signal processing, rendering it unnecessary to change effects settings by hand, as was previously required. The advent of MIDI-controlled effects lets you change from one reverb setting (for example) to another by placing the correct command in your sequence. The reverb setting changes every time the sequence is played back to the point of the embedded command; the effect box responds to the sequence as if it were a MIDI instrument, playing a different reverb setting. When that part of the piece is played back, the reverb setting changes automatically.

■ **Tape machines.** A new development is called MIDI Machine Control (MMC). Taking advantage of it requires a tape machine that understands the MMC protocol. With such a tape deck, it is easy to synchronize tape recorded parts with MIDI tracks. With the two machines (the MIDI sequencer, which is usually a computer, and the tape machine) hooked together, the tape machine responds to the sequencer's transport control commands. When you click the Play button in your sequencer, the tape machine begins playing as well. A timing code is used to keep the two devices synchronized, so the tape machine always knows where in the piece the sequencer is.

MIDI SWITCHERS

MIDI switchers are like the dispatchers in a large train yard. Usually used in complex MIDI studios with many instruments, they keep track of the MIDI data flow. MIDI switchers are rack-mounted hardware boxes that feature multiple MIDI In and Out jacks. By plugging the studio's sequencer and MIDI instruments into a switcher, you can determine which device will send MIDI data to which other devices. The switcher allows you to program different data-flow configurations. In one program, the sequencer might be playing back MIDI data to all the instruments in the setup. Switch to another program, and your master keyboard controller can send the data from a played part to the sequencer and the tone modules. MIDI switchers take much of the hassle out of a complexly wired studio; they don't eliminate the wires, but they allow a single wiring configuration to work in many ways.

7

HOW MIDI STUDIOS GROW

MIDI studios usually have humble beginnings, often starting out in a corner of the living room or in the basement. From there, like a planted seed, they can grow in different directions, and come to have different purposes and musical intents. They can be recreational or professional. They can serve outside clients or only the musical vision of their owners. This chapter looks at a few of the common growth directions of MIDI studios, and what the hardware/software requirements are. It also looks at upgrading priorities for those who are expanding their current setups.

THE UNEXPECTED STUDIO

MIDI studios are sometimes begun inadvertently. In those cases, the first unwitting purchase is an instrument, usually a home keyboard, whose MIDI capabilities are not part of the purchase decision. The MIDI ports on the keyboard's back are beside the point at first—understandably, because single-item buyers don't yet own anything to plug into those ports.

Acquisitions of this sort are usually not ambitious. The buyer might be a young person just beginning explorations into music and digital devices in general; an adult wishing that he or she attended to those dreadful piano lessons as a child, and who wants to start learning again without investing in a full-fledged piano; or a senior citizen interested in taking up music during retirement years. The intent is simply to acquire an inexpensive, functional, and fun musical instrument, without regard to its data-networking capacities.

In the process of learning the keyboard, there can be a dawning of greater possibilities. Even a cursory glance at the owner's manual of a typical home keyboard reveals the MIDI connectivity inherent in the instrument. Furthermore, many home keyboards contain rudimentary sequencers, and perhaps elementary synthesis (sound creation) buttons—features that, once experimented with, practically beg for more advanced implementation. If a home keyboard is fully explored, it's hard to resist the allure of better tools for playing, composing, and recording music.

Because home keyboards, the most common starting points for inadvertent studios, have less power than more advanced models, the urge to expand can hit in various ways.

Ways to Expand Your Studio

■ **Sequencing.** For composers, this is the most obvious first upgrade path. Built-in sequencers on home keyboards are sometimes single-track affairs, hardly taking advantage of MIDI's multitrack potential. Even the multitrack models don't embody the powerful composing and editing features of dedicated sequencing software, or even a standalone hardware sequencer. That choice, in fact, is a key decision at this point. Some MIDI novices, still unwilling (understandably) to invest heavily in a new hobby, accomplish a modest upgrade of their sequencing tools by acquiring a standalone sequencer; in many cases it is a substantial step up in track space and editing power over the rudimentary sequencer in a hobby keyboard. If the user already owns a computer, it might not cost more to buy sequencing software than it would to buy a standalone sequencer, and this option works as long as the computer and keyboard are in the same room. Of course, buying a computer just for managing a MIDI studio is a dramatic upgrade.

■ **Sound creation.** Some home keyboard models let you tweak the built-in sound patches. In some cases this amounts to nothing more than fairly sophisticated tone controls, affecting the **equalization** (balance of the sound), but in other models you can create simple changes to the envelope, such as altering the attack and decay times of any sound, or substitute one waveform for another. Such features are irrelevant to people who are satisfied with whatever sounds are built into the keyboard. For those who enjoy the sonic adventure of creating

Basic MIDI connections are covered in Chapter 5, "How MIDI Works."

new sounds, the simple programming features of a home keyboard might whet their appetite for more powerful tools. In that case, the upgrade purchase is likely to be another instrument, one that emphasizes a strong sound synthesis engine. It might be a second keyboard, or a sound module to be controlled by the first keyboard. In either case, a standard In to Out and Out to In cable arrangement would bring the second device into the loop.

■ **Playing comfort.** Home keyboards are small, with playing ranges of only four octaves in some cases. They may be fine for experimenting with new technology and for learning the basics of music theory and playing technique. More practiced keyboard players soon long for the extra elbow room of a typical five-octave electronic keyboard, or even the 76-note and 88-note boards available in higher-priced models. It's also worth noting that home keyboards invariably have unweighted, plastic actions, which are unsatisfactory for piano players. Many professional keyboards are likewise unweighted, and offer no improvement on that score, but digital pianos and advanced keyboard controllers do provide a more solid, pianolike feel. Upgrading to a larger keyboard usually involves an automatic upgrade of other features in the bargain; upgrading to a weighted action, however, usually involves a loss of certain features because digital pianos and advanced controllers are specialty devices containing few sounds and no synthesis capabilities.

■ **Sound quality.** The glow of a home keyboard that sounds great in the store can fade with continual playing. As the novelty of the built-in sound patches wears off, the ear can begin to crave more realistic, deeper, or more imaginative sonorities. Home keyboards generally cannot acquire new sounds with a software upgrade, so the solution is to buy another instrument. This doesn't mean the old one should be thrown away or stuffed into a corner to remain unused. Often, the tired sounds of a well-used keyboard gain new life when combined through MIDI with the fresh patches of a new instrument. The main upgrade path for getting a better-sounding MIDI system is another keyboard or a sound module.

Inadvertent studios are usually noncommercial, nonprofessional ventures that evolve for the recreational pleasure of their owners. They are used primarily for at-home performance and practice, and the recording of compositions not meant for commercial release. Without the aspiration of album-quality production values, they are free from the treadmill of compulsive, up-to-the-minute upgrades. As long as they work, produce

REAL WORDS

When all I have is "Oh, Susannah" in my fingers, and Beethoven's Fifth in my head (exaggeration implied), it's nice to have a computer and MIDI because with the computer playing all the hard parts, the music in my head finally gets out despite my fingers' lack of skill. I have a full MIDI-based studio at home, with three synths, two drum boxes, a sampler, various effects, direct-to-disk recording, and a Mac driving the whole thing. I use this to do original music and fully orchestrated classical pieces, including Beethoven's Fifth! Yeah, all the notes, thanks to some very patient souls who have created MIDI files available on Internet. That's it!

Neal Johnson
njohnson@uop.edu

pleasing sounds for their owners, and accomplish basic musical tasks, they can be modestly upgraded as a person's taste and musical discrimination evolve.

THE PROJECT STUDIO

MIDI project studios are based on flexibility, and are designed to accommodate a variety of musical purposes, or projects. Sometimes this design is the result of spontaneous evolution more than forethought. Often, project studios get started to serve a particular goal, such as making a demo tape, then grow in fits and starts as new projects demand certain pieces of hardware or software. Project studio owners typically serve as audio techs who stand ready to jump at any client's need, whether it be for a voice-over for a commercial, a scrap of musical underscoring for a corporate training video, demo production for a local band, or any number of other recording and composition situations.

Project studios are often semipro ventures at the beginning, housed in basements, garages, and spare bedrooms—spaces that are sometimes soundproofed for recording with microphones. Following the curve of greatest success, an aspiring project studio moves out of the spare room into a more spacious and dedicated area, such as an office suite. Presumably, at that stage, the studio is a full-time, professional occupation for its fortunate (and often stressed-out) owner. Project studios usually remain one-person operations, with the owner wearing all the hats of sound engineer, technical troubleshooter, composer, producer, bookkeeper, client account executive, and sleep-deprived entrepreneur.

Project studios are very often hybrid MIDI/tape setups. Because they must accommodate a range of production needs, such real-sound recording devices such as microphones, live tracking decks, sophisticated mixers, and mastering equipment are integrated into the MIDI rig. As mentioned, this often requires soundproofing the studio space. Project studios sometimes evolve from the humblest beginnings, and sometimes are created as fully functional, multicomponent entities meant to serve clients right from the beginning. The main ingredients of a productive, flexible project studio are

These components are discussed in more detail in Chapter 6, "The MIDI Orchestra."

■ **MIDI controller.** Because project studios need to accommodate many players of varying musical backgrounds, a keyboard controller is put to good use. A full-range keyboard with a weighted action is a welcome sight for clients who are primarily pianists. High-end project studios contain digitized acoustic pianos that act as the primary MIDI controller (there may be other keyboards that can be adapted to be controllers for the whole setup if the visiting artist prefers one of them). Digital electric pianos are another option, as are mute MIDI controllers that access piano samples in tone modules. One way or another, a professional-caliber keyboard is often provided.

■ **MIDI rack.** The project studio's MIDI rack consists of tone modules, percussion modules, and rack-mounted samplers accessed by the master keyboard controller. Other keyboards are sometimes present, but because space is often at a premium and the master controller is usually a good, all-purpose keyboard, rack-mounted units are very popular for providing most of the MIDI sounds. A good sampler (or any instrument that can play back high-quality samples, even if it can't record them as samplers do) is essential to a project studio that needs to sound like a symphony orchestra at one session and an acid-techno group the next day. Added to that are usually one or two (or more) current synths and a reliable drum machine. The rack typically also contains a MIDI switcher for keeping the data flow straight.

■ **Mixer.** The audio mixer is at the center of a versatile project studio, forging bridges between the MIDI instruments, the live acoustic instruments, and the multitrack recording deck. The mixer is the audio nerve center, through which passes every sound signal the studio generates. Good, full-featured mixers have been developed that require much less physical space than past-generation monsters with huge footprints that require half a large room. Desktop models now compete with compact floor units without skimping on the bells and whistles you'd expect in a classy console: lots of input channels, multiband equalization (EQ) on each channel, channel muting and soloing, channel switching between live and tape input, stereo **panning** (moving the sound side to side in the stereo field), and much more. Some mixers are even automated, and respond to MIDI volume signals with motorized faders that move up and down in ghostly fashion while a sequence is playing.

▪ **Computer.** Most project studios are computer-enabled. The computer handles MIDI sequencing, synthesizer programming, and sound librarian duties. Furthermore, if hard disk recording is used, the computer processes the live tracks as well as the virtual ones. In extreme cases, when the computer is handling every sound recorded by the studio, as well as background tasks related to MIDI data flow and sound program storage, it can be the most expensive and valuable piece of equipment in the room.

▪ **Multitrack recorder.** Fundamental choices must be made in this department, the first being whether to use tape or computer hard disk as the primary recording medium for multitracking. Hard disk recording carries the advantage of flexible computer processing, and requires a very large hard drive to accommodate the huge digitizations that such recording creates. Tape is messier but more portable, and has a much easier learning curve. If you choose a tape format, there is still the choice between digital and analog tape. Analog tape decks generate more line noise in the recording process, but some people think they sound warmer and fuller. Digital tape formats are more portable, and also more expensive. One way or another, every project studio offers a multitrack recording solution for both live tracking and printing multiple MIDI tracks.

▪ **Effects rack.** A studio's effects rack is filled with rack-mounted devices that process sound, as opposed to generating sound. Such racks are also known as signal processors or digital signal processing (DSP) racks. The reverb box is the best known effects device, and there are many others. Typically, a track is bussed into the effects box, then returned in its newly processed state into the mix. The mixer generally handles this chore, providing one, two, three, or even more bussing options for each input channel. Because the mixer is a conduit connecting the instruments, virtual tracks, and tape tracks of a composition, any track can be sent to the effects rack for processing. Of course, the round trip happens so fast that there is no delay in hearing processed tracks as the piece is playing. The more devices in the effects, the more tracks can be processed simultaneously and differently. In some studios, the effects rack is one of the most impressive, elaborate, and expensive segments.

- **Mastering deck.** Certain tape decks specialize in recording the end result of a music production. They produce the master from which copies are duplicated. In recent decades, the machine entrusted with this job was a reel-to-reel, quarter-inch stereo tape deck. Now, alternatives exist in the form of digital audiotape (DAT) and portable hard drives, in addition to the standby analog tape choice. DAT recorders are perhaps the most popular: A godsend to studios on a tight money and space budget, they are compact, and you can slip the master in a pocket when you're done recording it.

- **Software and samples.** Computers are useless without software, and MIDI instruments are limited without an expanded palette of sound samples and synthesizer programs. Software, being mostly invisible, is easily overlooked as an expense when planning a studio, but it should be treated as substantially as equipment. Of course, if you already have a computer to build the studio around, chances are you already have software you like and are comfortable using.

Analog vs. Digital vs. Tape vs. Hard Drive

Any studio that combines live recording with MIDI recording (sequencing) must take a stand on how to record "real" (not MIDI) tracks. A few fundamental options must be understood, and the possibilities are compounded by the blurring distinction (thanks to computers in general and sampling and sound digitization in particular) between real and virtual tracks. Three main formats must be considered by any ambitious, MIDI-based project studio.

THREE STUDIO FORMATS

- *Hard disk recording.* In the broadest terms, hard disk recording is any digital recording process in which the tracks are stored on a computer device, not on tape. Typically, a computer equipped with a very large hard drive and special recording software is used. The recording package includes both the software and an audio interface with input jacks. When modified with such specialty equipment, the computer becomes a multitrack recording device whose sophistication (such as the number of tracks) depends on the power of the software and whose capacity (the amount of music that can be recorded) depends on the size of the hard drive. Another option is a dedicated hard drive recording machine that is not associated with a general-purpose computer. Such devices are called platform-independent hard disk recorders. They are self-contained machines that include everything needed—audio inputs, built-in recording software, and audio outputs—to perform live tracking in the digital domain.

- *Digital tape recording.* Digital multitrack tape recording, once the province of high-end professional sound studios, has come within reach of the home, semipro, and project studio in the 1990s. Digital multitrack decks even use compact tape formats such as VHS and 8 millimeter (normally used for video recording) that are extremely portable. The most popular decks provide 8 tape tracks of digital recording. Adding to the appeal of the digital tape alternative is the modularity of the machines, which can be stacked to provide additional tracks in increments of 8. In this way, a growing project studio can evolve from an 8-track facility to 16-, 24-, or 32-tracks as the budget permits, without discarding any equipment. Traditional reel-to-reel multitrack digital recorders are still an alternative, but tend to be very expensive, with high tape costs to boot.

- *Analog tape recording.* There are a few good reasons to choose analog tape over digital. For one thing, it's less expensive, especially considering the well-developed market for used multitrack decks. For another, the reel-to-reel format for 8-track decks is easier to work with, if you like razor blade cutting and splicing, than compact, cassette-based digital tape cartridges. Finally, some musicians and producers prefer the sound of analog recording, attributing to it qualities of richness and warmth that, to their ears, are missing from the sterile result of digital recording.

Choosing among the above three main alternatives is a matter of balancing production needs, finances, and personal preference.

Reverb, Echo, and Other Audio Hauntings

When planning, assembling, or even contemplating a project studio, the need for high-quality effects devices can easily be underestimated. Even when that is not the case, it's a difficult area to make decisions in, partly because so many different products and product types are available. It's also hard to predict what specialized signal processing will be needed by the studio's clients. Some types of processing are necessary right from the start, others are useful but not required, and a few are indulgences or toys. Within each group is a wide range of brands, prices, and quality. Here are some considerations.

EFFECTS

- Reverb is essential; some individual tracks and overall mixes sound terribly artificial, ironically, without artificial reverb treatment. There are two good ways to get reverb into a young studio inexpensively: one or more small, dedicated reverb boxes, or a single multieffect box. The latter choice offers the advantage of other effects types, but choosing two or more less expensive reverb-only products gives you more bussing flexibility.

- Multieffect boxes usually offer a range of preset effects and gradations with which those effects can be applied. Often, you can combine two, three, four, or more effects into a single processing patch. The big question when considering such a device is whether the built-in effects are programmable or you must take what is programmed in at the factory. One example is whether the decay time of the reverb patches can be adjusted. Such programmability may not be important for those who want many good processing options without spending a fortune on adjustment features they may never use.

- If analog multitrack tape is the main tracking medium for live instruments, some kind of noise reduction is usually crucial in eliminating tape hiss. Dolby and dbx are the two main trademarks seen in most studios; they have different characteristic sounds in suppressing tape noise, but operate essentially the same way. Noise reduction is sometimes built into analog tape decks, but it can also be acquired in rack-mounted form and hooked into the musical path. Digital tape decks do not need noise reduction.

- Digital delay is a specialized effect that sounds like repeated echoes, and is used in both subtle and obvious ways. Multieffect boxes always contain digital delay patches, but may not let you program the delay time between echoes, or how long the effect continues, both of which are crucial to using the effect in some

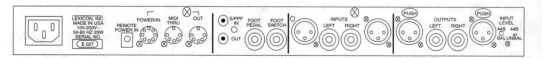

The back panel of a digital effects box, showing MIDI jacks, audio outputs, and audio inputs.

popular music genres. Having a dedicated, programmable digital delay unit is crucial to many project studios, and there are inexpensive products that get the job done.

• Aural enhancement can add sparkle and integrity to any recorded track, or to an overall mix, and can contribute to the sound quality by which a project studio becomes known and trusted. Aural enhancement boxes must be considered luxury devices for a new studio on a budget, but are sometimes necessities as the enterprise begins to grow.

UPGRADING A PROJECT STUDIO

Project studios typically make the most of their resources, emphasizing a lean approach when upgrading and expanding. They are often semipro enterprises run out of the home, and space and financial limitation keep their owners ingenious and resourceful. When it comes to buying new equipment, project studio owners are willing consumers, and just about the most savvy shoppers on the musical scene. Making full use of information resources available, they are the best-informed consumers on the music scene, staying abreast of new technological developments and hungrily absorbing equipment reviews by the hundreds. Typically, they buy something new only when it serves them broadly in a wide variety of production situations. Sometimes their upgrades are invisible to the inexperienced eye: They do not often buy the latest, hyped keyboard with a palette of glitzy new sounds, but they might spend almost as much money on an inconspicuous signal processor (such as a digital effects box) that elevates the overall sound of their mixes and helps give the studio a signature sound.

Project studio upgrades can be ambitious, but are never capricious. Here are a few main ways to augment a studio's usefulness to prospective clients:

More 'n' Better: A Project Studio

■ **Number of "real" recording tracks.** Recording studios are traditionally rated, first and foremost, by how many recording tracks they offer, as defined by the multitrack deck they use. So studios are broadly classified as 8-, 16-, 32-, and 48-track facilities. MIDI studios render such evaluations somewhat meaningless because virtual tracks (sequencer tracks) can be practically limitless in number, as a function of inexpensive software, not costly hardware. Because project studios are usually hybrid

MIDI–microphone setups, the live tracking capacity plays a fairly important part in attracting clients.

■ **MIDI sound palette.** One specialized request often made of project studios involves replacing MIDI sounds. Owners of small home studios record basic tracks for a project, using whatever synth patches and samples are at their disposal. Then those tracks are taken (on disk) to a better-equipped MIDI studio that can substitute higher-quality samples from a more professional sound palette. Studios with large sound libraries, either in the form of many MIDI instruments or sample libraries on disk, can offer a useful production service to owners of less ambitious, budget studios.

■ **Processing and sound effects.** *Sweetening* refers to processing prerecorded tracks and mixes with digital effects. Project studios with well-equipped signal processing racks can court clients who want to enhance already-recorded tracks or re-record certain lead tracks with better reverb and other processing.

■ **Video synchronization.** Soundtrack and underscoring projects are a staple for many video-capable project studios. Nonvideo setups can upgrade to video status by acquiring a playback deck of some sort (it could be as simple as a standard VHS videocassette recorder) and a synchronization box that links it to the studio's sequencer. Using such a setup, a video with **timecode** embedded on it can drive the sequencer's forward and rewind controls, keeping picture and music married in tight synchronization. The equipment isn't expensive but, as with anything, there are ranges of complexity, features, and cost.

■ **Alternative MIDI controllers.** The friendliest MIDI project studios offer MIDI controls for all kinds of instrumental players, from keyboardists to wind instrumentalists, from drummers to violinists. Granted, not many prospective clients need to have a MIDI violin at their disposal when making their band's demo; if they do, they are likely to bring their own. Perhaps the most important controller upgrade is a MIDI drum kit, as many keyboard-based producers want to bring a real drummer into the project but don't have enough tape tracks to adequately record a full acoustic drum kit. The best compromise is to leave the drums in the MIDI (sampled) domain but use a real drummer, playing a MIDI drum kit controller, to record the virtual drum tracks. That way, although the sounds themselves are short of absolute authenticity, the playing style and feel of the tracks are much improved from keyboard-based recording.

■ **Physical facilities.** Finally, the most massive upgrade undertaken by most project studios involves the studio space itself, and soundproofing it for more effective live tracking. This ambitious enterprise usually signals a drastic elevation of the studio's business operation and intent to acquire a certain kind of client. It sometimes involves relocating equipment from house to office, but often is a home renovation and the beginning of a more official residential business.

THE SOUNDTRACK STUDIO

When MIDI was first developed, small, efficient studios began encroaching on professional territory previously occupied solely by particular industry collaborations. Before MIDI, soundtracks to films and television shows were acquired in a couple of ways. Productions with large budgets could afford to hire a composer, contract musicians to play the composer's score, and hire a sound studio to record the soundtrack. Budget productions fell back on prerecorded ("canned") underscoring fragments taken from collections that were purchased and stocked by recording studios, or by the film production houses themselves. (This underscoring method is known as needle-drop production, named during the days of vinyl long-playing records that contained the music collections.)

MIDI changed everything. Suddenly, in the 1980s little studios appeared, often in homes, that could provide original-music underscoring at a reasonable price while eliminating several intermediate steps. The links in the production food chain that felt the pinch were instrumentalists (replaced by sampled virtual instruments) and sound studios (replaced by the sequencer). For several years, there was controversy about the revolutionary (and some said damaging) effect that MIDI was having on the industry and those on the front lines who made their daily living as versatile studio instrumentalists.

Most of this controversy focused on soundtrack MIDI studios, for two reasons. The ongoing need for underscoring production was a substantial career platform for many studio musicians, and MIDI studios provided an elegant, irresistibly cost-effective alternative to live musicians for film and TV production companies. As is usually the case with industry transitions, jobs were added as they were taken away. New career avenues have been opened for composers and producers who work in the digital realm and who master the new instruments of the digital age. Soundtrack production continues to furnish perhaps the broadest career path for the MIDI studio composer. Soundtrack studios, a subset of project studios, have particular equipment needs. Soundtrack studios differ from project studios in several ways:

- Soundtrack studios usually don't serve live recording needs, and so have little use for soundproof space, microphones, or multitrack tape recording. They also do not usually serve clients who are performers, as demo studios do, so there is no need for a variety of keyboard options.

- Soundtrack studios need specific tools of the underscoring trade that enable them to synchronize music to video very precisely.

This is not to say that a soundtrack studio will never produce a live track and has no microphones or multitrack tape decks. Conversely, many project studios have synchronization tools even if underscoring is not the primary activity. But generally speaking, soundtrack studios are MIDI-intensive environments that can link music and sound effects directly to moving-picture programming.

Soundtrack studios need several types of equipment specific to the task of underscoring, in addition to the racks of MIDI instruments, switchers, signal processors, and mastering equipment.

- **Synchronization hardware.** Certain devices do nothing but create a timing connection between tape decks and computer sequencers. These devices are called **synchronization** (synch) **boxes**, and come in rack-mount and standalone models. Their job is to receive the timecode imprinted on videotape, translate

Synchronization boxes lock the timing of sequencers to the movement of tape decks.

it into MIDI commands, and pass it along to the sequencer. In the other direction, the box receives MIDI timing signals from the sequencer, translates them into timecode, and sends the code to the video deck. There are a few kinds of timecode that can be used on videotapes, but **SMPTE** (Society of Motion Picture and Television Engineers) timecode is the most common, and is used on virtually all movie and television footage that needs underscoring. Once the video deck is synchronized to the sequencer, the composer can use the deck's transport controls (Play, Stop, etc.) to control the sequencer. This way, virtual music tracks can be recorded in the sequencer as the film footage is being viewed, and timed to events on the video screen.

■ **Video decks and monitors.** Naturally, if a studio provides soundtrack services, it needs to be able to play video programming. Advanced VHS decks allow for back-and-forth shuffling of the tape. Other types of video deck, such as Beta and 1-inch, are sometimes present to accommodate working tapes from film production companies that don't print on the VHS format.

■ **Specialized underscoring software.** The sequencer is the main software program in any MIDI studio. Soundtrack studios also use programs that place music and sound effects at precise points in the footage, measured by the timecode of the video. These effects can be inserted, moved, and removed by using "hit lists" based on the timecodes. These programs bookkeep the many hit points that exist in any film project, and trigger the sounds at the correct time. Such specialized software replaces the traditional stopwatch method used by composers for decades.

■ **Sampled instrument library.** MIDI underscoring has emerged as a viable alternative to live instruments because of its ability to mimic an acoustic orchestra or other ensemble. Busy soundtrack studios specialize in a chameleonlike ability to emulate real instruments and instrument groups. Accordingly, samplers are a major part of the MIDI rack, and sample libraries are a big part of the studio's inventory.

▣▬▬▬ Q & A: SYNCHRONIZATION BOXES

Q How are synch boxes hooked into a MIDI studio?

A Synchronization boxes have audio input/output jacks and MIDI jacks. You connect them between a video deck and the sequencer, using audio cables to and from the video deck, and MIDI cables on the sequencer side.

Q Are there different types of synch box?

A Different models embody a range of features. Because there are several types of timecode used on videotapes, and even SMPTE timecode (the most common) has a few different subtypes, some boxes handle all the variations better than others. In addition, you have a choice between rack-mount units and desktop boxes. Of course, there are price differences.

Q Are synch boxes used only in soundtrack studios?

A No, they are commonly found in other MIDI studios as well. The task of a synchronization device is to connect a tape deck to a sequencer, so the sequencer's transport controls can be slaved to the movement of the tape deck, and this can be useful in pure music situations. Timecode can be imprinted on audiotape as well as videotape. Many MIDI producers take advantage of this by **striping** (imprinting) one track of multitrack tape with timecode, then slaving the sequencer to the deck. Once that is done, live tracks or MIDI tracks recorded to tape can be synchronized with virtual tracks on the sequencer.

UPGRADING THE SOUNDTRACK STUDIO

Successful underscoring takes creative ability and a peculiar talent for reflecting the character of a story in music. The composer must elevate the show without attracting much attention to the music. The best soundtracks move the audience without the audience knowing it. Soundtrack composers must maintain a certain egoless quality. These personal and artistic qualities make a valuable soundtrack producer, and when such a person is well-equipped with studio gear, there can be little need to upgrade for long stretches at a time. However, when the need arises, soundtrack studios often evolve in the following ways:

▪ **Expanded sample and effects library.** New instrument **sample libraries** are the most cost-effective way to upgrade the general fidelity and realism of a soundtrack studio. They can be purchased on CD, ready to be input to a sampler, or on floppy disk already formatted for a specific instrument. Sound effects are available in (fairly expensive) CD collections. Such expansion is often done on a project-by-project basis, as the work's need requires.

■ **Video formats.** A soundtrack studio can get off the ground with a single VHS video deck, but as time goes on and a variety of clients are encountered, the need can arise for alternative formats and backup decks. Furthermore, standard VHS-format decks can be upgraded with features that ease the process of locating specific points in a video and dealing with timecode.

THE DEMO STUDIO

The arrival of MIDI has been a creative and financial gift from heaven for independent, unsigned bands and solo performers. Previously, creating a representative recording of your work required renting the expertise and equipment of a recording studio that was equipped from head to toe to serve all kinds of clients, large and small. This usually means paying high rates to support an unnecessarily fancy facility. The advent of 4- and 8-track home recorders helped the situation, but adding drum, piano, and other tracks to a stripped-down demonstration tape was still daunting and expensive.

When MIDI hit the streets, powerful production techniques became available to everyone from the unsigned rising star to the home hobbyist. Bands can now record backing tracks in their own time and space, then take them to a sound studio for vocals, acoustic solos, processing, and mixing. More ambitious bands can invest a bit more to accomplish the entire process without outside help. The demo studio, as a particular configuration of equipment, was born.

Very often, demo studios graduate from serving the needs of a single musical act to become businesses of their own. Such studios, often run by musicians who have transferred their dream of stardom to a dream of financial solvency, cater to the demo needs of local music acts. They are hybrid recording environments that blend live and virtual tracking, as project studios do. Unlike project studios, demo studios are ill-equipped to handle certain clients, such as film production companies. They provide basic live and MIDI tracking in the creation of songs, sometimes interfacing with other studios that provide finishing touches such as track replacement and mixing.

What Makes a Demo Studio?

▧ **A multitrack recording deck.** The deck can be of very modest proportions; some terrific and famous songs have been recorded in garages on 4-track systems. These days, 8-track decks are considered of minimum modesty in a demo studio that takes paying customers. The machine might be a digital tape recorder, or analog with noise reduction.

▧ **A MIDI palette.** Demo recordings don't need to be state-of-the-art masterpieces ready for global distribution. Their purpose is to convey a song within the industry. So racks of samplers and synths are not necessary, but some vanilla MIDI timbres can be used to add string sections, horn stabs, drum programming, and keyboard parts to songs.

▧ **A sequencer.** Preferably computer-based.

▧ **A quiet space for live tracking.** Song demos are rarely MIDI-only productions, or the composer would be composing in his or her own studio. A soundproof room (or at least very quiet), equipped with several microphones and some dividers, gets the ball rolling when recording a band. It's usually a bring-your-own-instruments situation.

▧ **A mixer.** Pure MIDI studios can get away without an advanced sound mixer, but demo studios need at least a lightweight model for separating and processing recorded tracks.

▧ **Effects.** Not necessarily an entire rack of effects, but at least a reverb box or a single multieffect unit must be present to sweeten live tracks.

From the above elements a demo studio grows, depending on the needs of its owners and their business aspirations. The most significant upgrade is the multitrack tape deck, because studios are judged on the number of tape tracks they provide. It's especially crucial to have lots of them when recording live drum kits, as is often the case with band demos. So upgrading to 16, 24, 32, or more tape tracks instantly elevates the status (and debt) of a demo studio.

THE MUSICIAN'S SHOPPING GUIDE TO MIDI*

MIDI is the most powerful creative tool available to musicians in the digital age. The universality of the MIDI standard, and its characteristic networking capacity, make it easy to start as a hobbyist and end up as a professional. This chapter is a shopping guide, useful to both beginners and experienced MIDI users. Brand names are not mentioned here, and the purpose is not to make specific recommendations. Rather, you can get a handle on what questions you should ask, whether to buy used or new, and what the price ranges are for basic types of MIDI equipment.

Computers, the center of MIDI studios, are covered in Chapter 4. Shopping information about computer sound cards can be found there, too.

SYNTHESIZERS

Keyboard synths are the most generic piece of MIDI equipment, so generalized that they are usually simply called keyboards, their synthesis capabilities taken for granted. But nothing should be taken for granted when shopping, especially for a product that has so many models to choose from. Synthesizers also come in keyboardless versions, called tone modules or sound modules. They are rack-mounted boxes that contain the same "brain" as

*Price ranges in this chapter are based on 1997 retail prices.

the corresponding keyboard model, and most of the same internal features. You can shop for a tone module with the same considerations as the keyboard version.

Keyboard synthesizers are distinguished from home keyboards, often found in general music shops, by the higher quality of sound, programmability, and lack of built-in speakers. They are purchased in music stores exclusively, not in department stores, computer stores, consumer electronic stores, office supply stores, or other retail outlets that carry computers and home keyboards.

There is a vibrant, evolving, and interesting market for used keyboard synths. More used trade occurs with keyboards (and keyboardless tone modules) than any other type of digital music equipment. This is partly because musicians love upgrading their keyboards, and partly because it is one of the safest used purchases you can make. Digital keyboards contain no moving parts except the keys themselves and the disk drives (if included), and as long as they are not defective when new, they tend to last very well. It's worth noting that keyboards used in performance could have been dropped, and if they were played in club gigs, who knows what might have been spilled into them. But studio keyboards make great used purchases.

Essential Shopping Questions: Keyboard Synthesizers

- **How does it sound?** This may seem like a no-brainer, but remember that you'll have to live with these sounds for a long time, trusting them to carry the spirit of your music. In the store, go through all the presets to see whether they inspire you.

- **What type of keyboard does it have?** This question has to do with both range and feel. Sixty-key, five-octave keyboards are the smallest in range, and most 'boards have a light feel, with plastic, unweighted keys. Players with piano backgrounds prefer weighted keyboards, and there is some variety in the degree to which keys are weighted. A short keyboard is not a terrible liability in the studio, where you have time to place passages outside the keyboard's range through sequencer manipulation. But if you're buying a performance instrument, make sure it has enough range to play your parts.

- **How big is the LCD screen?** Most keyboards have some kind of liquid crystal display (LCD) screen on the front panel for seeing what patch is selected, and even for programming new sounds. If you plan to program (even modest tweaking) your own sounds directly through the instrument, not using computer software, then the larger screens make life easier. Generally, you should prowl through the instrument's innards via that screen and see how well it delivers all the keyboard's options to you. The size of the screen and the efficiency with which information is displayed on it have much to do with how friendly the instrument is.

- What are the polyphonic and multitimbral limits? Find out from a salesperson, spec sheet, or published review the instrument's polyphony (how many notes can sound at once) and multitimbrality (how many different patches can play at once). Ideally, for complex playing and recording, 24 polyphonic voices are needed (but some keyboards have only 16) and you want to have access to 16 multitimbral parts simultaneously (some instruments deliver only 8). Your requirements depend on what kind of music you're involved with and whether you have other MIDI instruments in your setup. The more instruments you have, the less powerful each individual machine needs to be.

- Are there built-in effects? Are they programmable? Many keyboards have internal digital signal processors (DSPs) for adding reverb, digital delay, and other processing to a patch. This is desirable. But it's also desirable to control the processing. Ideally, the DSP portion of the instrument allows you to assign one (or more) effects to a patch, and even program those effects to some degree. The on-board processor doesn't need to be as sophisticated and feature-rich as a dedicated unit, but the more control you have, the better.

- Is software available for sound programming? If you want to accomplish sound design with the instrument, it's best to use a computer. So find out if there is a program that corresponds to the model you're considering buying, and make sure it's available for your computer's operating system. These programs are not always ready when the instrument first comes out, but usually they are soon thereafter.

- Does the keyboard accept external samples? Samples are the building blocks of new synth sounds, and every keyboard comes equipped with its own permanent palette of sampled waveforms. Many models also accept additional waveforms, either by floppy disk or CD-ROM. Such disks also can package new preprogrammed synth patches. In both cases, it's a good, inexpensive way to broaden the usefulness of the instrument and refresh its sound after you've been using it for a while.

Bottom Line

Keyboard Synthesizers

Synthesizers vary in cost depending on their sets of features.	
Low-end synth with rudimentary sound programming and low expandability	$800–$1,500
Basic pro-model synth with disk drive, sampled waveforms, expandability, and strong programmability	$1,200–$3,000
High-end synth with extravagant memory capacity, sound quality, audio output options, and expandability	$2,500–$6,000
Tone modules, deduct from above prices	$200–$500

SEQUENCING SOFTWARE

Software is hard to buy intelligently because it's hard to preview. It would be unthinkable to buy a keyboard without playing it first, but it's common to buy software without trying it. Of course, software costs less than a keyboard. Still, it's an investment, and if possible it should be demonstrated. Some music stores carry computers and music programs; this is your best bet. Otherwise, at least try to ask questions of other wired musicians. If you are online, ask for advice on music forum message boards. Some software companies also make slightly disabled demo programs available for downloading, which is probably the best way to try a sequencer before committing your money to it.

Perhaps surprisingly, used software exists. When upgrading to a new program, musicians sometimes sell what they were using. You might wonder why, because software can be copied so easily. Remember that distributing copies of commercial software is against the law and undermines the music community. Buying used software isn't a perfect solution either because you are not registered with the company as the owner, and will have trouble getting technical support. If you do buy software from a private seller, be sure to get all the printed documentation (owner's manual), boxes, and disks.

New programs cannot easily be found in general software stores. Computer-oriented music stores are good, and some software can be purchased on the Internet or through catalogs with a credit card.

Essential Shopping Questions: Sequencing Software

- **How many tracks does the program have?** Many software sequencers have more tracks than you'll ever need, but it's good to make sure there aren't too few. As a rough guide, go for at least 64. That may seem more than ample, but plan for the future. And if you're new to MIDI production, you don't yet know how easy it is to fill up virtual tracks with alternative takes, segregated drum tracks, and other necessary indulgences.

- **Are the screens comprehensible?** Try to find a program that is intuitively designed. You shouldn't have to puzzle over the screens or resort to the documentation very much. If you can't find a demo of the program, at least try to find screen shots to get an idea of how the windows are built. Reading product reviews in music magazines helps.

- **Does the program have a notation editing screen?** If you are a music-reading, traditional musician, a notation window makes you feel at home with the program. It's probably not the only screen you'll use for MIDI editing, but if you buy a program without it, you'll probably end up wishing you had it.

- **Can you print out sheet music?** Some sequencers are hybrid programs (recorders and notators). Find out whether you can notate your MIDI composition, edit the notation, and print it out. The notation portion of the program may not be as powerful, elegant, or easy as a dedicated notator, but it's a good way to begin. You can always upgrade later.

- **Does the program support more than 16 MIDI channels?** The MIDI specification delegates only 16 channels, but more can be added through software and extra MIDI jacks on the computer–MIDI interface. You may not see a need for more than 16 channels now, but if you continue to accumulate MIDI instruments, and your recording gets more complex, you will eventually feel cramped. The sequencer should have the ability to accommodate 32 or more MIDI channels (in increments of 16); you may have to purchase additional hardware to make the extra channels work.

Bottom Line

Sequencing Software

Freeware sequencers	Free!
Shareware programs	$10–$75

Commercial sequencing programs with moderately powerful features	$70–$150
Professional sequencers	$150–$500

DIGITAL PIANOS

Digital pianos are generally more expensive than other keyboards of similar quality, for a few reasons. They simply have more material to them, for one thing; they are heavier and bulkier than keyboards. They usually have weighted keyboards, which adds to the price, and are housed in a console that sometimes resembles a piano.

Used digital pianos can be found, but the marketplace isn't very active. This may be because most people invest in a digital piano for the long haul. Because the piano sample is the primary reason for buying one, if the instrument sounds good, advances in keyboard technology won't affect its value, and people don't trade up too often.

Essential Shopping Questions: Digital Pianos

- **Is the action weighted to your satisfaction?** Digital keyboards tend to have weighted actions, more so than portable keyboards, as they are meant to emulate a real piano in sound and touch. There is some range to the possible weight added to an action, and the instrument's playing feel is one of the biggest considerations.

- **Does it have a full-range keyboard?** There is a certain frustration in playing a great-sounding digital piano with only a 76-note keyboard, which is sometimes the case. Of course, it cuts the price, which can be a worthwhile tradeoff.

- **What other settings are included besides piano?** The grand piano samples are obviously the main feature of a digital piano, but most models include a smattering of other related instruments, such as a vibraphone, harpsichord, organ, and Fender Rhodes electric piano. Indeed, a few ambitious models carry a hundred or more virtual instruments of varying quality. Decide what you want this instrument to be. If you want the best possible piano sound, don't go for one that squanders memory on superfluous sounds; choose a model that contains a few excellent piano samples. On the other hand, if you want a general-purpose machine with a darn good piano sample on it (something most keyboard synthesizers fail to deliver), then a model with a larger orchestra makes sense.

- Is there a built-in sequencer? If you don't have a computer or hardware sequencer, and are slightly interested in recording yourself playing the digital piano, look for a model with a built-in MIDI recorder. Chances are, it won't be a sophisticated sequencer, but for simple recording of a performance, you don't need a multitrack powerhouse.

- Is there a disk drive and available software? Disk drives are usually found on the high-end, orchestra-enabled digital pianos. Such instruments often have sequencers built in, and disk drives to save your work. Additionally, the drive accepts extra software that includes prerecorded sequences for music-minus-one type of playing along.

Bottom Line

Digital Pianos

Prices for digital pianos vary according to three main features: how big they are, how many instrument samples are included, and how many extraneous features, such as a sequencer, tone controls, reverb, and disk drive, are on board.

Basic digital piano with only a few instrument settings and no tone control or reverb	$1,200–$2,500
Midrange digital piano with full keyboard, a number of good samples, tone control, and reverb	$1,800–$3,200
High-end digital piano with dozens of instrument settings, sequencer, disk drive, and extensive tone controls	$2,500–$4,000

DRUM MACHINES AND PERCUSSION MODULES

There is a surprising variety in quality and type of machine that delivers drum sounds. All such machines use digitally sampled sounds, of course, but there is an astounding range of samples available, and the hardware design varies considerably as well. Hardware and software (the software being the sounds inside the hardware boxes) are mainly what you need to keep in mind when shopping for MIDI drum sounds.

Drum machines are tabletop units with small, playable pads on the top panel. Each pad can be assigned to a single internal sample, creating a miniature playable drum kit. The sounds can also be played by an external controller, such as a keyboard, just like any other MIDI tone module. They have a certain type of built-in sequencer that specializes in recording drum patterns, and there are usually prerecorded patterns that can be used as the rhythmic basis of songs.

In contrast to the traditional drum machine, percussion modules are like sound modules in that they must be addressed by an external controller, because they have no pads. They are built differently, also, being rack-mounted units with only a slim front panel showing when screwed in place. They are meant to be used in multicomponent MIDI recording studios. There is no internal sequencer in percussion modules, or prerecorded patterns in most cases. They are pure sample-delivery machines.

Drum machines move well on the used market, thanks to their durability.

Essential Shopping Questions: Drum Machines and Percussion Modules

- **Does the machine have the type of samples you need?** Some models have a musical attitude, providing a characteristic sound designed for a certain type of music. Some machines are strong on bread-and-butter samples for simple pop songs, with very few nonkit percussion samples. Others specialize in world music percussion, with somewhat unsatisfactory basic kit sounds. It's best to know what you need the drum machine for, and go for the machine that gives you more of what you want.

- **How many audio outputs are included?** This is an important question for drum machines because in MIDI production it is very effective—some would say crucial—to process each drum sample differently. (That's how it's done with live drum kit recording.) So, when playing a drum sequence, if each sample can be assigned its own audio output, it makes it easy to separate the samples for individual processing at the mixer stage. Some machines provide an extra pair of outputs for a total of four individual jacks. Others go higher, which is gratifying (8 is nice, 16 is heaven).

- **Does the unit accept new samples?** Like some keyboards and tone modules, some percussion modules and drum machines can receive additional samples from an external source such as floppy disk or ROM card. This is a great way to get new sounds for little investment.

- **What is the drum machine's time signature range?** This question doesn't apply to percussion modules, which are controlled by an external sequencer. But drum machines, when using the internal sequencer, are subject to that sequencer's limitations. If it is a bread-and-butter, pop-oriented type of machine, you may not have much flexibility to use odd meters. If you like rhythmic experimentation and hate to be blocked in your creativity, be careful on this point. If you want complete freedom, it's always best to use an external computer sequencer, whether you buy a drum machine or a percussion module.

- **What nonpercussion samples are included?** Some drum machines also contain bass samples, sound effects, and orchestral hits, among other miscellaneous sounds and noises. You may not care to use that killer breaking glass sample very often, but it's nice to know it's there.

SAMPLERS

A sampler is one of the most technical of all MIDI purchases. Samplers are wonderful machines, and add a degree of realism to a virtual orchestra that cannot be obtained any other way. Along with their desirable features comes a complicated tangle of hardware–software configurations. Samplers require more internal memory than the average synthesizer, which adds a consideration when shopping. Additionally, there are compatible sample libraries to consider, as well as the sample processing power of the instrument. And after you've sorted through a maze of options, you have the privilege of paying more for the sampler of choice than a regular keyboard costs.

On the plus side, there are fewer model choices among samplers than among other keyboards. You can also look into sample-playback machines, which convey the realism of a full-blown sampler but without the built-in recording option. (This portion of the chapter deals only with actual samplers, with audio inputs.)

Samplers come in both keyboard and nonkeyboard versions. You can save money by forgoing the keyboard if you already have a keyboard controller. Like other sound modules, the keyboardless sampler usually has the same features as the keyboard version.

There is a market for used samplers, but it's not as active as for other keyboards. Samplers are such a substantial investment that musicians are reluctant to trade them in quickly, putting themselves through the process of researching and funding a new instrument. Also, the inevitable buildup of a sample library endows the original investment with even more value. A sample-based MIDI studio owes its sound, to a large degree, to its sampler and sample library, so ditching one instrument for another is a bigger decision than with other equipment.

When considering a used sampler, examine the bit rate. The bit rate represents the amount of data used to create each "audio snapshot" in the digitizing process. Modern instruments are 16-bit samplers, which deliver very good results. In the early years of consumer samplers, lower bit rates of 12 and even 8 were used. Some of these machines are on the used market, and are of a fundamentally lower quality than their 16-bit counterparts. They're not necessarily inadequate, and the low price might make it worthwhile as an entry-level, get-your-feet-wet kind of instrument.

Essential Shopping Questions: Samplers

- **Does the sampler come with a sample library?** Remember that a sampler is mute until you put something into it, unlike a synthesizer, which comes loaded with preset sound programs. With that in mind, make sure some kind of disk-based sample library is included with the instrument, or your first experience playing the sampler will be disconcertingly quiet.

- **Is it compatible with samples from other brands?** Advertisements for samplers sometimes carry the promise that sample libraries made for other brands can be used in the model you're considering. This is a good thing. It expands the range of your instrument, and gives you expandability options well into the future, supported by at least two companies.

- **What sampling rates are available?** The sampling rate is the frequency with which "sound snapshots" are taken of a sound wave in the digitizing process. Higher sampling rates deliver greater fidelity to the sound being sampled. The sampling rate used when making commercial CDs, which are essentially giant samples, is 44,100 audio snapshots per second (abbreviated as 44.1 kilohertz, or kHz). Some music samplers exceed that rate, reaching up to 44 kHz or higher. This is great for sampling sound with very high frequency (pitch) content, such as cymbals or rain. The important thing is to make sure that at least 44.1 kHz is available to you if you plan to do original sampling. Beneath that standard, there should be a selection of lower rates. They come in handy when trying to conserve memory while taking samples of lower-frequency content that doesn't require superb fidelity.

- What is the sampler's maximum sample time? This is a question about the instrument's internal memory. Every sampler has a limit on the length (in seconds) of a sample that can be recorded. Clearly, the longer the better. In some cases it can be extended by adding memory, which then becomes a cost consideration. Consult a knowledgeable salesperson about this important issue if original sampling is in your future.

- How much RAM is included? Is it expandable? RAM determines the size of the samples you can acquire. As in a computer (a sampler is basically a specialized computer), RAM is measured in megabytes (MB).

- What kind of sample processing is built in? Once you've recorded a sample, some tweaking and processing are usually required to make it optimally playable on the keyboard. Looping, inverting, and cross-fading are a few of the standard operations that should be included in all samplers under consideration. Other models place more emphasis on standard synthesis features, letting you acquire new waveforms through sampling, then process them extensively as if the sampler were a synthesizer. Appropriately, such instruments are sometimes called sampling synthesizers. This consideration is important only if original sampling and sound design are part of your creative process. If not, any basic sampler with a good sample library will suit your purpose.

- What kind of disk drives and interfaces are included? Samples take up lots of memory. The best samplers give you options for managing your own sample files without stressing your machine's capacities. There should certainly be a floppy disk drive. Hard drives are welcome; in some cases they are internalized, as in a computer, and other models simply provide a SCSI port on the back of the instrument into which an external hard drive can be connected.

Bottom Line

Samplers

Basic 16-bit sampler with starter library and floppy disk drive	$1,800–$2,600
Midrange sampler with library, floppy drive, and hard drive	$2,500–$3,800

High-end sampler with large
library, floppy and hard drives, extensive
processing, and state-of-the-art specifications $3,500–$8,000

WORKSTATIONS

Workstations are a launching point into the MIDI world for a lot of people, and they are promoted with hype and promises. They are not too difficult to shop for, and fun to try out, but it's important to separate the wheat from the chaff—that is, the hype from the reality. The problem is that many beginners don't know exactly what they want out of a nascent MIDI studio, so they are vulnerable to showroom demos and insistent salespeople. There is nothing wrong with buying an instrument in a spirit of experimentation and finding your MIDI niche through experience. As much as possible, try to anticipate what the workstation will be used for and what your musical ideals are. They may change over time, and shift as you become familiar with the possibilities of digital music production.

Because workstations are all-in-one solutions for the beginning producer, they are set up in stores to give impressive and complete demonstrations of their power and great sound, by playing finished productions prepared by the manufacturer and loaded in by floppy disk. Nothing sells an instrument better than blasting a CD-quality piece of music from its circuitry through a good sound system. Let yourself be impressed by this flagrant display, then get down to the task of discovering exactly how the machine will meet your needs. You may expand beyond the workstation eventually—maybe quickly—but it should satisfy you for the near term, and some of its features should endure indefinitely.

Used workstations are all over the place. They are sold in the private market almost as often as synthesizers. Many musicians buy workstations for their sound, even if they don't need the built-in sequencer or drum samples, which they simply ignore. They are a fairly safe purchase, and sometimes come with the patch library accumulated by the original owner.

Essential Shopping Questions: Workstations

- **How many tracks are included in the sequencer? The on-board sequencers in workstations don't compare to software sequencers in any way, but are still useful. The number of tracks included is sometimes limited to the number of simultaneous** parts (the multitimbrality of the instrument). In many cases this is 8 or 16 tracks. This doesn't allow for storing alternative takes on empty tracks, or any of the other standard techniques that burn up sequencer tracks.

- How powerful are the sequencer's editing features? Once you've done some recording, the sequencer's editing power (or lack of it) comes into play. Workstation sequencers are usually about as powerful as the old hardware sequencers (that is, not very powerful at all). Still, functions such as note correction and event editing should be provided. On-board sequencers haven't developed all that much over the years because serious MIDI producers invariably gravitate toward computer sequencing.

- Does the workstation contain all the sounds you need to create complete recordings? While shopping, treat the workstation as a simple keyboard synthesizer, and evaluate it strictly on the basis of its preset sound programs. Do they suit your playing style and musical vision? Then add in the drum samples and see whether the instrument as a whole inspires your creativity.

- How much memory does the sequencer contain? Most workstations do not have built-in hard drives, as computers do, so the size of the sequence you create is limited by internal RAM memory. Sequencer capacity is usually measured in notes or events (the number of notes or MIDI events you can record before the sequencer memory fills up). Thirty thousand notes is a minimum. (Keep in mind that a note equals at least two MIDI events, so thirty thousand events is half as many notes.)

- Are the drum samples satisfactory? Now it's time to treat the workstation as a drum machine. Does it contain a good selection of the type of drum samples you need for your music? This is perhaps the least important part of the instrument, regardless of the flashy demo you probably were subjected to, because you can always supplement the workstation with an inexpensive drum machine if needed.

- How many audio outputs are there? If a workstation is to be a one-stop production alternative, then it should provide multiple audio outputs for separating recorded parts at the mixer stage. This enables you to process the parts individually, as if they came from different keyboards. An extra pair of outputs, furnishing two additional audio lines out of the instrument, is minimally acceptable. Eight total outputs is much better.

- Are there built-in digital effects? The answer is *yes* in most cases. Make sure the workstation you're considering has built-in effects.

Otherwise, it's back to the store to buy an effects box within the month. Preferably, the effects should be user-assignable, enabling you to allocate them to any sound patch you're playing, then store the result as a new sound patch. The icing on that cake is to have combinable effects (at least two per patch).

Bottom Line

Workstations

Amazingly, the price range for workstations is similar to that of keyboards without sequencers and drum machines built in. Many keyboard models tack on sequencers and drum samples to enter the workstation marketplace. In other words, the dividing line between the two types of instruments has gotten blurred, which has only increased the appeal of getting a workstation for a first keyboard.

Basic workstation with 8-track sequencer, good basic sounds, and moderately powerful features	$1,500–$2,300
Advanced workstation with 16 or more tracks, high-quality sounds, and a strong feature set including powerful synthesis engine	$2,000–$3,500

Part Two
GLOSSARY

Controller See *MIDI controller*.

DAW Digital audio workstations (DAWs) are hard disk recording systems (see *Hard disk recording* in this glossary). Two kinds of DAW exist. One is based on a standard personal computer, and consists of an audio interface (input and output jacks) and software that controls the recording process. The other is self-contained hardware and software that don't rely on a computer.

Digital piano Digital pianos are electronic instruments that sound remarkably like pianos. They are alternatives to acoustic pianos, but not replacements. Their advantages have to do with economics and convenience: Digital pianos are more portable and less expensive than their acoustic ancestors. They attain their persuasive piano sound through the use of digital samples of real pianos stored on the internal circuits. Such high-level sampling requires a tremendous amount of memory, and digital pianos cannot do much else besides emulate pianos; they do not have a wide palette of other sounds onboard, nor do they have synthesis capabilities. Digital pianos by definition are keyboard-equipped instruments, and often feature elaborate stands and pedal attachments designed for semipermanent installation in a studio or living room. However, piano-based sound modules are also available as rack-mount items or desktop boxes.

Drum machine Drum machines and percussion modules provide a specific range of sounds to a MIDI studio. Stocked with drum and percussion

165

samples, they can be controlled over MIDI by external keyboards or sequencers. Traditional drum machines are equipped with small pads on the top panel to which selected internal samples can be assigned, enabling the user to play the machine in real time, if desired. They also come with built-in rhythm sequencers for recording drum parts to songs. Some performers use prerecorded drum machine tracks in place of live drummers. Percussion modules lack the pads and, often, the internal sequencer. Such devices are usually rack-mounted units that function exactly like other sound modules. They can be accessed only with external MIDI keyboards or drum pads, or a sequencer playing back recorded tracks.

Editor/ librarian Editor/librarians are MIDI software programs that help program synthesizers and organize and store sound creations. Some editors don't have library functions, and some librarians cannot edit, but generally, the two software features are packaged together. Ed/libs (as they are abbreviated) are authored for particular MIDI synthesizers, as well as for particular computer operating systems. Accordingly, they must be purchased with both functions in mind.

Envelope A sound envelope defines what happens to a sound over time. In MIDI, an envelope is a programming parameter found in synthesizers that affects how a synthesized sound behaves over time. Envelopes come in three basic types: amplitude (affecting the loudness of a sound over time), filter (affecting the sound's tone as it sustains), and pitch (affecting the wavering or stability of a sound's pitch). Synthesizer envelopes are broken down into stages representing portions of a sound's existence. The attack is the first portion, followed by sustain and decay. Other portions may be added, contributing to the fine-tuned control a programmer has over the sound's evolution.

Equaliza- tion Equalization is the studio technique of balancing frequencies in single recorded tracks and entire music mixes. Adjusting the frequencies changes the tonal quality in the same basic way as using the treble and bass controls on a stereo system. In fact, treble and bass controls are the most basic kind of equalization. Some stereo systems give you control over five or six frequency bands. In a studio environment, much more detail is attained by emphasizing or reducing very narrow ranges of frequencies. Equalization controls are found on mixers, and can be applied in different ways to different individual channels or to the mix as a whole.

Filter Filters alter the tone of sounds while leaving the volume and pitch unaffected. In synthesizers, digital filters work with envelopes and other settings to create new instrument sounds. Filters work by including and excluding certain frequencies that go into any particular sound. High-pass filters eliminate frequencies below a cut-off point; low-pass filters work in reverse. Excluding higher frequencies gives a sound a more bass-oriented quality, and excluding lower frequencies makes the timbre more trebly.

Hard disk recording Hard disk recording systems replace tape recorders in some production situations. Popular for their convenience and noise-free sound compared to tape, hard disk recording systems consist of computer software and an audio interface. Using such a system enables the producer to digitally record live tracks directly to a computer hard drive. Because digitized sound takes a lot of memory, very large hard drives are needed for a useful system.

Home keyboard Also called hobby keyboards, home keyboards are distinguished by the presence of built-in speakers. Generally speaking, they are less expensive than professional models, as well as less powerful and of lower sound quality. In recent years, the quality of home keyboards has steadily improved, to the point of blurring the distinction between home and professional models. However, the defining characteristic remains the presence of speakers.

Keyboard In the MIDI world, *keyboard* generally is assumed to mean a MIDI keyboard because virtually all keyboards made today are MIDI-capable. But strictly speaking, a keyboard is any electronic instrument whose tones are controlled by pressing keys arranged in the standard piano configuration. Synthesizers, digital pianos, home keyboards, samplers, workstations, older electric pianos, and organs are all keyboards.

MIDI The Musical Instrument Digital Interface (MIDI) is a universal software standard that allows digital music instruments to link to each other, to computers, and to other specialized digital music devices. MIDI is built into digital keyboards and other digital instruments, but is not usually included in general-purpose computers. (A special MIDI interface makes computers MIDI-capable.) MIDI instruments and other devices can share digital information that results from pressing keys, using sustain pedals, and other music-making events. Accordingly, MIDI devices can interface with each other, creating mega-instruments from individual MIDI components.

MIDI cable MIDI cables connect MIDI devices. Thus, the MIDI cable is the artery through which MIDI data flows from one digital instrument to another, or from an instrument to a sequencer. MIDI cables are connected according to the same principle as audio cables, using In and Out jacks, and they are bidirectional. Each end of a MIDI cable is fitted with a male five-pin plug that fits a female five-holed MIDI jack. Unlike various types of computer cable, MIDI cables are all the same. They come in various lengths, although they become unreliable if extended beyond about 30 feet. Different-colored cables help keep complex connections straight.

MIDI channel MIDI channels are part of the MIDI specification, and they separate the different parts of a MIDI sound setup. Each sound patch in a track is assigned to one of 16 different channels, so they will sound properly when receiving MIDI data from a sequencer or a played keyboard. MIDI channels are one of the most important parts of the MIDI language because they allow multitracked, multilayered compositions to be recorded; they are responsible for the virtual orchestra.

MIDI controller A MIDI controller is any device that controls another device by sending data through MIDI cables. Typically, keyboard controllers are linked to sound modules, controlling the internal sounds of the module as if they were inside the keyboard. MIDI keyboards can also control other keyboards, drum machines, samplers, or any equipment that receives data through a MIDI In jack. Sequencers are also controllers: They send recorded data through their MIDI Out jacks, over MIDI cables, and into MIDI instruments for playback. Controllers are used extensively in stage rigs, where one master keyboard controller might access sounds in several MIDI instruments.

MIDI data MIDI data consists of all the MIDI events generated when a MIDI instrument is played. It is transferred among MIDI devices through MIDI cables, and recorded by sequencers. Owners of MIDI studios are concerned with managing and processing MIDI data flow.

MIDI effects Audio effects processors have been around for a long time, contributing such artificial ambiance as reverb, flanging, and digitally delayed signals to modern recording. MIDI effects devices combine audio signal processing with MIDI data processing, bringing the control of the device into the realm of computers. Using a MIDI effects box, a MIDI musician can control the switching of effects programs by embedding simple commands into a musical sequence. Furthermore, the parameters of the effect, such as the length of a reverberation echo, can be controlled by the player's style on a MIDI instrument. Using the reverb decay example, the program might be set to deliver a longer, more echo-rich reverb when the instrument is played loudly. MIDI effects devices are usually rack-mounted hardware boxes that can be used in a recording studio or taken on the road.

MIDI event A MIDI event is any single movement of a control feature on a MIDI instrument. This can include pressing a key, releasing a key, depressing a pedal, or moving a pitch-bend wheel. In nonkeyboard instruments, it includes picking a guitar string, blowing into a digital wind instrument, smacking a MIDI drum pad, or squeezing a MIDI harmonica. Playing a MIDI instrument generates MIDI events, which are data translations of everything you do. These events can be recorded by a sequencer or transmitted through a MIDI cable to another MIDI instrument, which provides the sound that you hear.

MIDI file MIDI sequences that have been saved to a computer disk are called MIDI files. MIDI files can be saved in two ways, influencing how easily they can be shared. Every sequencing program has its own proprietary way of saving files, using a file extension (the part of the filename following the period) unique to that program. MIDI files saved in this fashion can be loaded only into that program, whether on the original computer or another that is running the same sequencing software. Most sequencing programs also allow saving in Standard MIDI file format, which can be read by most other programs. MIDI files saved in this manner (using the .MID file extension) can be shared by musicians using different sequencers, although trying to distribute sequence files between Mac and IBM-clone computers still presents problems.

MIDI instrument Digital music instruments that contain MIDI ports are MIDI instruments. They can be networked with other MIDI instruments, various MIDI processing devices, and MIDI-enabled computers for augmented recording and performance capacity. The most common MIDI instrument is the keyboard, of which a dizzying number of variations exist. Sound modules, which have no keyboards and can be played only by an attached MIDI controller (such as a keyboard), are nonetheless considered MIDI instruments because they produce sound upon demand. Other MIDI instruments include digital guitars, violins, wind instruments, drum pads, and accordions. Almost any acoustic instrument can be turned into a MIDI instrument by means of adding digital sensors and circuitry, but it's usually preferable to start fresh with an inherently digital version.

MIDI interface Most computers don't naturally understand MIDI data, and must be specifically outfitted to process it. (Atari computers are the exception.) MIDI interfaces are hardware devices that attach to computers, supplying them with MIDI ports. Computer sound cards with MIDI jacks are one type of interface. Dedicated interfaces (devices that don't offer any audio capabilities) sometimes include multiple ports that augment the MIDI processing ability of the entire system. MIDI interfaces are necessary for computers used in a MIDI studio, and use the sophisticated sequencing software common in MIDI production at all levels.

MIDI mixer MIDI mixers help merge the two domains of traditional sound recording and MIDI recording. MIDI mixers work just like non-MIDI mixers, with individual channels for each instrument or audio input controlling that input's volume, panning position, and tone. Their remarkable characteristic is that the channels are, to some degree, under MIDI command control. That means you can control an instrument's volume, or a channel's mute switch, by recording the mixer's movements into a MIDI sequence. This automates certain functions of the mixing process, which is really helpful to many home-recording musicians who don't have four hands. Adding to the certifiable coolness of MIDI mixers is the system of motorized faders seen on some. The space-age ghostliness of mixer faders moving around on their own adds to the panache of any digital studio.

MIDI pads MIDI instruments emulate acoustic instruments for the benefit of musicians who play those acoustic instruments. MIDI pads are generally used by drummers. Assembled into configurations that resemble acoustic drum kits, MIDI pads are played with drumsticks. Although they are not imbued with any innate sounds of their own, the pads are connected to drum machines of percussion sound modules that provide drum samples. Preferred samples are assigned to specific pads, and the drum-pad kit then can be played, either over speakers or through headphones.

MIDI port MIDI ports (also called MIDI jacks) define MIDI instruments. Any digital device with MIDI jacks attached to its panel is a MIDI device. In most cases, as with keyboards and sound modules, they are found on the back panel. There are three types of MIDI port: In, Out, and Thru. The In jack receives MIDI data, the Out jack sends MIDI data, and the Thru jack passes data from the In jack to the next device in the MIDI chain.

MIDI slave A MIDI slave is any device that is connected to a MIDI controller. MIDI slaves are sound modules and other instruments equipped with MIDI In jacks for receiving data. Controller data can be generated by playing a keyboard attached to the slave or by playing back a MIDI sequence in a computer connected to MIDI instruments. Any MIDI instrument can be a slave, even those that function as controllers some of the time.

MIDI studio When at least two MIDI devices are connected for the purpose of playing or recording sound, the result is a MIDI studio. Such studios can be rudimentary or complex, and are infinitely expandable.

MIDI studios are usually based on recording music, as opposed to performance rigs, although the setups can be similar. The most basic MIDI recording studio comprises a keyboard connected to a sequencer. Playing the keyboard with the sequencer in Record mode creates a sequence recording of the performance; playing back the sequence replicates the performance through the keyboard. Larger studios encompass additional keyboards, sound modules, drum machines, samplers, MIDI switching devices, and audio equipment such as mixers, speakers, and audio effects processors. Some MIDI studios are integrated with traditional sound recording equipment such as multitrack tape decks, microphones, and acoustic instruments. MIDI studios are remarkable for the amount of musical power packaged in a small, portable, and inexpensive assortment of hardware and software. The MIDI studio, in all its variations, has created a revolution in how, where, and by whom high-quality music is produced.

MIDI switcher Complex MIDI studios are a bundle of wires and cables, weaving an involved data flow between the MIDI In, Out, and Thru jacks of many instruments and other devices. It can be hard to keep track of how things are connected, and nearly impossible to change the connections around without leaving something out or jamming the data flow. MIDI switchers consolidate all the MIDI connections in a single hardware device that contains several MIDI In and Out jacks. Centralizing the MIDI data flow to a single nexus—like a MIDI nerve center—simplifies managing the data flow. Even better, switching devices let you make several programs determining how MIDI data will be directed among the various instruments and computers in the studio. This lets you use different keyboard controllers, for example, to address the entire studio, without rewiring cables.

Multi-sampling When a musical instrument is sampled (digitally recorded), the best result is obtained when many samples are taken throughout the pitch range of the instrument. This technique is called multi-sampling. Most instruments change in tonal quality from the bottom to the top of their range. If the instrument is sampled only once—say, in the middle of its range—then transposed, the transposed notes sound unrealistic. Ideally, every note throughout the range is sampled, but many samplers don't have enough memory for such aggressive multisampling. Typically, the instrument is sampled every three or four notes so that no sample must be transposed more than two notes up or down.

Multi-timbral MIDI instruments that can sound more than one sound patch at a time are called multitimbral. This is important because of the multitrack capability of MIDI. You can create a complex composition using several different sounds, all with one multitimbral instrument. When that sequenced composition is played back from the sequencer, the single multitimbral instrument can play all the parts at once. Multitimbrality is also useful when controlling a sound module with a keyboard controller that can transmit different MIDI channels from different portions of its range. In that situation, a bass sound from the sound module can be assigned to the lower portion of the keyboard, while a piano sound is assigned to the upper range. The sound module will sound both parts when this controller configuration is played. All modern MIDI instruments are multitimbral.

Panning Panning is a function of mixing a piece of music by adjusting the placement (left to right) of each part in the stereo field. Such adjustments determine what is called the stereo image, and is accomplished by means of dials on a mixing board, one panning dial for each mixing channel. Because each mixing channel normally represents a single instrument or part, it is possible to assign each part of a composition its own place in the stereo field, or move it around while it's playing. In MIDI instruments, panning is often a variable of the patch settings, enabling you to place each part of a multitimbral (see *Multitimbral* in this glossary) setup within the stereo image. This is important in instruments that do not offer multiple audio outputs, one for each multitimbral part, because the stereo imaging cannot be accomplished on the mixing board in such cases.

Patch A patch is a sound program in a synthesizer. Synths come with preset patches, and also allow the user to program new patches.

Percussion module Percussion modules are a specialized kind of tone module dedicated to percussion sounds and samples. Usually rack-mounted devices, percussion modules differ from traditional drum machines in a couple of ways. First, they have no pads by which the sounds are triggered, as drum machines do; the sounds in percussion modules are triggered by keyboards or other MIDI controllers hooked up to them. Second, percussion modules do not contain internal sequencers for recording drum patterns; instead, their sounds are recorded over MIDI in computer sequencers.

Polyphonic Literally meaning "multivoiced," *polyphonic* refers to a MIDI instrument's capacity for sounding more than one note at a time. All modern MIDI instruments are polyphonic to some degree. The ceiling of polyphony defines just how many notes can be sounded without any sounds being cut off; most instruments allow at least 16 simultaneous tones, and some go much higher.

When the polyphonic ceiling is exceeded, older notes are terminated to make room for the newest notes played.

Sample Strictly speaking, a sample is a digital recording of any length. Practically speaking, the word usually refers to a short sound sample for use in a digital sampling instrument. MIDI producers create two distinct forms of a sample, relating to the stages of creating an effective instrument sample. First, a sample exists in raw form as a new recording of an instrument tone. Several such samples are recorded, representing different notes throughout an instrument's range, and all those short recordings are bundled together to form the final sample. So a sample is both the raw recording and the finished product: an instrument sample (made up of several discrete samples) that can be played across a keyboard's range. In the larger perspective of digitizing sound, a sample can be a digital recording of any length, used for any purpose. Looked at that way, a CD of a Beethoven symphony is a gigantic sample.

Sample library Sample libraries contain prerecorded instrument samples for use with a sampler. They are usually packaged on CDs, but can also be found on cassette tapes and digital audiotapes, or in digitized form on CD-ROM. Creating good instrument samples is difficult, requiring silent studio conditions and excellent sound recording equipment. Many musicians therefore prefer to bypass the recording session entirely by purchasing sample collections, which they can feed into their samplers through an audio cable connected to the sampler's audio input jack. Sample libraries are grouped by instrument type or musical genre, and include not only individual instrument notes, but also short rhythm patters, drum hits, orchestral sections, sound effects, and special effects.

Sampler Samplers are a specialized kind of digital instrument capable of recording a sound and playing the recording up and down the range of its keyboard. (Some samplers don't have keyboards, and must be played by a controller connected to the MIDI In jack.) Samplers are equipped with a few unique features: an audio input jack and analog-to-digital (A/D) converters. A microphone may be plugged into the audio input for live sampling, or an audio cable for playing a prerecorded sound into the sampler. Either way, the sampler digitizes the sound and stores it in a playback buffer. After sampling, you can play the sound across the keyboard's range, transposing it automatically as different keys are pressed.

Sequencer MIDI data recorders are called sequencers because they register MIDI events in sequence. MIDI music recordings are sequences of MIDI events (such as a key being pressed on a

MIDI keyboard, then released) that can be recorded, edited, and played back. The first sequencers were hardware devices connected to keyboards and other MIDI devices. Then, as personal computing became popular and common in MIDI setups, software sequencers appeared and quickly outstripped their hardware cousins in power and ease of use. The word *sequencer* now refers primarily to software programs. Sequencers are also found as internal features of keyboard workstations and in drum machines. A special breed of sequencer, called a pattern sequencer, records patterns of musical material tailored to popular song recordings, making it easy to manipulate the music in blocks representing verses, choruses, and bridges.

Slave See *MIDI slave.*

SMPTE An acronym for Society of Motion Picture and Television Engineers, SMPTE (pronounced SIMP-tee) is known by MIDI musicians and producers as a brand of timecode (see *Timecode* in this glossary) used to synchronize a MIDI sequence to video playback. SMPTE timecode is used when composing a video soundtrack.

Sound module Sound modules are MIDI instruments that cannot play themselves; they contain no built-in controller. They must be played by an external device, usually a keyboard, that is connected to the module via MIDI cables. They fulfill the MIDI musician's need for multiple instruments but only one keyboard controller. With a single keyboard and a rack of sound modules, a MIDI studio can be equipped with a broad range of sounds and instrumental possibilities, without taking the extra space of several keyboards. Sound modules include synthesizers, samplers, workstations, and percussion modules.

Striping Striping is the process of recording timecode (see *Timecode* in this glossary) to a single tape track. Doing so links the sequencer of a MIDI studio to the transport controls of the tape deck, so the movement of the sequence is controlled by the movement of tape. Striping timecode is a basic recording process involving running the tape in record mode while playing the timecode from a synchronization box to one tape track.

Synchronization box Synchronization boxes generate timecode (see *Timecode* in this glossary) that, when recorded on a tape track, keeps the MIDI parts of a composition synchronized with tape parts. The synchronization box is a small piece of hardware, either sitting on a studio surface or mounted in a rack, that is positioned between the sequencer and the tape deck in the studio's signal path. It is first used to generate one of several types of timecode for recording to a tape track. Then, when that track is played back along with the musical parts recorded to other tape tracks, the audio timecode is sent back to the synchronization box, where it is translated into a digital format understandable by the sequencer. The sequencer's playback is then controlled by the movement of the tape, keeping all the parts (MIDI and tape recorded) in synch.

Synthesis engine Synthesis engines are so named because they "drive" the sound-generation features of digital synthesizers. Synthesizer sounds are created by a combination of settings—hundreds of settings in some instruments. Those settings make up the synthesis engine. Programming sounds in a synthesizer is a matter of adjusting the engine settings.

Synthe-sizer Synthesizers (synths) are electronic instruments that create sounds from built-in waveforms. Modern synthesizers are digital instruments, equipped with MIDI interface jacks and digital sound waves. Typically in keyboard form, but also available as rack-mounted sound modules, synthesizers come with many preset sounds, plus blank slots for storing original sound creations. Preset and original sounds (patches) may be used in MIDI compositions and performances. Synthesizers create new sounds by means of parameters whose settings affect chosen sound waves. The parameters include envelope and filter settings, among many other types of variables, that can change the timbre in a nearly infinite number of ways. Software programs make sound programming easier. Keyboard synthesizers are usually 60-key, unweighted-action boards.

System-exclusive data MIDI information can be transferred between MIDI instruments, and understood by them equally. But each digital instrument in a MIDI setup uses its own brand of information to accomplish its internal operations. These operations include creating sounds, storing sounds, sampling sounds (in samplers only), naming sound creations, and some other functions. The data that performs these tasks is called system-exclusive data, because it is exclusive to the system (particular MIDI instrument). It is essentially a MIDI instrument's operating system. As such, system-exclusive data is not meant to be conveyed from one instrument to another, and cannot be understood outside its host instrument. However, some system-exclusive information can be transferred over MIDI cables with the help of computer utility programs. In this fashion, a MIDI instrument's internal patch settings can be stored on a computer or reloaded into the instrument from a computer.

Timecode The synchronization of different components of a MIDI studio is accomplished with the help of timecode, a specialized audio signal. When timecode is recorded to a tape track, that track can be used to control the movement of a MIDI sequencer, thus keeping MIDI parts of a composition synchronized with the acoustic parts recorded on the other tape tracks. Several brands of timecode exist; the two most commonly used in MIDI studios are SMPTE (see *SMPTE* in this glossary), usually used in the production of MIDI soundtracks to video projects, and MIDI timecode, often used in pure music projects. Timecode is generated by synchronization boxes (see *Synchronization box* in this glossary), small pieces of hardware that play different kinds of timecode for recording to tape and also receive it back from the tape during production and convey the code to the sequencer for synchronization.

Tone module See *Sound module.*

Virtual track MIDI tracks are called virtual tracks because they are recordings not of sounds, but of MIDI events. Virtual tracking is the process of recording in a MIDI sequencer.

Workstation Two kinds of workstation inhabit the MIDI world. The first is a specialized kind of keyboard instrument that includes a built-in sequencer and drum machine. Such workstations are meant to include everything needed to produce multipart pieces and songs, and are popular first purchases for a home MIDI studio. The word *workstation* also refers to digital audio workstations, which are hard disk recorders. (See *DAW* and *Hard disk recording* in this glossary.)

PART THREE
MUSICIANS ONLINE

From her modest beginnings as a digital-age musician, Penelope Envelope has become the proud, sometimes frazzled owner of one of the hottest project studios in her region. Penny went the computer route to the max: Her studio is dedicated entirely to recording in the MIDI domain, and although she owns one or two microphones she never uses them. Bands don't come knocking on her door to record demos, but independent film producers come calling with requests for soundtracks, and she has just landed a gig scoring musical bumpers for a soap opera. Penny begins every day by checking her e-mail, then quickly visiting the sites on America Online and the Web where she gets her morning fix of industry and general news.

Pat Chedit enjoys cyberspace, too. He has a more recreational attitude about going online, just as his MIDI studio is less professional—but no less fun—than Penny's. He uses the studio as a hobby, creating complex, atonal musical layerings that make his bandmates scratch their heads. Pat goes online for epic surf sessions, cruising for obscure music sites on the Web, and he especially likes hunting for collections of MIDI files that can be downloaded. His best find was the complete collection of preludes and fugues by Bach: He downloaded them into his studio, strung them together into a single enormous piece, and key-shifted all the parts until it sounded like Baroque on hallucinogens.

9

ONLINE BASICS

This chapter acquaints you with the rise of online networks in the past 15 years, and how to jump on the still-burgeoning bandwagon. Chapter 10 follows up this background by describing exactly why a musician would want to get involved with cyberspace.

A BRIEF HISTORY OF CYBERSPACE

Cyberspace existed long before it was called cyberspace. (The term was invented as part of a science fiction novel.) A glamorous concept now, and one that even the modern online experience doesn't always live up to, cyberspace implies virtual reality, artificial intelligence, out-of-body electronic actualities, and other vague contemporary notions of transcendent experience that weren't even conceived, much less approached, in the early years of computer networking.

THE EARLY INTERNET

The **Internet** started things off, although most people weren't aware of it at the time. The Internet is commonly thought of as a modern invention, splashing into popular culture (or at least the fringe of pop culture) as a 1990s phenomenon. It's true that the modern Internet, which in its radical differences from earlier incarnations is almost a distinct and brand-new entity, has emerged to capture public imagination only in the last several years. But the Net, in a more primitive form, has existed for decades, indispensably so for academicians and military types. It was begun as a military safeguard, designed in the 1950s to withstand aggressive assault so that lines of communication would be maintained in a national emergency. The key to the Internet's invulnerability lay in its decentralized nature, and the fact that key components (network computers) could be located anywhere, invisibly, unpredictably. Tied to the telephone infrastructure, the system grew effortlessly across political borders of state and nation, becoming

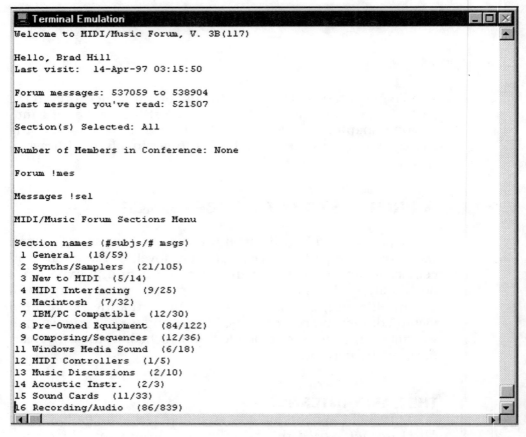

An ASCII online interface, rarely used these days. In the early days of online services, everybody's screen looked as uninviting as this. CompuServe still allows nongraphic, text-based access to some of its forums.

an international data networking resource, ungoverned by any regulating body, owned in bits and pieces by universities and other institutions that housed the computers.

So things remained for some time. During the early years musicians and most other people didn't have much experience with the Internet, or even necessarily know it existed. Computers weren't yet personal. The Internet was used mostly by academicians as a research tool. It probably would have been incomprehensible to anyone else, as the user interface was anything but friendly. The early Internet was user-hostile. Graphical user interfaces weren't even a gleam in any visionary's eye until the 1980s, and the Internet terminals of earlier decades featured a complex, thorny command language that required some degree of mastery if you wanted to go anywhere online. Once you learned your way around, it was a tremendous resource in which research papers could be accessed from computers around the globe and shared with the wired academic community.

NETWORKING FOR THE MASSES

Online networking moved from elite to populist circles with the advent of two things:

- The personal computer
- Online services

The personal computer brought computing into the home, and **online services** followed right behind with the lure of connecting to other, bigger computers. One of the earliest online services to offer accounts for home use was **CompuServe**, which offered a system of **forums** in which people of like interests could share information and even talk to each other by typing sentences on their computer keyboards. Like the Internet, CompuServe's new service was accessed by means of a distinctly unglamorous and arduous command-based text interface. Although the popularity of this service grew slowly, it caught the imagination of enough people to keep the word slowly spreading. CompuServe modeled its usefulness on the utilitarian values of the Internet. Prizing information over social interaction and technical information over entertainment, its online content was dry compared to what today's surfers are accustomed to. However, one attraction helped move this new medium out of the realm of research and into the domain of common interests: online customer support for computers and other electronic equipment. The early customers of online networking enjoyed logging on to ask a manufacturer questions about the operation of a computer peripheral, or to share technical solutions with other users on electronic bulletin boards.

The popularity of online networking from the home grew indomitably. Other services joined the party, giving consumers a choice of logon alternatives, each with its own online content and user interface. By the time the digital revolution skidded into the 1990s, a few developments had set the stage for an unpredicted tidal wave of interest in going online:

- Personal computers had evolved into much easier and attractive machines. The Windows operating system, the Macintosh operating system, and faster, more powerful computers allowed software designers to craft online access interfaces that buried the old command-text modes forever. Furthermore, modems (those essential devices used to connect computers with phone lines) were getting faster and better, making the online experience more rewarding.

- Interest in personal computing, as a general aspect of life, soared. The computer was on its long odyssey from being a luxury novelty to being a necessary household appliance. (It's still on that odyssey.)

- The landscape of cyberspace had become cluttered with companies competing for online customers, and they were beginning to turn the online universe from an informational venue into a medium of entertainment.

- One service in particular, America Online, was positioning itself to make waves.

CompuServe was the juggernaut service of the early 1990s. Additional contestants (Prodigy, Genie, Delphi, and a few others) were jostling to play second fiddle to the vast offerings of CompuServe's many forums. Musicians embraced online networking, on CompuServe and other services, in a big way. In the early days of digital music making, logging into a virtual community was one of the best ways to find other infatuees of synthesizers and MIDI. Software for the secondary music computing platforms such as Atari and Amiga was traded online, problems were solved through networking on virtual bulletin boards, and manufacturers and software developers were available for customer support.

One company had new ideas, and began offering a different kind of service. **America Online** manifested a populist approach, offering scads of online **chat rooms** in which members could talk to each other in real time, by typing sentences and viewing the typed sentences of others logged into the same virtual room. Though not an original invention, America Online's chat rooms were well designed, easy to use, and, perhaps most important of all, substantially less expensive than competing services. A meteoric rise was under way, that would change the online world.

Currently, America Online is the leading online service by a substantial margin, and live online chatting has become the preferred virtual activity of millions of new members. America Online brought the possibilities of personal online interaction into sharp focus. The innovative service also took an entertainment-based approach, in contrast to CompuServe's (and the Internet's) information-based approach, that made logging on fun. Musicians who relied on their modems to deliver resourceful networking and customer service stayed with the older services, but plenty of newly wired instrumentalists, performers, MIDI jockeys, and digitally wired composers headed for the bright, colorful, and sociable cyberspace of America Online.

THE NEW INTERNET

The early 1990s brought other developments as well, which would change the online landscape even more drastically. Two innovations affected the Internet, changing it forever in appearance, function, and possibility:

- Gopher was invented. Gopher was the first attempt to apply an organized interface to Internet terminals. Before Gopher (thought to be named for its "go-fer" capacity, but additionally honoring the mascot of the University of Minnesota, where it was invented), the Net was a rich resource, but a chaotically disorganized one. If you wanted to download a file you needed to know where it was located, or search endlessly, often in vain. Gopher was a directory service that could locate files. Internet users could now approach the vastness of the global network armed with a menulike system on their computer screens that guided them from the most general (topic headings) to the most specific (individual files). It was revolutionary. I remember visiting a Princeton University scientist soon after Gopher was available, and he couldn't tear himself away from the computer as he showed it off. He was an Internet veteran, but for the first time the Net was a coherent and enjoyable place. For him, it had even become recreational.

■ Great though Gopher was, its fame was short-lived. It was soon supplanted by a much more glamorous invention, one that would carry the Internet well beyond the walls of academia: the **World Wide Web.** The Web took Gopher to the next stage of evolution by rendering the Internet in a whole new interface, one that relied solely on the computer mouse. Web users navigate around the online globe by clicking on **hyperlinks,** certain screen elements that take the surfer to a new online location. The World Wide Web spawned several innovations important for musicians, which I'll describe in more detail later in this part.

Gopher attracted some attention, primarily among people already online, and the Web grabbed the spotlight for good, much to the detriment of most online services. The Web made the Internet colorful, fun, and available to everybody. As the members of these services found more attractive content on the World Wide Web and less appeal in their online service, they dropped their memberships in favor of being Internet "Netizens." In time, only two major online services survived: America Online and CompuServe. Each is finding ways to thrive in the new Internet-dominated online environment, and the future of each is unclear.

THE CURRENT SITUATION

The global online atlas is constantly shifting, as if its tectonic plates were hyperactive. Currently, the scene resembles an oceanic Internet whose omnipresence is broken by two major continents (America Online and CompuServe, the two remaining giant online services), a few large floating empires (other online services such as the Microsoft Network and Prodigy), and many small islands (local BBS services). This atlas metaphor also must take into consideration the hundreds of **Internet service providers** (ISPs) that provide access to the oceanic Internet.

The Internet, with its user-friendly World Wide Web, has attracted so much interest that it has become, in effect, the biggest online service in town. It's not really an online service because it is unowned, unregulated, and definitely unorganized. You do not "join" the Internet, you merely access it. Neither the Internet nor the Web provides anyone with software or customer service. However, these functions have been adopted by Internet service providers, and the ISP/Internet combination

REAL WORDS

AOL has its strong points. There is a forum on AOL called "SSS," or "Studio, Sound and Stage," which is run by Craig Anderton. This has discussions about almost anything to do with music, including song-writing techniques, equipment, musical philosophy, mastering, monitors, and the music business. Keyword "SSS" will get you there if you are an AOL subscriber.

can seem just like an online service. It stands to reason that ISPs with the most experience in the business accomplish this new model of online access better than others, and the companies that have been in the business longest are the online services. As a result, online services have dived into the ISP business in a big way. Even CompuServe and America Online are, in many people's eyes, little more than glorified ISPs. The fact that they also offer a huge amount of proprietary content—forums, online publications, message boards, file libraries, and so on—shouldn't be lost in the rush to surf the Net, but that fact is definitely secondary to someone who is mostly interested in the World Wide Web.

Other online services, once in competition to provide the best proprietary content, have retreated overtly to a stance of providing Internet access. In some cases, they have moved their private forums onto the Web, available to anyone. At the opposite end of the spectrum, ISPs that entered the field strictly as access providers, with no proprietary content, have in some cases begun developing Web-based forums and other sites for the private enjoyment of their subscribers.

The result of all this jockeying for position is mainly to blur the lines of distinction that used to be clearly etched in stone. Online services are no longer fortresses insulated against the Internet; on the contrary, they treat the Net (especially the Web) like annexed territory, providing access, software, and navigation assistance. ISPs are no longer simple onramps to the Net, whose lack of customer service or software made them suitable only for experienced hands; many of them are striving to become Web-centric online services, complete with content and friendly help.

The other result of exploding interest in cyberspace has been to make it easy to get on board. The next part explains exactly what you need to get started.

FIRST STEPS ONLINE

There is considerable excitement about online culture and the Internet. As we move from the academic to the practical, this part takes a look at what you need to get connected.

BASIC EQUIPMENT

You need three items to log onto the digital highway:

■ **A computer.** A Windows or Macintosh machine works, although you have many more software choices with Windows. Musicians using Atari and Amiga computers for music production have at least partially migrated to the Windows or Mac platform for online uses because there is little or no Web and online service software for the older music machines.

■ **A standard telephone line.** It's convenient to situate a wall jack reasonably close to the computer, but if that's not possible, long telephone extension cords are easily available.

■ **A modem.** The modem connects the computer to the phone line. They can be purchased independently of the computer, and installed internally or connected externally. The phone line plugs into the back of the modem and essentially becomes part of the computer.

With these components you are equipped to become a Netizen, as long as you have a couple of simple pieces of software. The software you use depends on what kind of online connection you have (online service or Internet).

■ Online service software is made by the service you log onto, and is provided free of charge. It sets up a screen environment designed by the service, with all the menus, toolbars, and other features you need to access the service's features. The program conveys the look and feel of the online service, and is the only way to access it. Except in the case of CompuServe, you cannot use generic, third-party software to log onto an online service.

■ Internet access software comes in two main parts: a modem dialer and a **Web browser.** Other programs, such as e-mail readers, Usenet newsgroup readers, and Web plug-ins, are options, and are often included in the browser package. The dialer is also integrated sometimes, depending on the company that provides the software. If not, it must be acquired separately. (The Windows 95 operating system has a built-in Internet dialer.) All this Internet software must be acquired by some means, if it is not furnished by the access company that provides your Internet connection.

HOW IT ALL WORKS

Eventually, it's time to log on for the first time. Once the hardware and software are in place, making the phone call that connects your computer to an online network is done by the computer, through software. You don't touch the phone or the modem. The computer dials the phone (you can hear it through the modem speaker), connects with a receiving modem located at the other phone number, some odd sounds indicate the two modems are forging their connection, and after a few seconds your computer is logged onto the remote network, and things begin appearing on your screen. If you've logged onto an online service, the first thing you see is a welcome screen with some menu options. If you've logged onto the World Wide Web with an Internet dialer, you must open your browsing program and direct it to a Web location.

Q & A: ONLINE SURFING

Q When I get online, do I need to do something?

A Yes. Being online is not a passive experience like watching TV. It's interactive, which means the online service (or Internet) won't do anything for you until you tell it to. Once you've logged on, you need to tell your software to go somewhere. In an online service, a menu appears on your screen with some starter choices. (America Online calls these channels, but it's still not TV.) Choose anything on that menu, and you'll soon be given other choices, and before you know it, you're exploring the nooks and crannies of the entire service. If you're on the Internet, you need to enter an address (called a **URL**) into your Web browser. Some browsers give you a bookmark list of addresses to start you off. Once you begin surfing the Web, you begin clicking hyperlinks to get from one site to another, building your own bookmark list as you go.

Q How do I find online sites about music?

A All the online services, and the World Wide Web, provide some kind of searching service or Find feature (called a search engine). In the online services, pull down the on-screen menus to find the searching pages, and in your Web browser pull down the Book-

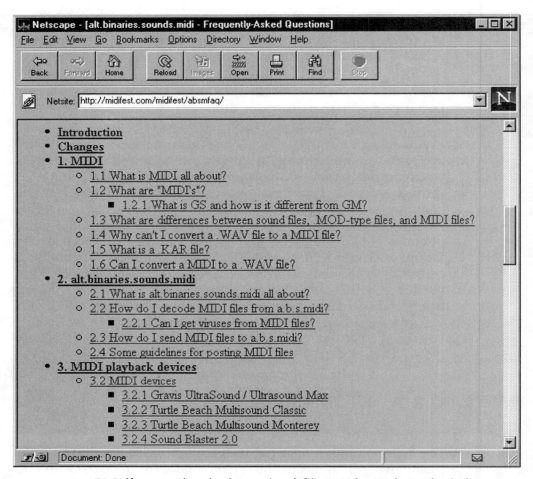

FAQ (frequently asked questions) files on the Web can be in hypertext format. Click on any question to see the answer.

mark list to find them. Once you are in a search engine, you are invited to type key words for what you're looking for. Obviously, *music* is a good one. On the Web, you can get much more specific, entering types of music, names of musicians, band names, composers, festivals, instruments, software titles, and so on. You can also (warning: incoming shameless plug) refer to my book *The Virtual Musician* for the locations of the best musical cyberspots in the online services and the Web.

Q What happens if I forget to log off and leave the computer?

A After a certain amount of idle time (10 or 15 minutes in most cases) your connection automatically times out and the phone connection is broken.

Q Can I make a phone call while logged online?

A No. When the modem is using your phone line, it cannot be used for any other calls. Incoming callers receive a busy signal. Call waiting, the phone service that allows you to receive incoming calls while talking on the phone, is troublesome with modem connections. Generally, it disrupts them, breaking the connection.

Q Is there a cost to use the World Wide Web?

A There is a cost to access the Web, paid to either the online service or ISP you subscribe to, but the Internet itself is a free domain. A few Web sites charge subscription access fees if they are offering very valuable information or services. But for the most part, aside from the access charge, the Web is free.

10

WHY GO ONLINE?

Everybody knows that the Internet has made a big splash, stoking the imagination and excitement of many people. It's not too much to say that online access has changed our society already, and that bigger changes are yet to come. Online culture has become a subset of our global consciousness. Still, there is a quality of hype to all the Internet publicity, especially as it appears to those who haven't yet taken the plunge into cyberspace. Many people who are not online wonder why anybody should be. What is its usefulness, what does it look like, what are its features, and how does it help with life? This chapter looks at basic features of the online experience and how these features apply to musicians.

SHARING STUFF

Digital musicians have an easy way to share files online with other musicians all over the world. There are two basic procedures for sharing a file:

■ **Uploading.** Sending a file from your own computer to a network computer is called **uploading.** You can upload a file to an online service to which you belong, to your own Web site, or to an upload site provided by a service organization catering to independent musicians.

■ **Downloading.** Obtaining a file from a network computer and storing it on your own computer is called **downloading.** You can download stuff from an online service to which you belong, from the World Wide Web and other portions of the Internet, and in particular from Web sites that specialize in music files.

What types of files are typically shared among musicians? The following kinds of file sharing are popular, with advantages that are sometimes balanced by challenges and specific requirements.

SHARING MIDI SEQUENCE FILES

Online service music libraries, World Wide Web sites, and Internet FTP locations are filled with MIDI sequences that have been uploaded. In some cases these files are useful as production tools, but in most instances they are contributed to the vast file repository of cyberspace in a simple spirit of sharing. MIDI musicians, especially hobbyists and semipros, upload and download files to and from all over the world to broaden their personal network and help keep the creative impulses sparking. Zillions (approximately) of MIDI renditions of popular and classical music can easily be found online, as well as original compositions.

After downloading a MIDI file, you can load it into your sequencer and play it through the MIDI synths, samplers, tone modules, and drum machines that are connected to your studio, if you have one. But one big advantage of multimedia computing is that elaborate MIDI studios are not necessary for playing back files. Any computer with a sound card can play back a MIDI file directly from the hard disk. Sound cards have MIDI sound patches loaded right onto them, and come with simple MIDI-playback software. The playback software falls into the utility category, and is not the same as a full-fledged sequencing application, but it gets the job done when faced with the simple task of playing a MIDI file. Simply call up the utility, select the MIDI file you just downloaded, and perk up your ears. (Of course, you must have speakers connected to the sound card, or use headphones.)

Most MIDI files found online are recorded using General MIDI to take advantage of GM's patch-assignment standard. When you play them back through a General MIDI sound card (almost all of them adhere to the GM standard), you can be sure you'll hear a correct approximation of the intended instrument assignments. If the file was recorded using piano, bass, drum kit, and trumpet samples (as assigned in General MIDI), those are the instruments you'll hear, and if your computer's audio card sounds different from the instruments used in the original studio, you'll probably never know.

MIDI files are small, especially compared to sound files. (MIDI files contain only keyboard command data, whereas sound files contain recorded music.) This makes them ideal for sharing online.

SHARING SOUNDS

For many people, creating sounds is almost as much fun as creating music. One of the delights of modern synthesizers is their programmability, or their capacity to fashion original, never-before-heard, sometimes unearthly timbres. Sound design can be a hobby or a profession. Computer programs dedicated to providing access to a synthesizer's inner workings have made programming less esoteric to the average musician, and more fun to try casually. But even musicians who choose not to learn the complex craft of sound programming want to stock their instruments with fresh sounds; it's usually preferable to buying a whole new instrument when you get tired of your studio's sounds!

Banks of new sounds can be uploaded to virtual libraries, and shared in a large pool of creativity. Keep in mind that sound patches are generally not transferable from one MIDI instrument to another; MIDI compatibility doesn't extend to the sound program level. Sounds are created within a certain synthesizer, and must be used in that same model synth (or a later, backward-compatible model from the same company). So when searching for free new sounds, Netizens seek out those for the particular instrument to be upgraded. When you find a bank of appropriate sounds, you can download it and place it inside your synthesizer. In some cases, the receiving computer (which downloaded the file) must have the same software that created the new sounds in order to load them into the synthesizer. In other cases, a simple (often free) system-exclusive dump program (isn't that a pleasant name for it?) can be used to load them in.

Samples are also found online. These are digitized sound recordings, often of acoustic instruments playing single notes, but sometimes of sound effects or other noises, that can be loaded into a sampling instrument for use in a MIDI environment. These can be created for a specific sampler, as sound patches are made for individual synthesizers, or they can be saved and uploaded using the Sample Dump Standard. The Sample Dump Standard creates samples that can be acquired and used by any sampler that uses the Sample Dump Standard.

SHARING SOUND FILES

Cyberspace is brimming with sound files. When it comes to fidelity and accuracy, sound files are the best way for a musician to share original music online. The drawback is the large size of a typical sound file, which makes it a time-consuming task.

The tradeoff between accuracy and convenience is illustrated in the case of someone who has recorded a beautiful MIDI composition in an advanced MIDI studio. No live tracks were used—nothing requiring a microphone. Great care was taken in crafting original sound designs to be used in the sequence; original sampling and synthesizer programming give the composition a unique sound that could not be exactly reproduced in any other MIDI studio, unless those original samples and sound patches were transferred to the second studio. How to share this composition? A MIDI file would be the most convenient way, as MIDI files are small and easily downloaded. But the quality of the piece would not be conveyed accurately. Playing the piece to tape and then digitizing it would create an accurate sound file, but it would be enormous, and would certainly enjoy fewer downloads.

Most people deal with this dilemma by digitizing and uploading excerpts of their music. The files are still big (much larger than a typical MIDI file of an entire composition), but more manageable. One technological development is helping to solve the predicament: audio streaming. **Audio streaming** eliminates the need to download sound files by playing them through your computer directly from the Internet computer on which they are stored. Handy though this is for the downloader, it is not so easy to implement for the person creating and uploading the file. The sound file must be digitized by a particular process, and the necessary program is not free. Furthermore, specific software (called **server software**) must be installed on the Internet computer, and the uploading musician may not have control over the server contents. Additionally, the downloading musician must have a particular program (**client software**) installed in his or her computer. Finally, audio streaming pays a price in fidelity: It just doesn't sound as good as a downloaded sound file. This whole equation is cumbersome, but worth it. Audio streaming is gradually becoming more visible on the Internet, and the sound quality is improving as the technology evolves.

No matter how they are handled, sound files are a musician's biggest ally in distributing music online. And online distribution of music is one of the most dramatic advances in independent musicianship. For the first time, recorded music can reach a large audience directly from the recording studio, almost free of charge.

REAL WORDS

Technology has changed my life for sure! I was an independent producer and recording engineer who got tired of great music not making it through the record company funnel (too many artists funneled down to too few good labels). So I opened the anti–record company, Artist Underground. We take the best music we can find, in all genres, and promote it and make available for sale on the Web—straight from the artist to the people!

Joe Seta
Artist Underground
http://www.aumusic.com

As technology evolves and as the bandwidth continues to expand (making download times shorter), distributing music over computer networks will become more ubiquitous, convenient, and cost-effective.

SHARING SOFTWARE PROGRAMS

Software presents a great online value for the downloader. Unlike MIDI files, sound files, and sound patches, computer programs are not likely to be uploaded by the average musician because most musicians are not programmers. But almost every digitally wired musician uses software, and cruising online for it is a popular activity. Two types of software can only be found online:

■ **Commercial demos.** Thinking of upgrading your shareware sequencer with one of the fancy professional programs, but are unsure which to buy? Music stores don't always let you try software extensively before buying it, and reading reviews in music magazines is only partly useful. Many of the big music software houses, for Macintosh and IBM clones, place demonstration copies of their programs online. These programs can be downloaded and used without limit to test their features. Demo programs have some crucial aspect disabled, and the only way to make them fully functional is to buy the official version. Often, it is the Save menu selections that don't work, making the demo program unproductive in the long run, but because all the other features work you can use it to test how the software operates and feels to work with.

■ **Programs for alternative computers.** Users of Amiga and Atari computers, once formidable music machines that have fallen out of the marketplace to a large extent, have difficulty finding software for their computers. It is almost never sold in general software stores. The online services and the Internet do store unusual programs, written for alternative computer platforms, in virtual libraries. Noncommercial programs can be downloaded free of charge, and commercial demos, from software houses still in business for unusual computers, is available.

In addition to commercial demos and software for unusual computers, there are two types of software to be found online:

■ **Shareware.** Shareware is free for the taking, but not for the keeping. You can download it without charge, use it for a certain period of time (the trial period varies, but is typically 30 days), and pay for it later, if you like it and decide to keep it. It's an honor system, but clever programming sometimes encour-

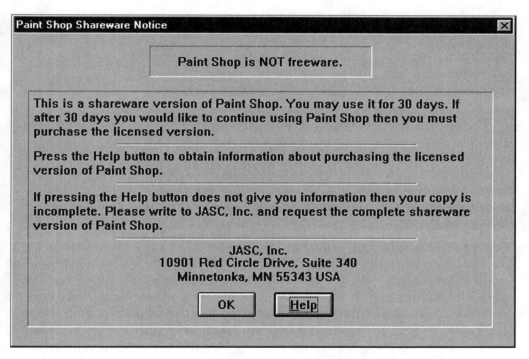

Shareware reminders encourage you to register and pay for the program.

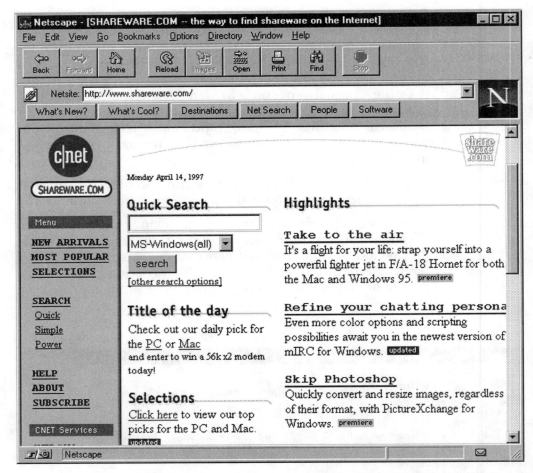

A shareware download site on the World Wide Web. Such "shareware stores" offer free downloads and huge selections.

ages your honest instincts. For example, the program might be disabled in some small way, like a commercial demo; this tactic is rare, but sometimes purchasing the program activates extra features that don't appear in the original, downloaded version. More commonly, it will flash reminders on your screen in an attempt to persuade you to register and pay for the software. In some sophisticated cases, the program will keep track of how long it has resided on your hard drive and stop working when the trial period expires. If by that time you have become enamored with its features, its sudden lack of cooperation will act as a fine motivation to buy a permanently functional version.

> ## REAL WORDS
>
> Because I have what can be called an alternative computer, the Internet is a vital resource for software and information. I have had so many questions answered and problems solved in the process of producing music. These days, anytime I see someone post a request where I know I can help, I always give back as much assistance as I can. Software updates, MIDI and audio utilities, hints on where to get hardware or wanted programs, discussions about getting more out of your music system, and many other things can be found on the Net. I proudly declare my Atari piracy-free and Microsoft-free! Shareware and freeware abound for alternative computers and there are still mail-order houses that know what I am talking about when I order something for my Atari. In fact, I am using my most valuable musical instrument on the Internet to write this.
>
> Paul Luscher, Insanity Void
> lenkel@ultra1.inconnect.com

■ **Freeware.** Guess how much freeware costs? That's right, it is free software, contributed to cyberspace by amateur and professional programmers, either in the online spirit of altruistic sharing or as a stripped-down ("lite") version of a more full-featured (and costly) program. Lite software accomplishes simple tasks, and for some people requires nothing more; it is also a fine advertisement for the more complex program. Less commercially ambitious programmers upload freeware simply to share a utility they wrote to solve a personal computing problem, and have no interest in making money on the product.

Shareware and freeware are abundant online. Online service music libraries and Web shareware stores are the best places to browse. Contrary to what you might think, inexpensively distributed software is not necessarily second-rate. Increasingly, software houses with long, successful track records are turning to shareware distribution of some of their titles as a way of cutting costs. Large, high-ticket, professional software, such as a hybrid sequencer/digital recorder, must still be purchased in a store or through the mail (or by using a credit card in an online store).

SHARING INFORMATION FILES

Cyberspace is traditionally a medium for sharing information, and modern cyberspace offers a wired musician ways of contributing and receiving information in several forms.

- **World Wide Web sites.** Web sites are the easiest and most attractive way to share information. Many musicians use them to convey facts about their band, such as album availability, performance schedules, and history. Even excerpts of recordings can be included as sound files. Some people go to great lengths to construct Web sites that are nothing less than authoritative multimedia publications on a certain subject, such as a classical composer's life and work.

- **Online service libraries.** The virtual libraries of services such as America Online and CompuServe are give-and-take environments in which anyone can participate. They can be browsed for all kinds of digitized information, from user's manuals to band photos. Anyone can contribute files, provided the uploaded file doesn't infringe on an existing copyright.

- **FTP libraries.** File Transfer Protocol (**FTP**) sites are the libraries of the Internet. They can be accessed through the World Wide Web interface (using a Web browser) and located using the antique but still useful Gopher system. FTP sites contain lists of files, including rich deposits of musical information, without the multimedia glitz of the World Wide Web.

- **Text files.** Informational texts are often uploaded to music libraries in online services. A typical file might include a performer's biography, a how-to file explaining how a particular synthesizer works, a press release for an upcoming performance or album release, or any number of other topics.

- **FAQ files.** Frequently asked questions (FAQ) files are texts that explain certain subjects in question-and-answer format. There is a FAQ file for almost any subject imaginable, located somewhere online. Anybody with knowledge on a particular subject, such as productivity tips for a certain software sequencer, is welcome to contribute a FAQ file to an online service library.

The Basics of Uploading

Uploading is the process of transferring a file from a personal computer to a network computer, from which other people can access it. To the uninitiated, this process seems mysterious and difficult, but in fact is quite easy. The specific instructions differ depending on software and the network you're uploading to, but the agenda remains the same in all situations.

Say you want to create and share a MIDI sequence file. Here is how the file is created, stored, and uploaded in a typical computer using the Windows or Macintosh operating system:

1. The MIDI sequence is recorded, perhaps over several sessions. After each session, the file is saved to the computer's internal hard drive. (The assumption here is that a software sequencer is used, not a standalone hardware unit.)

2. When completed, the MIDI composition is saved in final form to the hard drive. The composition is now a MIDI file, named according to the conventions of your computer's operating system. For this example, we'll say the file has been created in a program running in Windows 3.1, and the you've given it the filename CHASE.MID. It is saved in a hard drive directory (location) called MUSIC.

3. You decide to upload it to a file library in your online service, and you log onto that online service to execute the upload. You use the access program provided by the service to log on, then proceed to the file library (probably in a musicians' area) to upload.

4. In the library area, menu instructions walk you through the process of uploading. In most cases, a window is provided with blank slots for filling in information about the file you want to contribute. You must enter the filename (CHASE.MID) and a description of the file. It's helpful if you use the description to tell potential downloaders what equipment they need to play back the file.

5. When you're done filling in the window, you click on a button that initiates the upload, and a file selector panel opens on your screen. This is where you tell the system where the file is located on your hard drive (in the MUSIC directory), and point it to the exact file you are uploading.

6. At that point, everything becomes automatic. The network computer and your computer work together to copy the file to the online library. The file is not removed from your hard drive; it is merely copied. A window is usually displayed on your screen, informing you of the upload's progress as a percentage of the file remaining to be transferred, and also the estimated remaining time. MIDI files are small, and uploads usually take less than a minute.

A Help window for uploading files to an online service.

The Basics of Downloading

Downloading is the process of instant gratification. Almost instant, any-way; it's a quick way of obtaining software and other files without leaving your house, or even your chair. Downloading copies a file or a software program from a network computer (such as the Internet or an online ser-vice) to your personal computer. It places it directly on your hard drive, where you can access it anytime. The process is easy, and you really don't need to know much to start downloading as soon as you get online. Although the details vary among different online systems, here are the common main points:

1. While online, you see a file or program you want to obtain. It could be in a library of your online service, or perhaps a share-ware repository on the World Wide Web.

2. Whatever system you're on will prompt you to proceed. There might be a Download or Retrieve button to click.

3. A window displays on your screen, similar to your computer's file-selection window, asking you where to place the file. Use this window to select the directory or subdirectory on your hard drive that will store the download, at least temporarily.

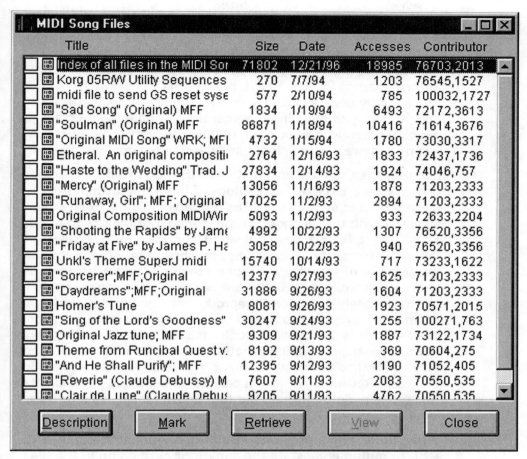

Title	Size	Date	Accesses	Contributor
Index of all files in the MIDI Sor	71802	12/21/96	18985	76703,2013
Korg 05R/W Utility Sequences	270	7/7/94	1203	76545,1527
midi file to send GS reset syse	577	2/10/94	785	100032,1727
"Sad Song" (Original) MFF	1834	1/19/94	6493	72172,3613
"Soulman" (Original) MFF	86871	1/18/94	10416	71614,3676
"Original MIDI Song" WRK; MFI	4732	1/15/94	1780	73030,3317
Etheral. An original compositii	2764	12/16/93	1833	72437,1736
"Haste to the Wedding" Trad. J	27834	12/14/93	1924	74046,757
"Mercy" (Original) MFF	13056	11/16/93	1878	71203,2333
"Runaway, Girl"; MFF; Original	17025	11/2/93	2894	71203,2333
Original Composition MIDI/Wir	5093	11/2/93	933	72633,2204
"Shooting the Rapids" by Jame	4992	10/22/93	1307	76520,3356
"Friday at Five" by James P. Ha	3058	10/22/93	940	76520,3356
Unkl's Theme SuperJ midi	15740	10/14/93	717	73233,1622
"Sorcerer";MFF;Original	12377	9/27/93	1625	71203,2333
"Daydreams";MFF;Original	31886	9/26/93	1604	71203,2333
Homer's Tune	8081	9/26/93	1923	70571,2015
"Sing of the Lord's Goodness"	30247	9/24/93	1255	100271,763
Original Jazz tune; MFF	9309	9/21/93	1887	73122,1734
Theme from Runcibal Quest v.	8192	9/13/93	369	70604,275
"And He Shall Purify"; MFF	12395	9/12/93	1190	71052,405
"Reverie" (Claude Debussy) M	7607	9/11/93	2083	70550,535
"Clair de Lune" (Claude Debus	9205	9/11/93	4762	70550,535

[Description] [Mark] [Retrieve] [View] [Close]

A portion of an online library of MIDI song files waiting to be downloaded. The *Accesses* column indicates how many times each song has been downloaded. The numbers under the *Contributor* column are the ISP account numbers of the uploaders.

4. **After you select the download location, the transfer begins. In most cases a window pops open on your screen indicating how much of the file has been transferred, and the time remaining.**

Once the transfer is complete, the file or program resides on your hard drive and can be used. Well, it's almost ready to be used. Many downloads are compressed, and must be decompressed (unpacked or unzipped) before they can be used. Compression, using a protocol such as Zip, makes the file smaller, meaning a quicker download time. This convenience is balanced by the need to decompress it offline, and to do that you need a decompression utility. Fortunately, such utilities are themselves easily downloaded and used.

Facts About Sharing Files Online

- Program files must be compressed before being uploaded. There are two reasons for this. First, it reduces the size of the file, which is universally done as a courtesy to prospective downloaders. Second, it's a way of bundling together the several files that make up a typical program. Compression utilities for every computer type let you compress your uploads and decompress downloads.

- Copyrights exist in cyberspace just as they do offline. Although certain gray areas exist, restrictions of fair use remain pretty much the same online as off. The burden of infringement generally rests with the uploader, or the manager of the site to which an infringing file has been uploaded. For this reason, system operators (sysops) of BBS systems and online service libraries are cautious about what they accept on their systems. Musicians, as uploaders, should be equally cautious about what they share indiscriminately online. MIDI reproductions of popular music, for example, infringe the copyright of the song. The same goes for copies of text works such as books, magazine articles, album liner notes, newspaper clippings, material from an online site, and any other published verbiage. Scanning and optical character recognition (OCR) technology make it easy to render a large published text work in digital format, but that doesn't mean it's any more legal.

- When uploading a previously published work, either music, text, or multimedia, state the copyright permission in the file description.

   In most cases, shareware can be redistributed by anybody, provided all the original files are included in the compressed package. It's a good service to everyone involved, when you find a good shareware program, to spread it around by uploading to your favorite haunts. You get to share it with cyberfriends, and the program's author gets new potential customers.

PERSONAL NETWORKING

Sharing information is one of the two primary reasons to go online, for musicians and all others. The other is personal networking. Information and community, the two aspects of cyberspace, balance each other in a rough equality of purpose. Some

REAL WORDS

E-mail is a tool, just like anything else. It can be used to great advantage when communicating with musicians or contacts around the nation and around the world, since there's no charge, but don't treat it like a marketing tool. You should never send someone unwanted e-mail in the form of an ad. This attitude may change over the next 20 years, but there's still a perception that a person's e-mail is much more personal than their regular mail.

Start off your e-mail escapade by responding personally to someone's post, instead of posting it to the whole group. Wonderful conversations and relationships (business and personal) are started that way. Take the opportunity to develop a business contact in private that looks promising and knowledgeable in a newsgroup or forum.

people are lone wolves in cyberspace, taking advantage primarily of its educational, informative, resourceful quality. Others mostly want to interact with people for friendship, promotion of music projects, career support, or a combination of reasons. Whatever your personal inclinations, the personal quality of cyberspace is as available as all the files and Web sites in the world.

Online community can manifest in a one-on-one approach of e-mail, or as the group community of a message board. There is also the variable environment of chat rooms to consider.

E-MAIL

E-mail is the most widely used feature of the online experience, as well as the most profoundly revolutionary (so far). E-mail is most often the first step into cyberspace, yet is likely to remain the most profound change in lifestyle. If you are considering taking the online plunge at least as far as getting an e-mail box, the addition of this seemingly innocuous feature to your life is practically guaranteed to change your routines of communication more drastically than you anticipate. It is great for networking with musicians around the globe, but you may also find yourself building and strengthening relationships closer to home and heart.

Why does e-mail have such a penetrating effect on a person's lifestyle and relationships? Three essential qualities of electronic mail give it power and tremendous appeal:

REAL WORDS

I've used e-mail and newsgroups to gain further knowledge about various equipment. My favorite newsgroup for this purpose, as well as for just browsing, is rec.audio.pro. Posing a question there can get quite a number of well-informed opinions by professionals working in the field. Several people who post there, including Steve Dorsey, Mike Rivers, Nick Batzdorf, and me, write for trade recording publications such as *Recording* and *EQ Magazine.* I've learned quite a lot about all aspects of recording, including digital audio editing, music software, CD-ROMs, microphone recording techniques, and effect processors (and, I hope, contributed something of value as well). Alt.music.4-track is also quite useful.

Ken Lee/Eleven Shadows
Burglar@primenet.com

■ **It's cheap.** E-mail boxes come with virtually all online service accounts, whether from America Online, CompuServe, or an Internet service provider. When you open the account, you get an e-mail address, and with the proper software (which may be provided free of charge) you can immediately begin sending and receiving mail to and from all corners of the globe. No matter where you write, regardless of the physical location of that computer, you are logging into cyberspace through the same local (in most cases) phone call. Some services offer e-mail absolutely free. Others charge about $10 each month, and include many other features and online sites. Internet accounts usually cost $15–$30 per month, and include unlimited access to the entire Internet in addition to e-mail.

■ **It's fast.** Really fast. It makes postal mail look like a percussion section of logs and rattles. In cyberspace, postal mail is called snail mail because of its glacial pace compared to e-mail. In many cases, e-mail letters are delivered to their destinations almost instantly. In extremely problematic delivery situations, a delay of a few hours might transpire. The speed of e-mail has given rise to an entire culture of communication, based on rapid exchanges of brief, informal notes. It is reminiscent of postal deliveries in New York City early in the century, when postal couriers made the rounds several time each day, and sending a response by return mail got an answer to a morning letter back in the afternoon. E-mail takes this ideal to an extreme, facilitating dozens of daily written round-trips when necessary.

■ **It's nonscheduled.** Like a postal correspondence, e-mail exists outside real time. Its faster delivery speed makes the correspondence more like conversational than snail mail, without the timing considerations of a telephone call. Whether you fulfill your part of the conversation at 4 p.m. or 2 a.m. makes no difference to the recipient.

Q & A: E-MAIL

Q What do I need to start using e-mail?

A E-mail requires hardware, software, and an online account. You need a computer with a modem, an e-mail software program, and a membership with an online service or Internet service provider. The online account gives you an e-mail box (address), and software is often included in the deal.

Q Who would I send an e-mail letter to?

A It's amazing how quickly you meet people online once you begin surfing around. Most Web pages have links to the e-mail box of the page's creator. Online services are full of people wanting to meet other people, and trading e-mail addresses. Also, once you have e-mail, you'll be surprised to discover many people around you have it also, and you may enjoy writing electronically to real-world friends, family members, and officemates.

Q How do musicians use e-mail?

A Many ways. Wired musicians keep electronic **mailing lists**, or **listservs**, just like postal mailing lists, for sending promotions, concert announcements, club date schedules, album release noti-

---

REAL WORDS

Another truly valuable tool is the mailing lists. You can subscribe to a list that deals specifically with what you are interested in. For instance, I subscribe to PC-DAW Digest, which deals primarily with digital audio workstations for the PC, as the name suggests. Another extremely useful one is the DAT-heads mailing list, discussing all things about digital audiotape.

Ken Lee/Eleven Shadows
Burglar@primenet.com

fications, and everything else that snail mail is used for. As e-mail becomes more of a multimedia phenomenon, using attached graphics and sound files, e-mail will become even more practical as a career tool.

MESSAGE BOARDS

Online electronic bulletin boards were one of the first features of computer cyberspace. Taking the principle of e-mail and broadening it to include more than two people, **message boards** foster community networking more than any other aspect of the online phenomenon. Called bulletin boards, message boards, or simply boards, they work in a dynamic of posting and replying. Anyone can post a message, initiating a discussion topic. In turn, anyone can reply to that message, and if it's interesting enough, several people will reply. Continuing, those replies will encourage their own responses, and in this branching fashion a virtual conversation is formed. The convoluted string of messages around a single topic is called a thread or a message tree.

Although this principle remains universal, boards differ substantially in how they work and how effectively they encourage lively, involved discussion. The native software that runs the board may thread messages with great sophistication and accuracy, including features such as addressing messages directly to another member of the board, notifying members when a message addressed to them has been added to the board, and keeping track of which messages are new for each member who logs onto the board. Less sophisticated boards house messages but make no

---

REAL WORDS

When trying to network with other musicians on the Internet, don't make the mistake of letting everyone know your opinion until you've gotten very used to the newsgroups you're in. It's an absolute guarantee that you'll be very, very sorry the first time you post an opinionated message. There are many on the Internet who take great joy in pointing out the inaccuracies and foibles of others. Those comments should be taken with a grain of salt; whether you were correct to post or not, don't take any attacks personally. Just imagine all the people who didn't attack you.

Craig Patterson
midigod@aol.com

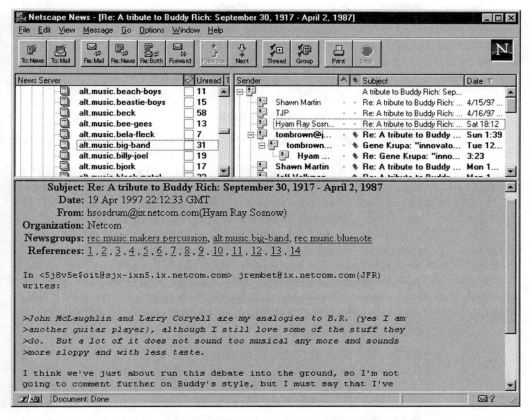

A Usenet newsgroup reader, displaying messages in the alt.music.big-band newsgroup. There are hundreds of musical Usenet newsgroups.

distinctions as to whom they are addressed to or what relation the messages bear to each other. In other words, the threading isn't as good.

There are thousands upon thousands of message boards in cyberspace located in a few main areas of the online landscape:

■ **Usenet.** The **Usenet** is one of the oldest portions of the Internet, and consists purely of message boards. There are several thousand boards in Usenet alone, each devoted to a particular topic. These message communities are called **newsgroups**, something of a misnomer considering that many of them have nothing to do with news anymore. In the Usenet's early days, newsgroups represented the underground communication network of academia, and did indeed function as transmitters of news, research developments, and industry information among participants in a certain field. Now that the Internet in general, and Usenet in particular, have sprawled into the wired world at large, the newsgroups fill functions distinctly removed from their original intent. Usenet newsgroups are unowned by any governing body, and are for the most part unmoderated forums for free expression. They are an adult environment, and even adults should thicken their skin before reading some of the more intensely confrontational groups.

■ **Online services.** Traditionally, all online services contain message boards committed to various topics. There are fewer online services now than there used to be, but CompuServe and America Online both have an involved system of message-based communities in place, and Prodigy, the Microsoft Network, and perhaps others still offer messaging environments. The tone of the discussion on these boards is tamer, more polite, and more friendly to newcomers than the Usenet newsgroups. Message content is policed to some extent by staff members of the online service, and any contribution that violates the communal well-being is removed. In some cases, members can be locked out of the message board if they cause consistent trouble.

■ **BBSs.** Considering that **BBS** stands for *bulletin board service,* it's not surprising that these small, independent online systems contain message boards. Whereas the large online services have struggled to retain their membership in the increasingly competitive online marketplace, smaller BBS companies are proliferating. Each of the hundreds of BBSs is usually devoted to a particular topic, sometimes narrowly focused. They provide a more physically local community than the big services because they are sometimes basement operations that offer only regional telephone access. They are a great alternative for message-based networking with people in your area who share a musical interest, and their download libraries often provide some of the best shareware collections in cyberspace.

■ **Web sites.** Although the World Wide Web was not designed with message boards in mind, inventive developers are getting around that design limitation. In an attempt to make the Web more community-friendly (it has always been information-friendly), large Web sites include message board forums on certain subjects related to the site's prime focus. Most of these are complex, corporate Web environments that strive to be miniature, self-sufficient online services that you can access for free. Web-based message boards usually do not operate with the speed or sophistication of their counterparts in online services.

The Message Board Experience

Understanding what a message board is and how it works theoretically isn't so hard. But how do you begin to get involved, and what does it look like on the computer screen? How do you fit a virtual community into your daily life?

Assuming you have an online account of some sort (an absolute necessity), the first step is to sample a few message boards and choose one (or more) in which to participate. Reading messages on any board is a telescoping process that begins with viewing a list of topics, choosing one and viewing a list of thread titles (subtopics), choosing one of those and viewing a list of messages, and finally choosing a message and reading it. Cumbersome as this sounds, it won't take you all night to sample a board (although it may prove so much fun that you can't tear yourself away).

Messages are displayed on your computer screen in plain text, framed in a window. The specific appearance of these screen elements depends on the system you're logged into and the software you're using. Online services provide access software that presents that service's message boards in a user-friendly design. The Usenet newsgroups have no official software, and must be approached using one of many available Internet programs, such as Netscape Navigator (the most popular, but my no means the only choice). Whatever system–software configuration you're using, every message window will present you with a couple of basic choices:

- You can reply to the message. Most boards in online services automatically address your reply to the person who authored the message you're viewing. (Not in the Usenet newsgroups, though.) The Usenet gives you the option of responding on the board, directly to the author's e-mail box, or both. Online service boards generally make you choose one or the other.

- You can move on to the next message in the thread. You may also have the option of storing the message in a software filing cabinet for later reference.

You'll know which communities to settle into by where you feel inspired to respond to messages. Alternatively, you might try beginning a few discussions of your own, and see which boards respond best to your attempts. Once you start meeting people online and pitching in to ongoing discussion threads, you'll find a certain level of involvement. A typical level, participatory but not addicted, is manifested with once-daily logons to read and respond to messages. Some systems and software packages allow the downloading of messages for offline browsing, reading, and responding. When you've gone through the board (while logged off) and written all the replies you care to, a second logon is required to post your messages. Some people develop enough attachment to the messaging community to log on in the morning and evening. More completely enthralled participants read messages

several times during the day. The most casual involvement requires only occasional visits to the board; weekly participation is about the most sporadic frequency that still provides a sense of membership in the community.

Wherever message boards are located, they serve a multitude of purposes, from social to utilitarian, from silly to grave, from flippant to life-saving. Even in the single field of music, messaging groups are varied in their intent. Here's a survey of the types you can find online and how you could expect to benefit by involving yourself in such a community.

- **Music appreciation boards.** Don't let this phrase evoke horrible memories of forced-listening experiences you might have suffered in your youth, as dry teachers tried to explain why you should like neoclassical string quartets. What I am calling music appreciation boards are messaging communities for people who love all kinds of music and enjoy talking with others of similar taste, exchanging tips and discographies of their favorite genres. Generally not oriented to professional musicians, but certainly not excluding them, such virtual socializing can be found in discussions of classical, jazz, folk, pop, techno, world, and just about any other kind of musical category ever invented. Many Usenet newsgroups are devoted to individual bands.

- **Artistic support boards.** Plenty of composer/performer/singer/songwriter message areas can be found. Mutual support for the sometimes lonely lifestyle of musical creation is a great thing, and these boards provide sympathetic and helpful virtual companionship, on call.

- **MIDI boards.** MIDI can be both frustratingly complex and rewardingly powerful, and messaging communities are great places for sharing problems, solutions, and delights with other MIDIfied musicians. Board divisions might run along the lines of MIDI tasks, such as sampling or synthesizer programming.

- **Music computer boards.** Problem solving is a valued feature on most computer boards, as brave souls attempt to merge the inner artist with the outer technology. Music computer boards are usually divided by computer platform (Macintosh, PC, Atari, and Amiga). Sometimes the subdivisions occur along lines of computer tasking, such as sequencing or hard disk recording.

- **Professional networking boards.** Message boards have been set up in online services and in the Usenet for music and entertainment professionals. Some are private and access must be applied for; others are public. Information about performing venues, professional organizations, personnel needs, contracts and royalties, teaching resources, financial planning for the freelance lifestyle, and other concerns of the working musician are discussed by voices of experience. Well-known figures in the industry can be found on these boards, and the opportunity to talk with them over time is one of the great benefits of message boards.

■ **Customer service boards.** A time-honored use of messaging resources, some boards are run by manufacturers and vendors of musical hardware, software, and instruments. There are situations in which customer service over the telephone doesn't cut the mustard, and messaging with a company representative can provide a more satisfactory experience. Granted, some of these message boards are so crammed with beleaguered customers, and so understaffed by company representatives, that only a sour experience can possibly result. However, in the best cases, exchanging messages with a customer service technician over a period of days, as you troubleshoot possible solutions and your understanding of the problem evolves, can be a godsend, and one of the most worthwhile adventures of the online musician.

Q & A: MESSAGE BOARDS

Q Are message boards private clubs?

A Usually not. Message boards are flagrantly public institutions that allow—even encourage—participation by anyone and everyone. The implicit ethic of a message board is that any posted message is available for reading and can be responded to. Message threads take on the ambience of a virtual cocktail party, in which clusters of people form impromptu discussion groups that anyone can join or listen to. Some boards provide private sections for topics that thrive on personal revelation, such as support groups. To access a private section, members need to apply to the board administrator with an e-mail or message.

Q Can sound files and pictures be posted on a message board?

A Online service message boards cannot accommodate multimedia postings, although this may change soon. However, the Internet newsgroups (Usenet) commonly contain pictures and sound files as part of their messages, and their are even entire newsgroups devoted to such postings. The ease with which this feature can be enjoyed depends largely on the software used to read the Usenet newsgroups. Some programs translate the encoded files immediately and automatically, letting you see a picture when you select the message, without any special download process. However, sound and video postings usually need to be downloaded and played with a separate software utility.

Q Do I need special software to read and post messages?

A Each online service provides an access program for using the message boards in that service. (In CompuServe, there are several software choices.) Reading the Usenet newsgroups is not so simple. Because they are not owned or governed by any organization, there is no official software, and users must find their own. Choices abound, and most Web browsers let you participate in newsgroups through a Web interface. Specialized newsgroup readers offer helpful features.

Q Do music industry pros participate in message boards?

A Absolutely!

CHATTING

Live, online chatting is a virtual activity that has gained in popularity during the mid-1990s. Thanks to the profligate chat rooms of America Online, typing in real time to other logged-on folks has ascended to the status of a national pastime. Other online services offered similar features, sometimes called conferencing, before the meteoric rise of AOL, but didn't succeed in capturing the mass imagination. However, popular or not, chatting or conferencing has only limited value as a networking tool for musicians. These two drawbacks limit its usefulness in this regard:

■ You can chat only with someone logged onto the same system at the same time, making it logistically inconvenient compared to e-mail and messaging. In this respect, chatting has no advantage over a phone call.

■ Chatting is slow, as all participants are limited to the speed of typing.

■ It's usually hard to create and save a file of the chat session for future reference, as you can easily do with e-mail or a forum message.

Because of these shortcomings, informal online chatting has evolved primarily as a social phenomenon. It's a good way to meet new people, though not as time-efficient as browsing through a message board. You can select new acquaintances only from among those who happened to be logged on at any given time, and it's generally more difficult to learn about a person in a chat room than on a message board, where they can write at greater length. Besides, if productivity and career networking are your prime goals in cyberspace, you may not be attracted to people who have a lot of free time to spend aimlessly chatting, nor might you be attracted to that activity yourself.

Live events in conference rooms, virtual convention centers, and online auditoriums are another story. This has been going on for many years in CompuServe, Prodigy, America Online, and other services, and presents a nifty way of meeting a well-known personality through the computer. At the time of this writing, hundreds of musicians and fans recently experienced conference events with David Bowie and Hootie and the Blowfish, in which participating Netizens could ask questions, or just sit back and watch the interview unfold across their screens. More productive for working musicians are conferences with guests whose expertise appeals to working pros in the trenches of the music industry. Manufacturer representatives, trade magazine editors, book authors, band members, live audio professionals, leaders of professional associations, and many other helpful guests often provide live, question-answering expertise in all aspects of the music business.

Live conferences (and informal chatting) used to be the exclusive domain of online services, and were not featured on the Internet. But times are changing online, and as the Internet strives to develop more of a community feel, chat sites and live events can be found scattered around the World Wide Web. How can you find live conference events and chat rooms?

■ If you are a member of CompuServe, America Online, or another closed-network online service, check out the system announcements that appear when you first log on. They usually advertise upcoming live events and point you to other announcements.

■ Visit the music forums within online services frequently, and keep up to date with announcements within those specific areas.

■ If you're on the Internet, go to the Yahoo! Web directory (at http://www.yahoo.com) and check the Live Event listings.

How Chatting and Conferencing Work

Chatting and conferencing are both means of talking in real time with someone, or a group of people, by using the computer. Traditional chatting is text-based, which is to say you talk by typing words and sending them by hitting the Enter key. Typing and sending in a series of short lines, you can fashion a conversation of sorts, although if too many people are in a virtual room at once, it can get chaotic and jumbled. Chatting occurs in two primary modes: formal and informal.

Informal chatting is a popular online hobby, and transpires on all subjects imaginable. Participation begins when you enter a chat room. This is done by choosing from a list of rooms, titled by subject, and clicking on your selection with the mouse. A window opens on your screen, within which you see the lines sent by participants, immediately after they send them. Everyone in the room sees everything typed by everyone else, almost instantaneously. The lines scroll upward as new lines are appear at the bottom of the window. Below the main chat portion of the window, a smaller area displays what you type as you are typing. When you send a line, it disappears from the bottom portion and appears in the main portion of your window and everyone else's.

That much remains constant in most informal chat systems. Beyond that, various features might be found to enhance the experience, depending on the service you are logged into. You may be able to call up a list of participants in the room and send side-windows to one of them for a private discussion parallel to the main group talk. Some systems let you type several lines into a buffer and send them into the chat room all at once. Internet chatting, sometimes called Internet relay chat (IRC) is usually a more cumbersome procedure, sometimes requiring that the entire window redraw on your screen every time you send a line. It's slower, but improvements are being made.

Formal conferencing works according to the same type-and-send principle, but the rules are different. A formal conference usually includes an invited guest speaker who delivers a prepared talk, then answers questions from the logged-in participants. During the conference, special guidelines are sometimes in place governing when people can talk. The conference's moderator gives the floor to one person at a time, and generally keeps order so that everyone doesn't talk at once, obliterating the guest's ability to be "heard" on the screen.

In special cases, loosely moderated guest conferences do not provide enough control, as when the conference is attended by hundreds of people. Then, special areas are used that can accommodate large numbers of participants without crashing the host computer. The native software of these virtual auditoriums usually enforces an orderly conference by making it impossible for anyone to send a typed line into the main conference window until they are cued by the moderator.

Evolving interactive technology is developing new formats for chatting, including nontext and multimedia-enhanced conference experiences. In an attempt to personalize the process of meeting people through typing, systems of graphic enhancement have been invented that allow users to adopt visual personas (called avatars) to represent them on-screen. Instead of viewing a plain window of upward-scrolling text lines, avatars let people view animated figures. Audio and video streaming are also being incorporated into conference adventures. Some musical conference events include simultaneous transmission of sound files and pictures. In this way, a recording artist can be answering questions about a new album release while participants receive audio feeds of excerpts from the album. Finally, and perhaps most exciting to sci-fi fans, video chatting using computer-mounted cameras and microphones promises to enliven chat rooms with full-motion, real-time multimedia.

Still, text chatting prevails, largely because of bandwidth limitations. Standard telephone lines, which carry chat and conference rooms into personal computers, cannot transfer video and audio data quickly enough to be effective. Happily for musicians, sound streaming requires less bandwidth than video streaming, but fundamental speed limitations make all multimedia chatting fairly unrewarding to all but cutting-edge hobbyists.

Q & A: CHATTING AND CONFERENCING

Q Is special software needed to chat online?

A Sometimes; it depends on the system you're using. When using a chat room, conference room, or virtual auditorium in an online service, you just use the same program you always use to log onto that service. It contains everything you need to chat, message, or use any other features of that service. However, the program won't work on any other network. When chatting on the World Wide Web, you need a special software utility that may or may not be included in your Web browser. Such utilities are called **plug-ins** because they plug in to your browser, and can be obtained as a free download. Different Web-based chat areas may have different plug-in requirements, and instruct you how to proceed.

Q Is live chatting private and safe?

A Yes, if you take sensible precautions. Nobody can get into your computer through a chat room. However, in most situations your e-mail address is exposed through your presence as a chatter, so you may get e-mail communication from people you've chatted with, and some of it might be unwelcome. It makes sense to be cautious about what you tell strangers online, especially when asked for personal or offline information. As a side note, public, unmoderated chat rooms are risky environments for kids, who are vulnerable to all kinds of approaches and don't have the adult sensibilities to fend them off. The big online services offer filtering options for parents who want to limit exposure to adult areas for their kids.

Q Can music be shared in a chat room?

A No, not effectively at this time. At some point, available data bandwidth will expand to allow real-time sharing of multimedia data, such as sound and video. Currently, most chatting is a words-only experience, although experimental sites are appearing that offer multimedia options.

Q Is online chatting expensive?

A It can be, if done frequently and for long periods. Most online service accounts are charged by the hour, and include a small monthly allowance of free time. Chat addicts pay large monthly bills for the privilege of socializing online. Internet users mostly pay a flat monthly fee for unlimited use. In those cases, the cost-effectiveness of free chatting is balanced by the lower quality of chatting on the Internet, compared to an online service.

Q Can I create my own chat room?

A Some systems allow this, and some don't. It is not possible on CompuServe, where preset conference rooms are provided. The America Online and WOW! Systems, by contrast, let their members create and name chat rooms, and invite others to join in.

PERSONAL PUBLISHING

In addition to sharing files and networking with other musicians, personal publishing is a third important reason to go online. Before the World Wide Web came into existence, there was no practical way of making a complete personal statement online. The closest an aspiring musician could come to that was accomplished by uploading a series of files to a music library in an online service. The Web has changed everything. Now anybody can create and publish a Web site, or **home page**, designed to promote a band, present research, attract advertising revenue, or serve many other purposes.

I use the word *publish* in this context deliberately, and it might sound like a peculiar choice of terminology. Online publishing is completely paperless, and therefore goes against our long-held ideas of what it means to be a publisher. Wired musicians who have made the mental shift to paperless, electronic promotion find themselves with an opportunity to control their promotional image to an unprecedented degree.

Musicians publish themselves on the World Wide Web for a few main reasons:

- **As an electronic business card.** It's increasingly common to hand out the URL (Web address) of a personal Web site on a business card or in a business letter. The Web site then provides background information on the musician's past and present activities.

■ **As a music distribution tool.** Web sites can contain music, and audio streaming technology makes it easier than ever to let a virtual visitor hear what you're up to. Some musicians even release entire singles online in support of their offline (real-world) distribution efforts. Increasingly, storing demo material online, at a personal Web site, may supplant the traditional method of sending tapes to a record company's A&R director.

■ **As a newsletter.** Bands, in particular, use Web locations to advertise upcoming events, concerts, tours, recording schedules, album releases, and so on.

■ **As a self-contained business venture.** Taken to the extreme, Web sites are business opportunities in themselves. Although Web-based business models are still in their infancy, and will no doubt evolve considerably in coming years, a few have already emerged and are being tested by entrepreneurial musicians. They include selling music albums online, as well as other musical merchandise; charging subscription rates to access the Web site; and selling advertising at the Web site to other companies.

Q & A: PUBLISHING ON THE WEB

Q Can anyone put up a Web site?

A There are no restrictions, criteria, or application procedures for participating in the World Wide Web by putting up your own site. This is partly why it represents an unprecedented opportunity for musicians to distribute their own music. It requires no permission or acceptance from a record label, distribution company, or anyone else.

Q Is it expensive to have a Web site?

A Placing a Web site requires space on an Internet computer (called a server), which is usually obtained in a lease arrangement with an Internet service provider. In many cases, such space is included with an access account for the Internet. In other situations, you must rent the server space separately for a monthly fee. Online services (CompuServe and America Online certainly, and perhaps others) include a certain amount of server space with a membership account; the amount of space may or may not be enough to hold your whole Web site.

Q What do I need to know to make a Web site?

A The first thing is to familiarize yourself with the World Wide Web by surfing it. Get acquainted with what a Web site is, the different types of sites, and how they are designed. Then you need to either create your own design with the help of software programs that produce the underlying code for you, or hire a Web design specialist. The decision is akin to designing your own album cover or hiring a graphic artist and layout specialist. Software makes Web design much easier, and there are many programs to choose from, but it still requires a good design sense and graphic sensibilities.

Q If I put up a Web site, how will people see it?

A Anyone with an Internet account, using a Web browser, will be able to access your site. No single Web site is more difficult to access than any other; they are all equal. However, it helps to promote your site so people find out about it.

Q How do I promote my Web site?

A You can spread the word online and offline. Include the URL (Web address) in all your official letterheads and business cards. Online advertisements include message boards and listings in Web directories, which are usually free. Also, friends and colleagues can include links to your site in their music-related sites, and you can do the same for them.

11

THE MUSICIAN'S SHOPPING GUIDE: ONLINE*

Shopping for the online experience is less hardware-intensive than buying computer or MIDI gear. In fact, there is really only one piece of specialized hardware you need (besides a computer), and that's a modem. Otherwise, it's a question of service and software. You need some kind of connection service, for which a monthly fee is paid and of which there are many alternatives. Once connected, you need software, some of which is specifically geared to a musical online experience. The good news is that much of the software is free!

In theory, the type of computer you have (Windows or Macintosh) doesn't affect the online experience. The Internet, or an online service, provides the same advantages no matter which computer is used as a viewing vehicle. But the reality is that Mac owners, blessed though they may be with high-quality music software, are at a serious disadvantage online. Online services do not provide the same service to Mac users as to Windows customers in terms of new software releases and updates. Macintosh options on the Internet are severely limited compared to choices for Windows users.

New online options are coming down the pike at a quick rate. Television display of the Internet, digital phone lines for faster access, and wireless satellite connections are a few that this chapter touches on. By the time you read these words, there will no doubt be other options. The online world itself is a good place to

*Price ranges in this chapter are based on 1997 retail prices.

get information about the quickly shifting world of computer connectivity, as are online magazines.

MODEMS

Modems are the crucial devices that connect your computer to a phone line, enabling you to log into the global online network. For such important little devices, they are satisfyingly inexpensive.

There are a few things you need to know about modems, but they're not complicated. First, if you have a computer, find out whether it already has a modem in it. If you can't tell by reading the owner's manual, just look at the back of the computer. Among the ports arrayed over the back panel, look for a standard telephone input jack. If you see one, you have a modem. Whether it's good enough to enjoy music online is another question, and to answer it you need to find the documentation that lists the modem speed. (Some Macintosh computers are sold with external modems that sit near the computer.)

MODEM SPEED OPTIONS

Speed is the main consideration when buying a modem. It is measured in bits per second (**bps**), and refers to how much data can rush through the modem in either direction (also called the modem's **baud rate**). The minimum acceptable speed for the Internet and World Wide Web is 14,400 bps, the capacity of a 14.4 modem. Better yet is a model that runs at twice 28,800 bps or faster. New 14.4 modems are nearly impossible to find, and 28.8 modems are becoming scarce, thanks to two new developments in modem speed that have hit the scene:

- **33,600 bps modems.** These models use compression and other hidden tricks to squeeze more speed out of standard phone lines.

- **56,000 bps (download) modems.** Once thought impossible, new technology has broken the 33.6 limit once thought to be the speed ceiling over regular phone lines.

Speed Limit Warnings!

There is some hype about modem speeds that entraps the gullible. It is tempting to believe that a 28.8 modem will deliver Internet access speed that is twice as fast as a 14.4 modem. Makes sense, right? Yes, but it's rarely, in fact, true. Many things can happen to drag down a high-speed modem, and they are out of the modem's (and your) control. Bad phone lines (not necessarily evident when you use the phone to talk), slow modems in the network you're connecting to, and even lots of traffic online all can combine to keep you out of the fast lane during any given online session. Quoted modem speeds such as 28.8 and 33.6 should be viewed as ideals, not minimums.

If you already have a 28.8 modem and are considering upgrading to a 33.6 model, take special heed. If you are not attaining a pure speed of 28,800 bits per second (your dialing program should tell you how fast your access is for each call), you probably won't get any faster with the new modem.

This is not necessarily the case with the 56,000 bps modems, however, because they use a completely different connection technology.

Why the infatuation with speed? Because the Internet is slow. Not slow so much as heavy with multimedia content; it's the modems that are slow in carrying it. There is a severe bottleneck in Internet access: the telephone system. Standard (analog) phone lines can move data only at a certain trudging pace. Meanwhile, the Internet has developed a rich environment of pictures, music, movies, and other multimedia goodies that require a huge amount of data to be moved very quickly if we are to enjoy the bounty of mixed media. In the future we won't be stuck with standard phone lines, and even now there are alternatives. But for most people, the only practical alternative is to get the fastest possible modem to squeeze every bit of speed through a regular phone line.

Ditching the Telephone

Some people invest the expense and effort to equip their home or studio with an alternative to standard phone lines for online access. This may seem exorbitant (especially when you find out how much it costs), but for musicians who are making the most of the Internet, it can make sense. Even if it is not professionally necessary to jack up access speed so dramatically, it is no more indulgent, and probably more useful, than buying a satellite TV system.

Here are the current options for home access:

- *SDN phone lines.* Integrated services digital network (ISDN) lines are provided by phone companies directly into homes, and provide Internet access about 10 times faster than a high-speed modem. There is an installation fee that varies drastically depending on the phone company, and a monthly line charge that is likewise unpredictable, but probably $30–$100 per month. You also need a special digital modem, which can cost $200–$500.

- *Wireless satellite connection.* This is similar to television satellite systems. You buy an 18-inch dish, install it on your roof, and connect it to your computer. You then use a regular modem to input information (upload) and the satellite to download information (the slowest part of the connection). This provides very fast Internet action, at a stiff price of about $700–$900. There is also a monthly charge of about $20.

In the future, wireless or cable modems will become common and analog modems will become antiques, representing the frontier days of cyberspace.

There is a small market for used modems, but because they are not too expensive new, many people don't bother trying to sell old ones. However, if you are tempted to buy a used modem, it is a safe purchase. Modems have no moving parts and are sturdy. As long as it's working when you get it, there isn't much room for hidden inoperability.

Essential Shopping Questions: Modems

There are only two questions you need ask when buying a new modem:

- Is it external or internal? Internal modems require opening the computer and plugging the modem (which is a circuit board attached to a phone jack) into the motherboard, then closing the computer. Internal modems are slightly less expensive than externals, and preferred by most people. The disadvantage to them is that you can't see the status of your connection. External modems have lights on their front panels that tell you whether your connection is open or has been broken, its speed (in some cases), and whether a download is proceeding or is stalled. Externals also offer the advantage of an On/Off switch, which caters to one of the primal impulses of the digital age: When in doubt, turn the damn thing off.

- How fast is it? This is not an area where you should cut corners. You need as much speed as you can get to take advantage of the music scene online. Get a 33.6 or maybe even a 56 modem.

ACCESS SERVICES

Once you have a modem, you need someplace to call with it. Access services connect you to online destinations, and take two main forms:

■ **Online services.** Companies such as America Online, CompuServe, Prodigy, and Microsoft Network provide numbers for customers who want to access the Internet, and also want the special online content stored within each service. America Online (AOL) members, for example, have access to AOL's private forums, electronic publications, message areas, and chat rooms, as well as to the Internet at large.

■ **Internet service providers (ISPs).** These companies provide simple access to the Internet, without private distinctions and features. Customers get a local number for getting on the Internet and World Wide Web.

Both access paths provide you with an e-mail address. Online services furnish the software necessary to log onto the system, plus a World Wide Web browser. ISPs sometimes provide a Web browser, but not necessarily. (Nationwide companies tend to; local companies tend not to.) Online services provide both the Internet access and a good deal of organized private content. In particular, music discussion groups and support forums abound in online services, and are easy to locate and participate in. Why, then, would anyone choose an ISP, and forgo the organized environment of an online service? ISPs have traditionally offered two main advantages:

■ **Cost.** In most cases, Internet service providers charge a flat monthly fee for unlimited or nearly unlimited use. Online services sometimes charge by the hour of connected time. (This is changing, though, and America Online, the largest online service, has dropped its hourly charge.)

■ **Phone access.** The big online services companies serve the national (and sometimes international) community fairly well, providing local access for people living close to a large town or city. But that leaves many people in rural areas who don't want to make a toll call every time they log on. Small, local ISPs serve out-of-the-way communities, giving rural residents Internet access with a free phone call.

On the other side of the coin, online services offer these advantages:

■ **Content.** Extensive valuable private content is available in the form of forums, virtual communities, technical help, music career support, file libraries, digital magazines and newspapers, financial services, and chat rooms.

■ **Customer support.** Unlike small, local Internet service providers, online services provide software and human support for their customers.

■ **Organization.** The Internet is a wild, chaotic place. Thrilling, but disorganized. Online services give you a rest from hacking your way through the vast digital jungle by organizing their content and presenting it coherently.

Chicken or the Egg?

In a bizarre catch-22 irony, the best place to research online access is—you guessed it—online. Finding a provider with the right combination of features for your situation is a little tricky, but here are some hints:

- Join America Online, CompuServe, or the Microsoft Network online services for the free introductory month, and use that time to discover whether you have use for the private content each offers, or whether you're interested only in the Internet. It's also a chance to test how the Internet access works for your location

REAL WORDS

Oddly, I've received more benefits from the little toys I buy because I want to than I have from the new technology I get into because I have to. If I see something that someone else has thrown away, I'll have fun using it. But when I have to get on a bandwagon because "everyone" is using a new item, like audio clips on the World Wide Web, I find that it doesn't give me the return I would like. And yet, if I leave it out, I'll be behind. I don't like that feeling too much.

But having said that, by far the most satisfying piece of the whole digital/technological puzzle is that, because I'm so involved with it, I feel comfortable right away with new ideas and equipment. People who haven't kept up can't say that. They find themselves sinking quickly when trying to understand what's going on today, but I'm so far ahead of them that I can put up my own Web page, put up the audio that goes with it, and even do the graphic design for my own brochures! It's nice to know that technology has progressed to the point where it's easier for me to do things on my own. That's really the way I prefer it.

Craig Patterson
midigod@aol.com

through the service you joined. While you're online, you can research other options.

- Browse through computer and online magazines, looking for advertisements for national access providers. Call their toll-free information numbers to get details.

- Become attuned to radio ads in your area; many local ISPs use radio promotions to spread the word.

Essential Shopping Questions: Access Providers

Whether you decide to hook up with an online service or a dedicated Internet service provider, there are a few points you should be clear on before forking over your credit card number.

- Does the company provide a toll-free access phone number? Check your phone company for the exchanges that are free calls from your location.

- Does the company provide unlimited access for an unchanging monthly fee? Or does it provide a certain number of free hours, followed by an hourly charge? Beware of "prime time" plans that give you free unlimited access, but only during certain (undesirable) portions of the day.

- Does the company provide software? Obviously, *yes* is the right answer. Many local ISPs don't, however, and then you may have to buy a Web browser in a store, which is a shame because one of the best is available free online. Another catch-22. (Online services always provide free software.)

- Does the company provide customer support, and if so, what kind? Small ISPs usually are the most accessible in terms of technical help; you can just call the office and speak to someone. The larger the company, the more complicated it gets. Ideally, an ISP provides live telephone support, a Usenet newsgroup that is monitored a few times per day by a service representative, e-mail support, and a Web site with complete explanations of basic questions. Online services also sometimes host live chat rooms for interactive online questions. The more dedicated an access company seems to be to customer service, the better for you. Chances are very good you'll need it at some point.

- Are customer referrals available? Ask whether you can have an e-mail address or Web URL for a few current customers.

- Does the service allow space on its computer for a Web site? You may not think you'll be creating a Web site now, but in time the urge hits people unexpectedly. If the answer is *yes,* find out how much memory is allocated per account (1 or 2 megabytes is minimal, 5 is decent, and 10 megs is very nice). There should also be a provision for leasing more space at a rate of no more than $1 per megabyte per month.

- How many customers per line does the company serve? This is a technical question, but what you're really asking is: How often will I get a busy signal? Busy signals are the bane of ISP customers. All ISPs advertise freedom from the dreaded busy signal. If a company is serving more than 30 customers per line, you may be in for trouble. There's no assurance you'll get a straight answer with this question, but listen to how glad the representative seems to be that you asked. Companies that upgrade their lines often and are determined to give their customers a good experience will relish the chance to talk about this issue. You might also ask when they last added modems to their system.

Bottom Line

Access Providers

America Online: Various monthly plans including flat-rate with and without Internet access	$10–$20
CompuServe: Two monthly plans involving a monthly fee, hourly charges, and a monthly allowance of free hours	$10–$25 or more, depending on usage
The Microsoft Network: Various monthly plans including flat-rate with and without Internet access	$10–$20
Internet service provider	$15–$25 per month for unlimited access

ONLINE SOFTWARE

You don't have to spend a lot of money to acquire online software. Of all the types of software available in the computer experience, online programs are the least expensive (in many cases, free). The software situation is more troublesome in its complexity than in its expense. Just as with music computing, where you might choose to use several programs (sequencer, synth programmer, hard disk recorder) to produce your music, you may need a few specialized programs to make the most of the online opportunities.

■ **Online service programs.** These are free, and provided by the online services themselves. CompuServe, America Online, and Microsoft Network provide the latest versions of their access programs to Windows (and Windows 95) users, with Mac programs bringing up a distant rear. Often, the services' newest features remain unavailable to Mac users for a long time after they are introduced to the Windows population. Online service programs are loaded into new computers and given away on disks mailed to the general population and attached to computer magazines.

■ **Web browsers.** Of the most-used Web browsers, only one costs anything: Netscape Navigator, which is the most popular. (That's why they can get away with charging for it—at least, so far.) Microsoft Internet **Explorer,** which is gaining popularity, is free and downloadable from the Web and the three big online services. Additionally, members of CompuServe and America Online have Web browsers bundled into the free access programs for those services.

■ **E-mail readers.** Specialized programs for reading, organizing, storing, and writing e-mail are available in great numbers as freeware, shareware, and store-bought programs. However, these standalone programs receive stiff competition from the free e-mail readers included in the Internet software suites Netscape Navigator and Internet Explorer or those provided by online services.

■ **Usenet newsgroup readers.** Usenet readers are likewise specialized programs for accessing the Usenet newsgroups and reading and replying to messages. There are many free readers floating around cyberspace, but most people use the utilities included with Netscape Navigator and Internet Explorer or provided by their online services.

■ **Web plug-ins.** Here's where it gets really complicated, but fun! There are many dozens of plug-ins (small utility programs that display a particular type of multimedia file on the World Wide Web) and virtually all are free for the taking. They are downloaded from the Web and incorporated into the Web browser, and they do their work invisibly and automatically, in the background of a Web session. When you encounter a Web page that needs a certain plug-in to be most effective, and that plug-in is not found in the browser, you are directed to a download location should you choose to get it.

There are no Essential Shopping Questions when shopping for online software because the generally free acquisition makes the whole selection experience pressure-free. Shopping for online service software is the same as shopping for an online service. Trying out a Web browser or plug-in is an experiment, but you've lost nothing by dumping one and using another. Likewise, there is no Bottom Line here, or, rather, the bottom line is zero. Which is good news for everybody.

Part Three
GLOSSARY

America Online The largest and most popular online service. America Online (AOL) provides a vast array of special-interest forums, chat rooms, electronic editions of magazines and newspapers, financial and shopping services, and music and entertainment sites.

Audio streaming An Internet technology that plays music and sound files through a logged-on personal computer without downloading them. Before audio streaming, in order to hear a sound file on the Internet, you had to download it—which could take hours for a long high-fidelity file—and then play it from your hard drive with special software. Audio streaming cuts out the download process by playing the file directly from the hard drive of its host Internet computer, through your computer speakers. This technology is a breakthrough for musicians, who can now promote their recordings online more effectively. Applications of audio streaming include previewing albums before buying them online and listening to live radio broadcasts, cuts from unsigned bands, live concert events, recorded interviews, and much more.

Baud rate See *bps*.

BBS An acronym for *bulletin board service*. BBSs are small, usually local online services that provide a virtual meeting place for people who share an interest. There are BBSs for owners of a particular computer, fans of certain types of music, *Star Trek* devotees, and residents of local communities. Although BBSs don't get the media attention that online services (such as America Online) and the Internet do, there are hundreds of them enjoying a small, loyal customer base.

bps An abbreviation for *bits per second,* it is a measurement of how fast a modem transfers data. So-called 28.8 modems, for example, transfer data at 28,800 bits of data per second. The measurement is sometimes called the baud rate, even though the two measures are not exactly equivalent.

Cable modem Cable modems may be common in the future, but are rare now. They are devices that connect a computer to a coaxial cable (the same kind used to receive cable TV programming) for high-speed Internet access.

Chat room One of the most visible phenomena of the online generation, chat rooms are virtual meeting places in which participants can talk to each other, in real time, by typing on their computers. The room is designed to display every line typed in, on every participating computer screen. In this fashion, discussions can transpire in which everyone sees what all the others are saying. (In some cases, private chatting is enabled as a background feature.) Chat rooms originally developed within online services such as America Online and CompuServe, then migrated to the Internet. The online services still attract many chatters, but they must compete with the new chat applications on the World Wide Web.

Client software Software programs that are used on a personal computer to communicate with a network computer are called client programs, or just clients. The most famous example of a client program is a Web browser, which interacts with Internet computers that store World Wide Web sites. Other famous clients include the America Online and CompuServe programs, and the RealAudio player for Internet music files. Client programs are usually free or very inexpensive.

Client–server The client–server relationship describes the interaction between personal computer programs (clients) such as Web browsers and network programs (servers) accessed by the clients. Client and server programs work together to provide some kind of online experience for the home user. It could be displaying a Web page, playing a multimedia file, or accessing an online service.

Compression Online files are often compressed for quicker downloads. After downloading, they must be decompressed before they can be read or used. In most cases, a decompression utility is required. The decision to compress a file before uploading it is made by the uploader, but in the case of shareware programs there is no convenient alternative because shareware programs consist of several files, and compression not only makes them smaller, but bundles them into a single package that can be downloaded in one transfer. ASCII text files are not often compressed, unless they are really huge. MIDI files sometimes are, but tend to be on the small side, rendering compression unnecessary. Sound files (such as WAV-formatted files) may be compressed, but the compression does not reduce their size much.

Compu- Serve Once the dominant online service, CompuServe now plays second fiddle to America Online, but still has a healthy membership of several million people who appreciate its well-established communities and forums. Very deep informationally, CompuServe offers many areas for musicians, producers, MIDI enthusiasts, and entertainment buffs.

Down- loading Downloading is the process of transferring a file from a network to a personal computer. The PC must be connected to the network by means of a modem connection through a telephone line. Downloading files is a way of acquiring software, music, text, movie clips, and many other types of digitized material. It is one of the primary online activities—for many people, the most important. Software purchases are increasingly transacted online through customer downloads, which is convenient and immediately gratifying. There is also much free software to be acquired through downloading. Technically, any data transfer from a network to a PC is a download, and it's common to refer to accessing a Web site as downloading it. Practically speaking, however, a download places a file on your computer's hard drive, rather than just displaying it on your screen.

E-mail Electronic mail (e-mail) is the most used application of the Internet. E-mail links everyone in cyberspace with a common standard for sending and receiving communication. It has thousands of applications from personal to professional, and recent developments have made it ever more useful by enabling it to send non-text files in addition to regular text letters. *E-mail* is also used as a verb, as in, "I'll e-mail you later in the week."

Explorer Explorer (its full name is Internet Explorer) is Microsoft's widely used Web browser program. The first and only challenger to Netscape's dominance with its Navigator browser, Explorer offers a slightly different view of the Web, offering certain private HTML extensions (just as Netscape does) to Web page designers that can be viewed only with Explorer. Explorer and Navigator are the two primary browser choices, and some people use them both.

Forum An online meeting area for people who share an interest. Online forums often consist of three main areas: message boards, chat rooms, and file libraries. The message boards provide involved discussions over days and weeks. Chat rooms are for quicker, briefer communication. File libraries store computer files for downloading by members. All this is tied together by a common topical thread, and there are forums devoted to all kinds of interests, professions, and hobbies.

Frames Frames are a coding technique used by designers of World Wide Web pages that divides those pages into sections that behave independently of each other. For example, one segment may have a table of contents for the whole site, whereas a larger segment contains the actual content. Frames take longer to display on the screen than frameless pages, and some Web sites offer a selection by which the frames can be turned off.

FTP File Transfer Protocol (FTP) is the digital standard by which files are uploaded and downloaded to and from the Internet. FTP sites on the Internet are file storage locations from which programs and other files can be downloaded.

Home page The first, or main, page of a Web site. The term originated from the early days of the World Wide Web, when people would contribute to the Web by placing single pages of personal information on the system for anyone to access. Because the pages tended to be of a personal nature, as if inviting visitors into a virtual home, the were called home pages. The expression has stuck, but now that most Web sites contain multiple pages, the home page refers to the site's first page, which links to all the others.

HTML Hypertext Markup Language (HTML) is the bedrock of the World Wide Web. All Web pages are encoded in HTML, and the consistency of that standard is what links the Web together. HTML features hyperlinks, which connect with other HTML pages. Web browsers understand HTML and can interpret it to display Web pages on the screen as they were designed. HTML is a text-based language that is easy to learn (as computer languages go), so anyone can design HTML documents (Web pages) and put them on the World Wide Web.

Hyperlink Hyperlinks (often just called links) are the means of navigation on the World Wide Web. A hyperlink is any item on the screen that, when you click on it with the mouse when using a Web browser, makes something happen. Usually, what happens is the browser goes to another Web location directed by the link. Hyperlinks can be individual words, groups of words, a picture, or a link embedded in a large image.

Internet A vast connection of computers, linked by the planetary telephone system. The Internet is an open system, which means that anybody can add a computer to it with the right hardware and software. It is not owned or regulated. The Internet consists of four main portions: e-mail, FTP, Usenet, and the World Wide Web (see those entries in this glossary). The Internet is accessed using personal computers equipped with modems and a phone line. Originally a library-based information resource tied to a community of academicians and professionals using message boards and e-mail to communicate, the Internet has grown enormously during the 1990s with the development of the World Wide Web. The Web has brought a commercial influence to the Internet, changing its character and demographics considerably. Musicians now have access to an electronic distribution and promotion system for advertising and sharing music.

Internet service Internet service providers (ISPs) connect home computers with the Internet. Customers receive a phone number to use, plus an Internet e-mail address. Usually charging a single flat monthly fee, ISPs offer unlimited access to the World Wide Web and other aspects of the Internet. In some cases they provide the necessary software, plus some memory space on the ISP's computer for putting up a Web site. ISPs are either nationwide companies offering a large network of telephone dial-up points, or local enterprises serving a smaller community of phone exchanges.

ISDN Integrated services digital network (ISDN) is a type of digital phone line offered by most phone companies. It provides a higher rate of data transfer when using the Internet, which is useful on the World Wide Web, whose multimedia content displays very slowly over standard phone lines. An ISDN phone line can be about ten times faster than a regular (analog) phone line.

Java Java is a programming language developed for use on the World Wide Web, with possible applications beyond the Web. Java creates Web content that is less static than a typical Web page. Early Java demonstrations were simple animations. Currently, Java shows itself in a variety of interesting ways on cutting-edge Web sites, including interactive jukeboxes for listening to new music, games, chat rooms, and much more. Java creations are small applications called applets.

Listserv See *Mailing list.*

Mailing list Mailing lists, also known as listservs, are unique functions of e-mail. They are group communities of people who share an interest and who talk with each other through e-mail. An automated system housed on an Internet computer, the mailing list receives each e-mail from every participant, and forwards it to every other member of the list. It functions like an e-mail party line, with everybody chipping into the group discussion. For all their value as a networking tool, mailing lists can also deposit an unwieldy amount of e-mail into your mailbox every day.

Message board Message boards are electronic bulletin boards. Using a modem-equipped computer, users can post, reply to, and receive messages on a public bulletin board. These boards are found in online services and in the Usenet portion of the Internet. They are one of the main community-building aspects of the online experience, enabling participants to develop involved discussions about virtually any topic. Most message boards are organized along topical lines, so the members all have an interest in common. Musicians use message boards to communicate with other musicians and to get technical help with digital products.

Modem Computer peripherals used to connect a phone line to a computer. Modems are the devices that allow computer users to access online services, the Internet, and the World Wide Web with specialized software. They come in external and internal models, and operate at different rated speeds. Faster modems enable the quicker availability of music and other multimedia online content.

Netscape One of the cutting-edge Internet companies, Netscape developed the first Web browser to gain almost universal popularity. That program, Netscape Navigator, is still predominantly used among Web users, although it is no longer as dominant as it once was. Netscape also developed many extensions to the HTML code that underlies the entire World Wide Web, creating attractive formatting options for Web designers that could be seen only through Navigator. (Now you know why it became so popular.)

News-group Something of a misnomer, a newsgroup is an Internet message board, part of the Usenet system. The term is a holdover from the early years of the Internet, during which time the Usenet message boards were more "newsy" than they are now. Once the domain of academicians and professionals in various fields exchanging news, research, and professional companionship, the newsgroups have become popularized and in many cases trivialized by the influx of new Internet users. They operate in bulletin board format, allowing users to post messages (called articles, another throwback term) and reply to others. There are thousands of newsgroups, divided by subject area, representing professional, entertainment, and social categories.

Offline browsing Getting what you want from the World Wide Web can be a time-consuming activity. For most people, using standard phone lines, there are many small delays that add up to a lot of wasted time. A number of programs deal with this crisis by offering automated logons and surf sessions. The software goes where you tell it to (or searches out locations based on key words you give it), downloads the latest versions of the Web pages you like, and lets you explore them offline. These programs are perfect for getting the entertainment news, for example: You can have it waiting for you when you get up in the morning or get home from work. It also provides a low-cost solution for people who must make a toll call to access the Internet, because the offline browser is never tempted to stick around online reading things or following hyperlinks for hours on end.

Online In a generic sense, an online service is any company that provides access to a computer network. More specifically, it refers to a handful of organizations that serve a nationwide audience with Internet access and private online content. The most well known of such companies are America Online, CompuServe, Prodigy, and Microsoft Network. Customers of these services are given an e-mail address and a phone number to access the system. Within the service, many forums, electronic publications, chat rooms, and other features greet members. Additionally, each online service provides access to the Internet and World Wide Web.

Plug-in A plug-in is a small, specialized utility program that works with a Web browser to access a specific type of multimedia content on the World Wide Web. One prominent example in use by musicians (and almost everyone else) is the RealAudio plug-in, which plays sound files through your modem in real time. Another is called Crescendo, which plays MIDI files in the same way. Other plug-ins give real-time playback of video files, animation, and other multimedia manifestations. Plug-ins are usually free, and can be downloaded. When installed, they work seamlessly with your Web browser, and pop into action when needed during a Web surfing session.

Real-Audio RealAudio is a brand name for a type of audio streaming technology. Audio streaming is the means for hearing music files online in real time, without having to download them first. RealAudio helped develop this technology, and is the foremost provider of audio streaming software. Most of the audio streaming on the Internet is in RealAudio format, and requires a (free) RealAudio client program, which can be downloaded. Once a computer is equipped with that, clicking on any RealAudio music file initiates instant playback through the computer's speakers. RealAudio (and other formats) is one of the great boons to online musicians, and makes it easy share music with the global community through online networking.

Server software Software programs that are used on network computers to communicate with personal computers are called server programs, or just servers. Server programs interpret commands issued by a client program (instructions from a home user logged onto the Internet) and initiate an event based on those commands. Server programs are used by musicians designing Internet Web sites. For example, the RealAudio server creates sound and music files that can be played in real time by the client (visitor to the site), which is more convenient for customers and other visitors. Server programs are usually not free, and sometimes are expensive.

Shockwave Shockwave is one of the most prominent and ambitious plug-ins on the Web, enabling users to see moving pictures, hear music, and play games on the World Wide Web in real time. The plug-in is a free download, and integrates with the Web browser so that whenever a Shockwave site is encountered on the Web, the plug-in pops into action to display whatever is there.

Uploading Uploading is the process of transferring a file from a personal computer to a larger network. The PC must be connected to the network by means of a modem connection through a telephone line. Uploading files is a way of sharing digital material with the world at large. The material can be a text document, piece of digitized music, graphics, or any other type of multimedia computer file. Typical upload destinations are topical libraries within online services (such as a library devoted to MIDI compositions), FTP libraries on the Internet, and Web sites constructed by the uploader.

URL Uniform Resource Locators are the addresses of the World Wide Web. Every URL follows the Hypertext Transfer Protocol (HTTP) standard, which simply means they all can connect with each other when addressed by a Web browser. You can recognize a URL because they all begin with the HTTP locator, followed by a colon and two slashes, followed by the rest of the Web address (for example, http://www.realaudio.com).

Usenet One of the oldest parts of the Internet, Usenet is a collection of thousands of message boards (called newsgroups) on different topics. In earlier years it was devoted primarily to professional and academic subjects, and the message boards were serious environments used for networking within various disciplines. Currently, there are newsgroups devoted to all kinds of capricious subjects and entertainments. Hundreds of music groups have their own Usenet message board for fans. Anyone with an Internet access account can view Usenet messages and participate in the electronic communities.

Video streaming An Internet technology that plays moving picture files through a logged-on personal computer without having to download them. Before video streaming, in order to view a movie file on the Internet, you had to download it (which could take a long time, as the files are usually quite large) and then play it from your hard drive with special software. Video streaming cuts out the download process by playing the file directly from the hard drive of its host Internet computer. Applications of video streaming include live television broadcasts, prerecorded news reports, music videos, and more.

Web browser The most important Internet software, Web browsers allow viewing of the World Wide Web. There are several different browsers to choose from, each of which provides a slightly different view of the Web. Notwithstanding the differences, all browsers are similar and have the same features, allowing you to view, scroll through, and link between destinations on the World Wide Web. Some browsers integrate easily with small utility programs that bring out the multimedia content of the Web. Web browsers are sometimes part of an integrated series of Internet programs that access e-mail and the Usenet newsgroups.

Web site Web sites are collections of related pages on the World Wide Web. In the Web's early days, Web locations were mostly single pages, called home pages. Over time, these simple sites evolved into complex, multipage presentations connected by hyperlinks. Now, the largest Web sites contain many hundreds of pages—they're virtually small online services available to anyone with an Internet connection and a Web browser. The most ambitious Web sites may contain interactive features such as message boards and chat rooms, as well as multimedia elements such as music, animation, and movies.

World Wide Web The Web is a software invention of the 1990s that has transformed the Internet. Essentially a collection of files written in the same software language (called HTML code), the Web allows easy navigation by means of hyperlinks that connect each of the nearly one hundred million Web pages together. Users of the World Wide Web are attracted by its ease as well as the colorful multimedia content. Anybody can contribute to the Web by designing and coding their own page or Web site (collection of pages), and placing it on an Internet computer. People have taken advantage of the system to self-publish pictures, music, and text. Corporations have taken advantage of it to advertise themselves, and even transact business. The Web is viewed with a software program called a Web browser, and can be accessed through any Internet connection.

Zip Zip is the most common compression protocol. Most online programs files are compressed so they can be downloaded more quickly. There are a few ways of accomplishing that compression, but Zip has become almost universal, and has the advantage of working on both PCs and Macs. (Compressed files created on the Macintosh use Mac-only compression protocols because they can't be run on a PC anyway.) Compressed files are sometimes informally called zipped files, and decompressing them is known as unzipping them. A Zip utility is always in the software toolbox of the online enthusiast, and such programs enable the compression and decompression of files.

RESOURCE LIST

MUSIC MAGAZINES

Music magazines have evolved dramatically in the last 15 years, reflecting the technological changes that have swept through the music world. Publications once devoted to acoustic instruments and playing techniques now are filled with equipment and software reviews, as well as articles on getting the most from a home studio. Music magazines are a tremendous resource of information about digital music tools, and subscribing to one or more of them is highly recommended. The following periodicals deal mostly with keyboard-related music production and generic MIDI equipment.

Keyboard Magazine
20085 Stevens Creek Blvd.
Cupertino, CA 95014

Electronic Musician
6400 Hollis St. #12
Emeryville, CA 94608

Mix
6400 Hollis St. #12
Emeryville, CA 94608

EQ
P.S.N. Publications
2 Park Ave., Suite 1820
New York, NY 10016

Home and Studio Recording
22024 Lassen St.
Suite 118
Chatsworth, CA 91311

Music Instruments and Software

Akai Professional
U.S. distribution by IMC
Box 2344, Fort Worth, TX 76113
(817) 336-5114; fax (817) 870-1271
Web site: http://www.akai.com/akaipro
MIDI instruments, samplers

Alesis
3630 Holdrege Ave., Los Angeles, CA 90016
(310) 558-4530; fax (310) 836-9192
E-mail: alecorp@alesis1.USA.com
MIDI instruments, effects boxes, recording gear

ART
215 Tremont St., Rochester, NY 14608
(716) 436-2720; fax (716) 436-3942
Digital effects boxes

Big Noise
Box 23740, Jacksonville, FL 32241
(904) 730-0754; fax (904) 730-0748
Music software; DOS/Windows

Buchla & Associates
Box 10205, Berkeley, CA 94709
(510) 528-4446; fax (510) 526-1955
MIDI instruments

Cakewalk
44 Pleasant St., Box 760, Watertown, MA 02272
(617) 926-2480; fax (617) 924-6657
MIDI and digital audio software

Coda
6210 Bury Dr., Eden Prairie, MN 55346-1718
(800) 843-2066, (612) 937-9611; fax (612) 937-9760
MIDI software

Digidesign
3401-A Hillview Avenue, Palo Alto, CA 94303
(415) 842-7900; fax (415) 842-7999
Customer service (415) 842-6699
Digital audio workstations

Dr. T's
100 Crescent Rd., Suite 1B, Needham, MA 02194
(617) 455-1454; fax (617) 455-1460
MIDI software

E-Magic
13348 Grass Valley Avenue, Building C, Suite 100, Grass Valley,
CA 95945
(916) 477-1051; fax (916) 477-1052
E-mail: emagic@emagicusa.com
Web site: http://www.emagicusa.com
MIDI software

E-mu Systems
1600 Green Hills Rd., Box 660015, Scotts Valley, CA 95067-0015
(408) 438-1921; fax (408) 438-8612
MIDI instruments; samplers

Ensoniq
155 Great Valley Parkway, Malvern, PA 19355
(610) 647-3930; fax (610) 647-8908
Web site: http://www.ensoniq.com
MIDI instruments

JLCooper Electronics
125000 Beatrice St., Los Angeles, CA 90066
(310) 306-4131; fax (310) 822-2252
MIDI switchers, synch boxes, other devices

Kawai America
2055 E. University Dr., Compton, CA 90224
(310) 631-1771; fax (310) 604-6913
MIDI instruments

Korg
89 Frost St., Westbury, NY 11590
(516) 333-9100; fax (516) 333-9108
E-mail: literature@korgusa.com
MIDI instruments

Kurzweil/Young Chang America
13336 Alondra Blvd., Cerritos, CA 90703
(310) 926-3200; fax (310) 404-0748
MIDI instruments

Lexicon
100 Beaver St., Waltham, MA 02154
(617) 736-0300; fax (617) 891-0340
Digital effects boxes

Mark of the Unicorn
1280 Massachusetts Ave., Cambridge, MA 02138
(617) 576-2760; fax (617) 576-3609
MIDI software

Opcode
3950 Fabian Way, Suite 100, Palo Alto, CA 94303
(415) 856-3333; fax (415) 856-3332
MIDI software

Passport Designs
100 Stone Pine Rd., Half Moon Bay, CA 94019
(415) 726-0280; fax (415) 726-2254
MIDI software

Peavey
Box 2898, Meridian, MS 39302-2898
(601) 483-5365; fax 601 486-1172
MIDI instruments

Roland Corp. U.S.
7200 Dominion Circle, Los Angeles, CA 90040
(213) 685-5141
MIDI instruments

Steinberg
9312 Deering Ave., Chatsworth, CA 91311-5857
(818) 993-4091; fax (818) 993-4161
MIDI software

Turtle Beach Systems
52 Grumbacher Rd., York, PA 17402
(717) 767-0257; fax (717) 767-6033
MIDI software

Voyetra Technologies
5 Odell Plaza, Yonkers, NY 10701-1406
(914) 966-0600; (914) 966-1102
MIDI software

Yamaha
6600 Orangethorpe Ave., Buena Park, CA 90620
(800) 322-4322, (714) 522-9011; fax (714) 527-9832
MIDI instruments

World Wide Web Resources

The MIDI Farm
http://www.midifarm.com/
A supermarket of MIDI information and links

Harmony Central
http://www.harmony-central.com/
A comprehensive resource for musicians

If I may be permitted a bit of self-promotion, readers might want to check out my previous book published by Schirmer Books: *The Virtual Musician: A Complete Guide to Online Resources and Services*. It lists hundreds of World Wide Web sites in several musical categories, and contains chapters describing the best ways to get online in the first place.

INDEX